D0204802

ROBERT MANNING
STROZIER LIBRARY

SEP 2 1994

Tallahassee, Florida

BEYOND CHRYSANTHEMUMS

Beyond Chrysanthemums

PERSPECTIVES ON POETRY
EAST AND WEST

Stephen Reckert

CLARENDON PRESS · OXFORD
1993

PN
6101
R425
1993

Oxford University Press, Walton Street, Oxford OX2 6DP
Oxford New York Toronto
Delhi Bombay Calcutta Madras Karachi
Kuala Lumpur Singapore Hong Kong Tokyo
Nairobi Dar es Salaam Cape Town
Melbourne Auckland Madrid
and associated companies in
Berlin Ibadan

Oxford is a trade mark of Oxford University Press

Published in the United States
by Oxford University Press Inc., New York

© Stephen Reckert 1993

All rights reserved. No part of this publication may be reproduced,
stored in a retrieval system, or transmitted, in any form or by any means,
without the prior permission in writing of Oxford University Press.
Within the UK, exceptions are allowed in respect of any fair dealing for the
purpose of research or private study, or criticism or review, as permitted
under the Copyright, Designs and Patents Act, 1988, or in the case of
reprographic reproduction in accordance with the terms of the licences
issued by the Copyright Licensing Agency. Enquiries concerning
reproduction outside these terms and in other countries should be
sent to the Rights Department, Oxford University Press,
at the address above

British Library Cataloguing in Publication Data
Data available

Library of Congress Cataloging in Publication Data
Reckert, Stephen.
Beyond chrysanthemums: perspectives on poetry East and West/Stephen Reckert.
Includes bibliographical references and index.
I. Title. II. Title: Perspectives on poetry East and West.
809.1—dc20 PN6101.R425 1993 92-26818
ISBN 0-19-815165-9

Typeset by Best-set Typesetter Ltd., Hong Kong

Printed in Great Britain
on acid-free paper by
Bookcraft Ltd.
Midsomer Norton, Bath

Acknowledgements

ACKNOWLEDGEMENT is made to the following for permission to reproduce illustrations or quote from works written, edited, or published by them:

Haags Gemeentemuseum and Cordon Art, Baarn, Holland (M. C. Escher, 'Bond of Union'); National Palace Museum, Taipei (Lěng Méi, 'Ladies in a garden pavilion'); Ō-oka Makoto ('Kage no naka de'); Penguin Books Ltd. (Dan Pagis, 'Written in pencil in the sealed goods van', *The Penguin Book of Hebrew Verse*, ed. and tr. T. Carmi, 1981, © T. Carmi, 1981, 575); Philip Sherrard (Giorgos Seferis, *Collected Poems 1924–1955*); Weatherhill, Inc. (Loraine Kuck, *The World of the Japanese Garden*).

Preface

THIS book has taken shape over several years, and parts of some chapters have previously appeared in Portuguese, Spanish, French, or Italian, as well as in English. Since every language carries with it a cultural context of allusions and assumptions, previously published material has been extensively rewritten as well as much expanded.

Apart from an overall emphasis on the relevance for the West of East Asian poetic techniques and the aesthetic principles underlying them, the unity of the book derives in varying degrees from three sources: one philosophical (the concept of the reconciliation of dualities); one philological (the method of the hermeneutic circle); and one semiotic (the foregrounding of signifiers). Concentration on minimalist verse (meaning, in principle, poems of not more than thirty-two syllables) provides the space needed for translation of the texts and for 'close-reading' analyses accessible to readers unacquainted with one or other of the various Eastern and Western languages concerned.[1]

In the transcription of early and orally transmitted Iberian poems, punctuation and graphic accidentals are tacitly modernized: early texts being practically unpunctuated, quotation inevitably means interpretation. Non-etymological *h* in definite and indefinite articles is deleted and etymological *h* in forms of the verb [*h*]*aber*/[*h*]*aver* restored, and abbreviations are resolved. Chinese is transcribed in the now usual Pinyin spelling except for some words with familiar English forms (e.g., Peking and Hong Kong, rather than *Běijīng* and *Xiānggǎng*). The diacritics [´], [`], [ˇ] indicate the 'inflected' tones: rising, falling, and 'dipping' (falling + rising); I have departed from common Western practice in using these regularly to represent the modern pronunciation of Chinese words and names,[2] of which they are as much an integral part as the accents on *élève* or *théâtre*.

---

[1] Translations, except those from Persian (translated from the Italian of Bausani), Hebrew, and Welsh, are my own unless otherwise stated.

[2] Those of Chinese authors of works in Western languages are cited in the form used in the respective publication, and that of the goddess Nü Gua is printed without umlaut to allow indication of tone.

Special thanks are due to José María Aguirre and Yvette Centeno for references to Rilke and Liè Zǐ; Alan Deyermond for reading draft chapters and alerting me to points that needed defending (and others that were indefensible); George Doris for conversations on Algarvian beaches or the banks of 'limpid River Wey' that always started more hares than I could hope to catch; Peter Dronke for a reference to Bernardus Silvestris; Elżbieta Hrankowska and Maciek Jura, who led me to Szymborska's metaphorical stone (and Olga Zakrzewska, who found Zbigniew Herbert's real one for me in the primeval Mazovian forest); Michael Loewe for the portrait of the Countess of Dài; Czesław Miłosz for clarifying points in 'No more' and 'On reading the Japanese poet Issa' (and Ewa Dzierzba for her Portuguese versions of Miłosz); Thomas Fitzsimmons for comments on Ō-oka Makoto's 'Kage no naka de' and for providing the text of the poem; José Cardoso Pires for *Jin Píng Méi*; Bogusław Zakrzewski, who literally charmed the birds out of the trees to perch on his shoulder and hear his wise words about Chinese poetry; my daughter and son Victoria and Nicholas for references to Scott Fitzgerald and Chaucer; and my wife Dídia for a quarter of a century's guidance through the minefield of her native language. Other debts are acknowledged in the notes and chapter dedications.

S.R.

Lisbon, January 1993

Contents

List of Plates

(between pages 146 and 147)

Abbreviations

ACA   J. A. Carrizo, *Antiguos cantos populares argentinos* (Buenos Aires, 1926)

AMRP   F. Lopes Graça and M. Giacometti, *Antologia da Música Regional Portuguesa*, i (gramophone record; Lisbon, 1961)

CBN   *Cancioneiro da Biblioteca Nacional*, facsimile (Lisbon, 1982)

CGD   S. Baud-Bovy, *La Chanson populaire grècque du Dodécanèse*, i (Paris, 1936)

CI   *Critical Inquiry*

CMP   Higini Anglès, *La música en la Corte de los Reyes Católicos*, iii. *Cancionero Musical de Palacio*, ii (Barcelona, 1947)

Cop   Gil Vicente, *Copilaçam de todalas Obras* (Lisbon, 1562). *Don Duardos* is quoted from the diplomatic edn. in Reckert (1977).

CPA   A. Viana, *Para o Cancioneiro Popular Algarvio* (Lisbon, 1956)

CPB   S. Romero, *Cantos populares do Brasil*, ed. Câmara Cascudo (Rio de Janeiro, 1954)

CPBA   M. J. Delgado, *Subsídios para o Cancioneiro Popular do Baixo Alentejo* (Lisbon, 1955).

CPE   F. Rodríguez Marín, *Cantos populares españoles* (2nd edn., Buenos Aires, 1948)

CPG   J. Pérez Ballesteros, *Cancionero popular gallego* (2nd edn., Buenos Aires, 1942)

CRHJ   A. de Larrea Palacín, *Canciones rituales hispano-judías* (Madrid, 1954)

CV   *Cancioneiro Português da Biblioteca Vaticana*, facsimile (Lisbon, 1973)

GL   Federico García Lorca, *Obras completas*, ed. A. del Hoyo, i (2nd edn., Madrid, 1980)

Hk   R. H. Blyth, *Haiku* (Tokyo, 1949–52)

HR   *History of Religions*

ICL   Liu Wu-chi, *An Introduction to Chinese Literature* (Bloomington, Ind., 1966)

IETS   J. C. Cooper, *An Illustrated Encyclopaedia of Traditional Symbols* (London, 1978)

IH   Harold G. Henderson, *An Introduction to Haiku* (Garden City, NY, 1958)

JCP   Robert H. Brower and Earl Miner, *Japanese Court Poetry* (London, 1962)

JT   Anne Birrell, ed. and tr., *New Songs from a Jade Terrace (= Yù Tái Xin Yŏng*, 6th c.) (London, 1982)

LTT   Dámaso Alonso and José Manuel Blecua, *Antología de la poesía española: lírica de tipo tradicional* (2nd edn., Madrid, 1964, with frequent reprintings)

MYS   *Man'yōshū*, ed. Nippon Gakujutsu Shinkōkai (3rd edn., New York, 1965)

NYRB *New York Review of Books*

TLS   *Times Literary Supplement*

'The tension between stars that are poles apart
is what keeps this tree dancing',
the woman says, who came
from far beyond chrysanthemums and November mist.

.   .   .   .

Surely the tree once grew beside a stream
in my first homeland on the Dark Lord's star;
the pulsing of that planet's mystery
compels me to become the other pole.

(Before me and the woman,
the tree keeps slowly dancing.)

Ō-oka Makoto

INTRODUCTION: WRITING IN OTHER LANGUAGES

SOME definitions are called for at the outset. Is 'writing' the act of putting signs on paper? Or the signs themselves, as organized in texts?[1] Or both? And 'other'—but other than what? The missing antecedent only becomes clear when we remember that 'languages' are sign systems—which, as structural anthropology has taught us, are not confined to the linguistic, but shape entire cultures. The 'other' is thus whatever falls outside one's own cultural frame of reference, or canon.

When I went up to Cambridge in 1946 I found that the Modern and Medieval Languages Tripos included an option called, precisely, 'Other Languages', and taught in part by a benign and eclectic philologist, N. P. Jopson, just returned from war service in Postal Censorship as Head of *Uncommon* Languages. His seminar met at five in St John's, and regularly began with China tea and charcoal biscuits, which were unrationed. One of the crumbs of incidental information I picked up but cannot vouch for was that any reasonably bright Lithuanian peasant could understand simple sentences in Sanskrit, while his equivalent in Sardinia (then even more off the beaten track than Albania today, but the Professor was determined to go there in the next Long Vac) would be as little fazed by Latin—at least by the kind to be found in the seven densely printed volumes of Du Cange's great *Glossarium Mediae et Infimae Latinitatis* ranged on their shelf in the Jopsonian study.

My sense of linguistic decorum as well as my transatlantic egalitarian sensibilities had already been bruised when I arrived in England three years before as an American sergeant attached to the

---

[1] A vogue word of the Eighties, but useful if carefully defined: e.g., as 'a combination of elements leading to semiotic events . . . [and] structured enough to be perceived as a whole and . . . presented as complete. Thus defined, novels, poems . . . , and paintings are texts' (Mieke Bal, 'De-disciplining the Eye', *CI* (Spring 1990), 511.

RAF, and found the sanitary arrangements provided for our use labelled 'Other Ranks'; but by now I was inured to the Antecedent-less Other, and in any case the language we were supposed to be studying, being neither Lithuanian nor Logudorese, did not technically qualify as Other: Old Spanish, after all, came under the respectable umbrella of Romance Philology. Not being French or German either, though, it was clearly Uncommon—as were also, *a fortiori*, oddities like Portuguese or its northern variant, Galician. Writing in such outlandish tongues, one nineteenth-century Galician poet said, came to much the same as writing on cork-tree bark, like the Arcadians:

> Escribir nada mais pr'ũa provincia,
> ou, com' os povos árcades fixeron,
> escribir sobr' a casca dos curtizos,
> cáxeque todo ven a ser o mesmo.[2]

Canons may be either collective or personal, and either synchronic (like European Modernism, or the Spanish 'Generation of 1927') or diachronic (like the English canon from Chaucer to Eliot[3]). To lead in to the general theme of this book, I shall begin by exploring and exemplifying these different aspects of canonicity; and since it is poetry that specifically foregrounds language, by exemplifying them with specific relation to poetry.

Starting from the Euro-American canon tacitly regarded in the West until not long ago as The Canon, I shall work inward, by way of a typical national canon—that of Portugal—to my own personal one, based on over four decades' professional concern with the poetry of the Iberian languages and an equally long-standing if dilettantish attachment (in the etymological sense of *diletto*) to that of East Asia.[4]

I shall then move outward again, bypassing the national and Western canons, to one as yet only potential: that of the *Weltliteratur* desiderated by Goethe from 1827 on, and now at last foreseeable in the writing of a number of poets both Western and Eastern (though

---

[2] Curros Enríquez, *Aires d'a miña terra* (3rd edn., Corunna, 1886), 3.

[3] For an analogy to Eliot's canonicity see n. 17, below.

[4] A keen eye will detect other influences: an early introduction by my mother to poetry in the form of FitzGerald's *Rubaiyat*; a philhellenism inspired by my first French teacher (whose pedagogical activity overflowed into unofficial tuition in her native Cretan demotic) and afterwards confirmed by personal and family involvement with Greece going back more than thirty years; and a Polonophilia dating from 1939 and ultimately vindicated by the Polish friends who five decades later organized my lectures at the universities of Cracow and Warsaw.

Goethe seems to have envisaged a homogenized literature in which national differences would wither away: a quite different position from the one to be advocated here).

I say 'at last'; but the narcissistic self-containedness of Western literary culture is in fact more recent than we tend to think, as are the various linguistic nationalisms that have conspired, since the decline of Latin as the common second language of that culture, to keep it fragmented like bits of some vast and ill-restored mosaic whose lost continuities can now only be guessed at.[5]

Moreover, both these parochial attitudes have lately been looking dated. Among contemporary Western poets who have gone 'beyond chrysanthemums and November mist'[6] to find something more in the East than mere quaintness, the names of Antonio Machado, Borges, and the Nobel laureates Seferis, Miłosz, and Paz (all of which will recur in the following chapters) come to mind. Earlier, Yeats was influenced by the classical Japanese Nō drama; Pound made free with the poetry and even the name of Lǐ Bó (preferring, for reasons best known to himself, to call the great Táng poet 'Rihaku': the Japanese reading of his name); Brecht used Chinese themes as a deliberately anti-exotic distancing device; and Britten, following Yeats's lead, based the libretto of *Curlew River* on a Nō play. More recently the vogue of Mishima Yukio has, if nothing else, at least brought Japanese fiction to the notice of the West; Indian novelists writing in English have been readily assimilated by the mainstream if not always by their own compatriots; and Nobel prizes have gone to Egypt and Nigeria as well as India and Japan.

Cultural chauvinism is by no means a Western monopoly. The modish pseudo-science of *Nihonjinron*, proclaiming the uniqueness

---

[5] Martin Bernal's controversial *Black Athena: The Afroasiatic Roots of Classical Civilization* (New Brunswick, NJ, 1989–91; 2 vols. to date) is a politicized bid to redress the neglect, since the early 19th c., of these roots. Arabic (and, via Arabic, Indo-Persian) influence on medieval Europe has been more generally recognized; and quite apart from the faddish excesses of *chinoiserie*, China, followed by Japan, sporadically engaged the serious attention of individual Western philosophers, artists, and writers, from the 16th-c. Jesuits to the Gautiers and Goncourts of the 19th. For a condensed but wide-ranging survey of the subject see Zhang 1989: 200–10.

[6] Ō-oka Makoto, 'Kage no naka de' ('In the Shadows'), in Ō-oka Makoto and Thomas Fitzsimmons, *Yururu kagami no yoake/Rocking Mirror Daybreak* (Tokyo, 1982), 20 f. 'The Dark Lord's star', in my version in the epigraph, is the Japanese for Pluto. Ō-oka (1930–), a poet, dramatist, and critic of art and literature, has lived in the West and translated Éluard, Breton, and Euripides. The poem was set to music by Tōru Takemitsu and performed at the 1987 Almeida Festival. While the tension and polarity it refers to are evidently sexual, they make an equally appropriate metaphor for East–West relations.

of all things truly Japanese, is a money-spinner for market-wise Tokyo academics and their obliging publishers; and China has never wavered in its conviction that the Middle Kingdom is the 'unwobbling pivot' of civilization.[7] But the traumatic humbling of both countries in the nineteenth century by the West compelled them to recognize the technological superiority of the barbarian periphery and undertake a selective acceptance of its material benefits; and while the immediate success of this policy in Japan was spectacularly confirmed by the Russo-Japanese war of 1905, in China it has led to a still-continuing series of convulsions. The title of Kurosawa's film *Ran* is the Chinese *luàn* ('chaos'): at once the historic nightmare of all Chinese regimes in the face of any threat to an ever-precarious established order and the pretext for the panic violence they meet it with; Deng Xiǎopíng, indeed, explained just before the Tiananmén massacre of 1989 that the students' sole aim was 'to create *luàn* under heaven'.[8]

Nor is East–West traffic only one-way: if Peter Brook's productions of the *Mahabharata* in French and English have been applauded in theatres from Paris to Sydney, Ninagawa's of the *Medea* of Euripides—in Japanese and with a Japanese setting—has been an equal revelation to audiences from Athens to New York; and Kurosawa's *Ran* itself is a samurai version of *Lear*, following his adaptation of *Macbeth*. It would be hard to find a Japanese poet of any note who was not conversant with Western poetry from Baudelaire to Seamus Heaney;[9] and Chinese poets such as Běi Dǎo or Duoduo, a survivor of Tiananmén, are as much at home with it as the Japanese Ō-oka or Takamura—whose 'Comic verses for the kind of Western poet who amuses himself with the East' reject fashionable exoticism as impatiently as any of the Western contemporaries I mentioned:

---

[7] On the persistence of historic Chinese ethnocentrism see Frank Dikötter, *The Discourse of Race in Modern China* (London, 1991). A contrary reaction to the West's 'cultural appropriation' of the East (for which Edward Said has in turn appropriated the once respectable name Orientalism) is the complex Chinese 'counterdiscourse' of Occidentalism studied by Xiaomei Chen, contrasting forms of which are cultivated by the regime and dissidents alike. Its more purely cultural equivalent in Japan is dealt with *en passant* by Kitagawa; Zhang (1992) demystifies Western and Chinese ideologies alike with impartial astringency.

[8] See Roderick MacFarquhar, *NYRB* 20 July 1989.

[9] Even today, however, while 'any reasonably literate Japanese could rattle off the names of [a dozen or more] living Western authors, and . . . expect to . . . buy their latest works in Japanese . . . , at . . . least a hundred novels are translated from English into Japanese for every one . . . in the other direction' (James Melville, *TLS* 16–22 Nov. 1990).

... When you get fed up with the Parthenon and Notre Dame,
fine, go on to sing the praises of lanterns, 'Fujiyama',
Hiroshige, Harunobu, Bashō, Buson—
. . . .

and the blank paper, too.
Choose *haikai* or *tanka*,
suit yourself.
. . . .

Only don't count on me to play chic with you.
. . . .

You can ... do your best to set me on the Way to instant Enlightenment,
but I beg to be excused.
. . . .

To tell the truth,
your *Ja-pon*, *Ja-pon*, *Ja-pon*, *Ja-pon*, *Ja-pon*—
well, it's just a crashing bore.[10]

(Japanese has always delighted in onomatopoeia; and *Japon*, to a Japanese ear, sounds like the *kerplunk* of the frog jumping into the old pond in Bashō's best-known haiku.)

Κανών comes from κάννα: a reed, hence a rod or (literally and metaphorically) rule. It is the source of our word *canal*, and is cognate with the Arabic *qānāʰ*, also meaning a reed, which by extension gave Persian *qanāt*: underground streams or canals.[11] Κανόνες were also the reeds of a loom, which lead the weft in an orderly course through the warp and press it down in even lines (the word 'order' itself, it is worth recalling, comes from Latin *ordīrī*, 'to weave', as 'text' comes from its synonym *texere*).

Paradoxically, the earliest recorded form of the character *luàn*— 'chaos' or '*dis*order'—shows two hands winding silk from two cocoons over a loom:

---

[10] Takamura Kōtarō (1883–1956), an aesthetician and sculptor as well as a poet, studied in France; his best-known work is a moving collection of love poems and elegies for his wife, the sculptress Chieko (*Chieko's Sky*, tr. Soichi Furuta, (Tokyo, 1987)). My version is based on that of Hiroaki Satō (in *A Brief History of Imbecility* (Honolulu, 1992)), who kindly supplied me with the Japanese text (cf. the Textual Appendix). *Fujiyama*, a name used only by foreigners for the Japanese *Fuji-san*, appears in the equivalent of italics in the original to emphasize the solecism; 'instant Enlightenment' translates the Zen *satori*, referred to below in Ch. 1.

[11] The Persian *qanāt*—inhabited by blind fish—might appeal to such critics as Professors Terry Eagleton and Jonathan Culler as an apt metaphor for canons.

HANDS   SILK   LOOM

But an alternative meaning in ancient times was the exactly contrary one of 'order': the hands were seen as either tangling or untangling the skein of silk, depending on context (an etymographic knot unravelled by my Chinese teacher Arthur Cooper on the analogy, precisely, of the verb *ravel*, for which the *OED* gives, along with 'tangle', the meanings 'disentangle' and even '*un*ravel', both in Shakespeare).[12]

In China and Japan the idea of a canonical classic is conveyed by the character *jing*, as in the *Shi Jing* ('Canon of Odes'), the *Yi Jing* ('Canon of Changes'), etc. The earliest recorded form of *jing*, dating from 390 CE, has the meaning—fortuitously the same as in Persian—'underground stream':

The top stroke is a covering; the three wavy lines under it are waves in the stream; and at the bottom a man, bent over like Atlas supporting the heavens, firmly stands his ground:

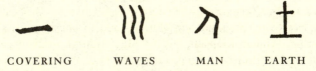

COVERING   WAVES   MAN   EARTH

The canon can thus be pictured as the outward and visible manifestation of a hidden underground current of tradition, from which it

---

[12] 'That the . . . meanings "order" and "disorder" both belong to [this] character has been so puzzling that attempts at emendation have been made where the first and now obsolete meaning appears in early literature. [But] one need only think of *let* (= "allow" or—also obsolete—"hinder"); *stalk* ("stride brazenly" or "creep stealthily"); and *ravel* . . .' (Cooper 1985). The contemporary scholar Qian Zhongshu mentions other characters with opposite meanings: e.g., *yi* ('change' or 'changelessness') in *Yi Jing* (the 'Book of Changes', which could as well be called 'The Book of Constancy', being 'about changeless presence in a world of always changing configuration' (Zhang 1985: 386)). Similar cases are studied by Empson as the seventh type of ambiguity.

draws its strength and resilience. But the modern character adds the modern form of 'silk' or 'thread' as a semantic indicator:

THREAD   +   UNDERGROUND STREAM   =   CANON

—and as well as signifying a specific kind of canon, the Buddhist *sutra* (a Sanskrit word meaning a thread, line, or rule), also denótes both the warp in weaving and the verb 'to pass through'. Once more, then, as in Greek, we find a straight, orderly 'passing through': a temporal process eventuating in an end product which, by progressive semantic drift, has come to mean something firmly established in the past: a precedent elevated to the status of a rule. In short, a canon.

Any discussion of the Portuguese national canon necessarily begins with Camões. But 'who, today,' asks George Steiner (1978: 178), 'reads Camões's *Lusiads*, that bracing pageant...?' (Not Steiner, apparently; which is a pity, since despite a sometimes gratingly magisterial tone he is among the more perceptive readers now writing.)

No doubt part of the trouble is the language problem: after all, Camões in English—or so Pound said—tends to sound like sub-Milton. It was perhaps the only relatively sensible thing he did say about him; but whatever Camões may sound like in English, which he did not write, he is no sub-Milton—and in any case, as another poet-critic, William Empson, put it: 'The language problem, but you have to try'[13] (Professor Empson was in bed with a Japanese lady during an earthquake when he had to try, but the principle also applies more generally). What happens, then, when we try with that bracing pageant, the corner-stone and touchstone of the Lusitanian canon?

'Tous les États', de Gaulle said, 'sont des monstres froids'; and the first instinct of any nation-state confronted with the subversive ambivalence of a truly national epic is to downgrade it from an *œuvre scriptible*, demanding the reader's active collaboration, to the altogether more comfortable and innocuous status of the merely

---

[13] *Collected Poems* (1955; London, 1984), 48 f.: 'Aubade'.

lisible, so as to convert it to the uses of the State and incorporate it in a canon less national than nationalistic.

Predictably, then, no effort has been spared to domesticate, appropriate, capitalize on, and mummify, *The Lusiads*. It has been quarried for lapidary lines to be carved on monuments and stirring sentiments to be slotted into Tenth of June orations. Generations of schoolchildren, obliged to parse its sentences and forbidden to read Canto IX, have been shielded from the danger of ever suspecting it was poetry, and possibly failing to be braced. It has been instrumentalized, neutralized, and emulsified into what the poet Jorge de Sena called a 'classico-patriotic mishmash' or dog's dinner: consistently by the Establishment and sporadically by successive Oppositions: a policy that still continues, after four centuries, to mislead (and thus either alienate or gratify) unwary readers who take it at face value.

These are all ways of *not* trying. If we do try—with the once New Critics' techniques of close reading, say—we shall not have far to look for irony and paradox. If we opt for a slightly more modern semiotic approach we shall discover intricate networks of macro-signifiers—myths, symbols, metaphors—subliminally buttressed by phonemic microsignifiers, all joining to create a vast, disquieting, and profoundly ambivalent total signified. If, finally, we deconstruct the triumphalist rhetoric of Empire and the blare of martial trumpets (I have tried all three approaches[14]), we shall find at the heart of Camões's poem the lonely whistling of the wind in the yard-arms of the caravelles, the Virgilian *lachrymae rerum*, and the Ovidian conviction that nothing is what it seems—or if it is, it will shortly turn into something else. And the disconcerting climax not only to this insistent subtext of 'chance, and death, and mutability' but to the text itself of the so-called *Bíblia da Nacionalidade*, is the gloriously anarchic and pagan celebration, in Canto IX, of Eros as the key to Gnosis. It seems likely, then, that the language problem that allows *The Lusiads* to be consigned to a patronizing throw-away line as a rattling good yarn is not any hypothetical sub-Miltonic diction, but the fact that it is written in an 'Other Language', and therefore canonical only in the context of a literature itself uncanonical.

Like most national canons, that of Portugal is now in a state of flux; but while everyone knows the Anglo-American canon is under

---

[14] For examples of each see Reckert 1973 and 1984, and Ch. 5, below; for microsignifiers, Ch. 1, n. 9 and corresponding text.

beady-eyed scrutiny from several quarters, the Portuguese, as far as the outside world is concerned, might have been put in deep freeze a hundred years ago. Everyone also knows by now that the mere observation of a phenomenon can be enough to alter it. But a phenomenon that remains *un*observed can also be affected by its very failure to be observed. Lack of outside feedback has hindered both the formation and the revision of the Portuguese canon, turning it in on itself as a closed system, with admission granted to some works and authors either as makeweights (a balanced canon being felt to require all genres to be fully represented in all periods) or because some peculiarly indigenous themes—psychological motivations, cultural or historical references, local allusions, and the like, without much resonance for a wider public—may quite legitimately strike a responsive chord in Portuguese readers.[15]

These tendencies are partly due to the 'cultural belatedness'[16] of Portugal itself up to the first World War. If Oporto is neither Rouen nor Boston, and its hinterland no Wessex, it still comes as a shock to realize that the novelist Castelo Branco was younger than Flaubert, and the naïve and sentimental Júlio Dinis the same age, give or take a couple of years, as Henry James and Hardy (while it may be possible to get by on one or the other of Schiller's antonyms, when they coincide they cancel out).

The converse of the inflated canon meant for home consumption is the ruthlessly deflated export model, with foreign readers coerced into taking notice by a hard sell of Fernando Pessoa, implying that (apart from Camões, whose bracing pageant, it seems, no one reads anyhow) Portugal has only ever had one poet: a marketing strategy at

---

[15] Makeweights would include most drama between Camões and Garrett, fiction from Bernardim Ribeiro in the 16th c. to Castelo Branco in the 19th, and 18th–19th-c. poetry up to Cesário Verde (1855–86), except for Tolentino (1714–1811), Bocage (1765–1805), Garrett (1799–1854), and Quental (1842–91). Candidates for the second category, from an outsider's point of view (insiders being unlikely to grant that it exists at all), would be the 19th-c. historian Herculano when wearing his other hat as a writer of historical fiction and verse; the novelists Dinis and Castelo Branco; and among poets, the narcissistic António Nobre (1867–1903) and (in, but hardly of, the 20th c.) the bard of nebulous and ineffable abstractions, Pascoaes (1877–1952).

[16] The reference is not to Harold Bloom but to Curtius's term for pre-Enlightenment Spain. A conspicuous feature of Peninsular Renaissance literature is the coexistence of works whose essential medievalism is masked by an overlay of stylistic and thematic Italianism with others still medieval in form but in whose content elements not only of renovation but of innovation transcend the formal moulds they have not yet succeeded in breaking.

once demeaning to the literature as a whole and unjust to such predecessors and contemporaries of Pessoa's as Cesário Verde and Camilo Pessanha[17]—to name two who are surely his peers, and not to mention the half-dozen or so major poets of the past half-century.

Apart from lack of feedback, one reason for such anomalies may be the hothouse atmosphere of a milieu where everyone knows everyone else, knows what everyone else is writing, and is in competition with everyone else for critical attention. This certainly looks like observation altering the phenomenon observed; but it might be expected to apply even more to countries and languages with a shorter or less continuous literary history: Czech, for instance, with fewer speakers than the population of Portugal, has at least half a dozen well-known living writers.[18] But a better match might be Greece, even more macrocephalous and peripheral than Portugal, with a comparable population and degree of underdevelopment and the same uneasy sense of having stockpiled more history than can be consumed locally. Pessoa's Greek counterpart is his contemporary Kavafis; but unlike Pessoa in his solitary eminence, Kavafis coexists with—among other poets—two Nobel laureates.

Is Portugal, then, unable to field a comparable team? It seems more likely that Portugal does not choose to. The failure of the literature to achieve a projection appropriate to the third most widely spoken of all the originally European tongues is a likely cause of its withdrawal into a shell of defensive self-sufficiency; and one cause of that lack of projection may in turn be that, having had an unconvincing canon foisted on them (along with unconvincing reasons for its canonicity), some Portuguese find it hard to take their own literature seriously—or at any rate, with characteristic Portuguese diffidence, to conceive that anyone else could.

This diffidence traditionally grants only History, in Portugal, the honour of not being automatically suspect of provincialism; and is itself due both to the complexities of History and to the historical complexes they give rise to. The voyages and conquests 'emprisèd

---

[17] It is even truer of Pessoa than of Eliot that his 'primacy . . . diminishes the importance both of his contemporaries and of the historical milieu which conditioned the work. . . . criticism [of his work] needs the voice of a heckler' (Vincent Sherry, *TLS* 19–25 Aug. 1988). That Pessoa, a poet of ideas, is relatively easier to translate than Pessanha—a pointilliste painter in sounds, and hence even more untranslatable than most poets—must be granted.

[18] Havel, Holub, Hrabál, Klíma, Kundera, Škvorecký, and the Nobel laureate Seifert—like the Spanish *Generación del 27*—exemplify a synchronic national canon.

by the Portingales' in the fifteenth and sixteenth centuries have so awed and intimidated their descendants (and here, perhaps, Bloom's 'anxiety of influence' might properly be invoked) that they automatically tend to assess all cultural phenomena as historical. Hence the importance attached to the fiction and verse of the historian Herculano, for example; hence too, no doubt, the temptation to view *The Lusiads* almost more as historiography than as poetry.

I began by calling the Portuguese national canon typical. It might rather be thought atypical, in being open to the influence of other national literatures in the same language—but then so are those of England, France, and Spain. It is weak in both drama and, until the late nineteenth century, the novel—but so is Italian, which with English and French makes up the Holy Trinity of the Western canon. As for poetry—Portugal's strongest suit—even French, for the two and a half centuries from Ronsard to Baudelaire, has to make do (as Gide sighed) with 'Victor Hugo ... hélas!'

If the Trinity as model for a canonical élite was at first religious, so was the contrary principle of generous openness: for Pope John VIII, writing in 880, 'qui fecit tres linguas principales, hebraeam scilicet, graecam et latinam, ipse creavit et alias omnes ad laudem ... suam'. Pope John was reassuring a Slav co-religionist that his own language was not uncanonical; and it accordingly became usual in the Slav lands to replace either Latin or Hebrew, in the triad of sacred tongues, by Slavonic;[19] but even so, Russian was one of the last two of the *aliae omnes*, along with German, to become *principales* as literary languages.

Whether Portuguese literature, with eight centuries of existence and modern offshoots in Brazil and five Portuguese-speaking African countries, counts as the most minor of the major literatures or the most *principalis* of the minor ones, is a moot question: from the late twelfth to the early fourteenth century, at least, Portuguese poetry was unrivalled by an Italy still with no Dante or Petrarch, a France with neither Villon nor Ronsard, an England without Chaucer, or a Spain with not one lyric poet whose name has survived. Of the two undoubtedly minor literatures mentioned before, on the other hand,

---

[19] *Apud* Riccardo Picchio, 'Questione della lingua e Slavia cirillometodiana', in *Studi sulla questione della lingua presso gli slavi* (Rome, n.d.), 68 ff. Despite John VIII, 'le posteriori discussioni sulle lingue ... resteranno ancorate al numero tre, simbolo ... di arcana perfezione. L'opposizione vera non sarà contro il principio delle "tre lingue" ma contro l'esclusione ... di una determinata parlata.'

Czech poetry, from the fourteenth to the late nineteenth century, went under ground; and Modern Greek prose—owing to a 'language problem' of a special kind—never got off it till the twentieth. The gaps in the Portuguese canon thus seem in fact to be just what makes it typical; so if the ideal canon, with each successive genre appearing promptly on cue and flourishing happily ever after, is ideal only in a Platonic sense, there is neither any reason for embarrassment at not having achieved it nor any need for makeweights.

Before returning to this point I shall focus down briefly (and self-indulgently, it may seem; but I hope only at first sight) on the nebulous realm of the personal canon, where subjective and sentimental judgements compete—and combine—with objective critical evaluation.

Tolle, lege, Augustine said; and a book is at once the tangible physical object we pick up and the intangible and infinitely repeatable text[20] we read in it (or into it, a post-structuralist would say). At the core of my own canon are five books, each linked to a time, a place, a person, or all three. My first published article,[21] which I wrote in my final year as an undergraduate, was on the *Divine Comedy*, read in the *testo critico della Società Dantesca Italiana*; that *testo* is still on my shelves, and Dante still turns up regularly in more or less everything I write (including, as will be seen, the present book).

The 1562 *princeps* of the works of Gil Vicente, six of the seven extant copies of which I worked with in 1956–8 in the Portuguese archives, the National Libraries of Madrid and Lisbon, the palaces of Mafra and Vila Viçosa, and the Widener at Harvard, is also both a text and an object (or rather, six; but my only memento is a copy of the facsimile). My third text *qua* text is my teacher Dámaso Alonso's anthology of Iberian traditional lyrics (*LTT*), a main source of my inaugural lecture a decade later (and of the first three chapters of this book); but my tattered copy of the standard anthology of Táng dynasty poetry, the *Táng shi sanbǎi shǒu*, printed on cheap paper by the Mass Education Press (Shanghai, 1932), is once again a book in both senses: a going-away present from my other teacher, Arthur Cooper, when I returned to Yale from Bletchley at the end of the war

---

[20] On the vexed question of repeatability see Ch. 7, below.
[21] 'Alcuni parallelismi fra i simboli concreti della *Divina Commedia* e del *Pilgrim's Progress*', *Italica*, 25: 3 (Sept. 1948).

(to unravel a Táng quatrain now, alas, takes me as many hours as it has lines).

Alexander the Great had the *Iliad* carried before him into battle in a jewelled casket; and whenever a Cooper went off to the wars, so Arthur told me, the *Chanson de Roland* was in his kitbag. What had been in mine when I embarked for European shores in 1943 was a less martial text-cum-object: A. F. G. Bell's little *Oxford Book of Portuguese Verse*, which had not long before introduced me to the enchanted world of the medieval *cantigas*, and now brings us back to the national canon I began by proposing to transcend in our outward move towards an ideal *Weltliteratur*.

To transcend is not necessarily to deconstruct. If a private canon so flagrantly based on a mixture of defensible aesthetic criteria and arbitrary sentimental considerations of time, place, and person, is legitimate,[22] a similarly based national one can hardly be less so: the Portuguese too are entitled to their subjective canon, provided its writ is understood to run only on home ground.

Mutatis mutandis, the same applies in a wider context: even if the much (and not unjustly) disparaged Euro-American canon and its various national components were indeed originally devised as ideological props for a ruling class, control over them has long since passed from the Gentlemen to the Players (if that is the word for professional academics), and 'this tricky and rather fashionable subject', as it has been called,[23] now subsists largely in the fossil form of a syllabus. Its very demotion to a mere subject of academic study, however, allows us to consider it in the light of an analogous discipline.

History, at the end of the millennium, moves in simultaneous systole and diastole. As the first quarter of the century saw the breakup of the great land empires, in the last quarter the one-time principalities whose absorption or merger gave rise to the historic

[22] 'Defensible criteria' for the inclusion of Gil Vicente are proposed in Reckert 1977 and below in Chs. 1–4; Iberian traditional lyrics, medieval Portuguese *cantigas*, and Táng quatrains are also among the objects of study in the following chapters. (For Dante presumably no defence is required.)

[23] Kermode 1989: 287; for confirmation of both adjectives see the Prologue, and cf. *Comparative Criticism*, 1 (1979) ('The Literary Canon'), and *CI*, Sept. 1983 ('Canons'), Dec. 1983, Mar. 1984, Summer 1988, and Winter 1990. For a Marxist rejection of The Canon see Terry Eagleton, *The Ideology of the Aesthetic* (Oxford, 1989; rev. Sebastian Gardner, *TLS* 30 Mar.–5 Apr. 1990. Frederick Crews, *NYRB* 27 Oct. 1988, analyses other similarly ideological attacks on 'ideology').

nation-states of Europe have confidently or defiantly reasserted their autonomy. But even as nations turn into confederations, these gravitate towards a broader unity in what ex-President Gorbachev, gazing wistfully over the garden fence, called 'the common European home', whose attraction—as yet understandably weaker in the East, where the last empire has only recently crumbled away—is already felt in the successor states of the Baltic and *Mitteleuropa*, and may just conceivably one day even make itself felt again in the Balkans.

This historical process suggests a potential model for a two-tier literary canon, in which the internal legitimacy of each cultural community would be recognized and guaranteed, but within a wider frame of reference. I have seen castles in Poland and medieval Swedish towns whose names I had never heard (and cannot now remember without looking them up), but which are canonical cultural and historical references—and rightly so—for Poles and Swedes to whom Glencoe or Évora would be as unmemorable as Nidzica or Vadstena to a Scot or a Portuguese. It is a Scots poet, Edwin Morgan, who has said that 'out of respect for itself, a country must collect its resources, and look at its assets and shortcomings with an eye ... both sharp and warm: see what is there, what is not there, what could be there'.[24]

In parallel with History itself, specialists in the academic discipline known by the same name increasingly address both supranational and microcosmic themes: the Mediterranean or Montaillou. The equivalent in literary studies would imply the study of a foreign language from the beginning of school (with another later on for able pupils, so that all school leavers were competent in at least one, and the abler could go on to some of the *aliae omnes*), while at the same time opening the 'English' syllabus fully to other literatures in translation —which in turn would mean according translators incentives comparable to those of such other interpretative artists as actors or musicians.

An impossibly Utopian programme, no doubt. 'Imagine, then, by miracle' (as Empson says) 'what could not possibly be there'; for 'what is conceivable can happen too'.[25] That there is, at least, a new

[24] 'The Resources of Scotland' (1972), in *Crossing the Border* (Manchester, 1990).
[25] Op. cit. (above, n. 13), 32 f.: 'This Last Pain'.

receptiveness to the extra-canonical on its own terms—an openness to the experience of the Other, and of 'other languages'—is now beyond question. In the end it comes down once again to the language problem—but you have to try.

I. LYRA MINIMA

STRUCTURE, STYLE, AND SYMBOL
IN TRADITIONAL VERSE

For Charles Boxer

1

A MINIMALIST POETICS

Εὐθύς οὖν πρώτη ἐστὶ χάρις ἥ ἐκ συντονίας

Demetrius, *Περὶ Ἑρμηνείας*

In der Beschränkung zeigt sich der Meister

Goethe

Small is beautiful

E. F. Schumacher

IT is sobering to reflect that the oldest and westernmost body of lyric poems in any continental European vernacular (for the even older and metrically more sophisticated verse of the Celtic bards belongs to a very different cultural world, insular and Atlantic) is written not in a European script but in Hebrew and Arabic characters, and has an Arabic name. Though the *kharjas*, as they are called, were all transcribed on what is today Spanish soil, the earliest of them date from a time when it was not yet possible to speak of such a thing as a Spanish language. The form of Peninsular Romance they employ is Mozarabic: a *lingua franca* for most Iberian Moslems,[1] both Arab and

---

[1] 'Moslems in Spain were generally bilingual. The conquerors...brought no women..., and the mothers of the first...generations were...slaves from the North...[who] taught their children the mother tongue' (J. B. Trend, *The Earliest Spanish Poetry* (Oxford, 1959), 2). Cf. W. D. Elcock, *The Romance Languages* (London, 1960), 276–7; 427: 'From the first there was produced a mixed stock from... Arabic-speaking males and...Romance-speaking females...Most of the Mozarabic population must...have been bilingual....The frontier of Mozarabic Spain was established...towards the end of the 10th c. along the...Douro. To the north... evolved...Galician-Portuguese.' 'Los dialectos mozárabes desaparecieron conforme los reinos cristianos fueron reconquistando...el Sur....La cuña castellana... quebró la...continuidad de las lenguas peninsulares' (Rafael Lapesa, *Historia de la lengua española* (Madrid, 1980), 191; 194). A modern example of a native language used by colonial rulers 'to buy groceries or give orders to the servants—a "language of the bazaar", as the modern Indian...languages used to be called' (Keene, 34), is Swahili.

Berber (many of whom had had native nursemaids, and all of whom did business with native tradesmen), as well as the everyday speech of their Christian and Jewish subjects; and one which, as it happens, is closer to Portuguese than to Castilian, the former being lexically, syntactically, and morphologically so much the most conservative of the three main Iberian languages that Venus herself (as Camões observed in *The Lusiads*) 'took it for Latin, if a bit corrupt'.

This fortunate paradox highlights the inseparability of the sister literatures of Spain and Portugal from their beginnings in these early lyrics, some of them almost certainly dating from as long ago as the end of the tenth century, to the middle of the eighteenth. As the great Spanish scholar and poet Dámaso Alonso said (1958:29 f.) when they began to be deciphered in the 1940s, the kharjas—especially those transcribed or composed in Hebrew characters—not only are the fountainhead of the traditional lyric, but stand 'al frente de toda la tradición lírica peninsular'.

By 'traditional' I mean either orally transmitted or simply inspired by oral tradition, since attempts at marking the distinction have proved incapable of dispelling the notion that the latter kind is also 'popular' (or trying to pass itself off as such). Hispanists, following Alonso, generally speak of 'poesía *de tipo* tradicional'; for the truth is that in any purportedly traditional lyric text published before the nineteenth century, when the earliest folk-song collections compiled on more or less scientific ethnographical principles appeared, the only strictly traditional part (if any) is likely to be the semi-independent stanza that provides the poem's thematic point of departure, such as the initial refrain or *mote* of a typical Spanish *villancico* (of which more will be said later). Or such as the kharjas themselves.

The most immediately striking feature of these miniature poems, ranging in length from two to six lines and from twelve to thirty-two syllables, is precisely their brevity. By making a diachronic cut through the nine centuries of traditional verse in the Iberian languages to find other poems falling within these same narrow limits and, for the sake of more relevant comparison, treating a single common theme, I shall first try to arrive at a rudimentary 'poetics of the micropoem'. To this end I shall be considering three questions: whether such diminutive lyrics can really work as poems at all; if so, how; and finally, what methods have been devised to make them workable when it was felt they were not.

The first question is in the broad sense critical (that is, evaluative); the second belongs to the more restricted domain of stylistics; the third to that of literary history. For perspective on all three I shall draw freely on similarly minuscule poems in a number of non-Iberian and indeed non-European languages, while concentrating in general on the furthest West and the furthest East: the Iberian and Ibero-American countries on the one hand, and China and Japan on the other. I shall then go on in Chapter 2 to a closer study of the second question, substituting for the initial single theme a pair of related symbols.

WEST TO EAST: *KHARJA* TO *JUÉ JÙ*

To begin, then, it will be convenient to look at a kharja: as it happens, one with the maximum thirty-two syllables.[2] This octo-syllabic quatrain was written (or at least written down) early in the twelfth century by the greatest of medieval Hebrew poets, the Aragonese Yĕhuda ha-Levi, who placed it on the lips of a young woman symbolized in Oriental fashion as a gazelle (the Semitic root *ghzl*, corresponding to *gazelle*, is also common both to the word for 'lover' and to the generic term, in Arabic and Persian poetics, for a love poem: *ghazal*):

> Vai-se meu corachón de mib:
> *ya Rab*, si se me tornarad?
> Tan mal me dóled *li 'l-habīb*;
> enfermo yed: quand sanarad?
>
> Stern, 9

Once the initial hurdle of the Arabic and Hebrew words has been surmounted, this, at least, certainly does seem to work: the best indication that it does is that it cannot be translated, only laboriously paraphrased. The subject of all five verbs, and the leitmotiv of the poem, is *corachón*: 'heart'; but in the first couplet this word—expressed in the first line and understood in the second—represents the tender euphemism *habīb*: 'friend' (as in the Galician-Portuguese *cantigas de amigo* of the next century); and only in the second half of the poem, when the *habīb* has appeared in his own right, does it

---

[2] In view of the differing prosodic conventions of the various languages to be quoted, syllable counts will be on a phonetic rather than a metrical basis.

become literal. The meaning of the poem can thus be no more than approximated:

> My love is going away from me:
> ah God, will he come back?
> So sore aches [my heart] for my friend;
> it is sick: when will it be cured?

The rest of Yĕhuda ha-Levi's poem shows that he himself took this kharja to be a lament by the 'gazelle' for her lover's illness; but another Jewish poet, Todros Abulafia, retranscribing it a century and a half later at the court of the Castilian king Alfonso the Wise in Toledo, added the unequivocal gloss 'my heart is sick, and flies in search of him' (an interpretation which as well as being clearly preferable also makes it appear unlikely that Yĕhuda ha-Levi was the original author). The inherent ambiguity of the poem[3] is incidentally enhanced by the variant reading *meu doler*, 'my grief', for *me dóled* (the Hebrew letters ד = *d*, and ר = *r*, being easily confused). What is very likely the oldest (*c*.1000 CE) of all the extant kharjas, at least of those in Hebrew characters, offers a close analogy:

Tant amare, tant amare,	So much love, so much love;
habīb, tant amare:	*habīb*, so much love:
enfermiron welyos [nid]ioš (?)	eyes that shone (?) have fallen sick
e dolen tan male.	and ache so sore.

Stern, 18

To return to Yĕhuda ha-Levi: the form of his poem, with its reduplicated pattern of statement → question/statement → question, each question arising out of the statement preceding it, underlines the alternation of parallelism with cause and effect in the meaning: while 'Vai-se meu corachón de mib', in the first line, *explains* the heartache in the third, 'when will it be cured?', in the last, is simply another way of formulating the question already asked in the second: 'will he come back?'; and this to-and-fro movement between causal logic and the pure emotion of the parallel questions effectively mirrors the girl's trapped feelings of bewilderment and distress.

---

[3] See Helen Boreland, 'Ambiguity—and Troubadour Influence?—in a Thirteenth-Century *Kharja*', *La Corónica*, 5: 2 (1976–7), 77–84, with relevant bibliography. On ha-Levi's use of kharjas in the common domain see Ángel Sáenz-Badillos, 'Las moaxajas de Yĕhudah ha-Levi', in *Actas del VI Simposio de la Sociedad Española de Literatura General y Comparada* (Granada, 1989), 124.

The same 'gazelle' reappears in more resolute mood in another kharja likewise transcribed by Yĕhuda ha-Levi:

Garid vos, ai yermanellas,	Tell me, oh sisters,
com contenirei meu male?	how shall I contain my grief?
sin *al-habīb* non vivireyu:	Without my friend I cannot live:
advolarei[4] demandare!	I'll fly to seek him!

Stern, 4

If the previous quatrain could be said to have a zigzag shape, this one is in the form of a square. The speaker, after begging her sister gazelles in the first line to answer a question she is about to ask, next puts the question; then explains her reason for asking it; and finally (having now, in Socratic fashion, got it clear in her own mind) herself deduces the answer she had asked for in the first place.

A similar quadratic structure can be found in many later four-line traditional poems, and indeed in earlier ones: at the further end of the Arab empire, where another new literature in the conquerors' alphabet had already begun to take shape even earlier than in the West, theorists of the quatrain known as a *robā'i*, which in due course was to become one of the four classical verse-forms of Persia, maintained that its technical secret lay precisely in knowing how to give the third line a conceptual twist that enabled the fourth to close the square (Bausani, 37), coming out by that same door where in it went.

The robā'i traditionally considered to be the oldest poem in post-conquest Persian, however, works in a rather different way. Its relevance at this point is both thematic and formal:

Ahū-ye kūhī: dar dašt,	A mountain gazelle in the wilderness:
če-gūné davad-ā!	how she runs!
Ū ná-dārad yār: bī yār,	She has no friend: without a friend,
če-gūné bovad-ā?	how shall she live?

Bausani, 308

This quatrain displays the most characteristic method of comparison used by all traditional poetry. I shall call it symbolic equi-

---

[4] The absence of vowel pointing in the Hebrew transcription of *'dbl'ry* makes two other readings possible: *ad ob l'irei* or *adoblarei* ('where shall I go [to seek] him?' or 'I will redouble [my search]'). Decipherment of the kharjas is still far from consensus; the prevailing temper of discussion is suggested by S. G. Armistead's title 'Pet Theories and Paper Tigers: Trouble with the *kharjas*', *La Corónica*, 14 (1985–6), 55–70 (with a bibliography that has been called 'surely a case of overkill'). In those quoted I have tacitly used what seemed the likeliest of the various readings so far proposed.

valence; and the device that embodies it, a symbolic equation. Formally, it consists in hypotactic parallelism of the symbolic and proper terms of comparison; and this inseparability of symbolic content from parallelistic form compels recognition that parallelism itself is by nature as much a comparative as a formal device. Christine Brooke-Rose, in her analysis of the 'grammar of metaphor' (91), was in fact able to treat it simply as a form of comparative imagery, in which the mere juxtaposition of syntactically similar expressions implies their similarity or equivalence in other respects.

The typical quatrain—whether a robāʿi, an Andalusian *seguidilla*, or a Portuguese *quadra*—is particularly suited to the making of two-line statements that appear innocently literal until revealed as symbolic by the remaining two lines, which comprise the proper term of the equation and explain the 'real' meaning of the symbolic one. Except for the asymmetry artfully created in the third line by the poignant aside 'she has no friend', that is roughly what happens in the robāʿi quoted.

But once a symbol is sufficiently familiar—as that of the gazelle is to any reader brought up in the poetic tradition of Islam—it becomes possible to go a step beyond the normal symbolic equation by economically omitting the proper term altogether and stating only the symbolic one. It is this method of simple replacement (as Brooke-Rose calls it), depending for its comprehensibility on a previous acquaintance with the symbol involved, that our robāʿi uses. Both the wilderness itself and the gazelle's frantic coursing (like the to-and-fro movement or the flight to seek the lover, in the kharjas) reflect the girl's anguish at the loss of her friend; but as symbol and reality have become totally fused, we can be touched by her plight without being deprived of our first vivid mental picture of a real gazelle in a real wilderness.[5]

That wilderness, naturally, is Omar Khayyam's (and no one who has seen the parched, salt-crusted stream beds of the Persian *dašt*, with its swirling columns of dust towering into a milk-white sky, will have any difficulty in accepting it as an objective correlative for

---

[5] Seamus Heaney shows how extraneous factors can frustrate such a fusion: as a schoolboy he could not see Eliot's 'three trees on the low sky' (in 'The Journey of the Magi') as an objective correlative because he 'knew its [Christian] correlation . . . but not its artistic objectivity. Those . . . trees were never allowed time to manifest themselves . . . as images of trees before they . . . turned into images of Calvary' ('Learning from Eliot', *Agenda* (Spring 1989), 25).

the wastes of despair). By the time Omar wrote his *Robā'iyāt*, however, Persian metrics, under the influence of Arabic, had become quantitative, and a minimum length of forty-four syllables had placed the robā'i outside our terms of reference.

It would be rash to try to assess how far such parallels as those we have seen represent cases of polygenesis, deriving perhaps from permanent, universal archetypes of human psychology, and how far they are the products of cultural interchanges, begun and kept up over the centuries along routes that time and the desert sands have long since effaced, across the vast but by no means trackless expanses of Central and Western Asia. What is certain, though, is that the robā'i had arisen, together with post-conquest Persian literature itself, in the easternmost domains of the crumbling Abbasid caliphate, where the native Iranian population had for hundreds of years been infiltrated by Turkic tribes.

Frontiers as shifting as the desert sands themselves, and uncouth tribal names—Uighur and Oghuz, Kirghiz and Jagatai, Uzbeks of Tashkent and Azeri of the Caucasus—make it all too easy to forget the essentially homogeneous ethno-linguistic bloc that stretches from the tundra of the Siberian north-east to the oases of Iraq and from western China to eastern Thrace, and was until not long ago peopled in the main by highly mobile nomads. Iranian and Mesopotamian influences dating from palaeolithic times have been found among the Turanian peoples of the steppes:[6] it would be surprising indeed if they had contributed nothing at all in return.

Now Persian verse—except precisely for the early robā'i—was not only quantitative but non-strophic, like its revered model Arabic. But the characteristic form of Turkish poetry, in its oldest texts (and of Turkish folk poetry to this day), is a heptasyllabic quatrain; and it is in fact altogether probable that the earliest form of robā'i, exemplified by the one transcribed above (and which traditionally dates from the seventh century) was inspired by metrical models of Central Asian origin.

The horsemen riding out from Samarkand and Kashgar watered

---

[6] See Eliade 1964: 500; cf. E. G. Pulleyblank, 'Prehistoric East–West Contacts across Eurasia', *Pacific Affairs*, 47: 4 (Winter 1974–5), 500–8. J. S. Major ('Research Priorities in the Study of Ch'u Religion', *HR* 17: 3–4 (Feb.–May 1978), 233 f.), pointing out that 'it is reasonable to suppose that cosmological myths ... could have entered China via the steppe', relates such contacts to the ancient Chinese songs 'incorporating myths ... from those regions'.

their mounts in the Yangtze as well as the Danube; and it has even been suggested (Bausani, 533 ff.) that the great vogue of the *jué jù* or classical Chinese quatrain in the Táng dynasty, beginning precisely in the seventh century, was also due to their influence. Lǐ Tài Bó (otherwise known as Li Po or Li Bai), the recognized master of the jué jù in the following century (and by canonical consensus one of the two greatest Chinese poets of all time, with his friend and contemporary Dù Fǔ) was probably born in what is now Kirghizia or Tadjikistan, and is more than likely to have had Turkish blood in his veins.

By Lǐ Bó's time the traditional Chinese quatrain, which had originally been heptasyllabic like those of the Central Asian nomads, had become pentasyllabic. His own most celebrated jué jù is thus only twenty syllables long; but having lived with it for rather more than twice as many years as it has syllables, I ought to say before offering an attempt at translation that it is not simply, like all poetry, untranslatable: it is something approaching a paradigm of untranslatability. The best I can hope to do is to show how, and why.

Like our other three poems, it is about loneliness for an absent lover; but in its economy of expressive means, and above all in its deliberate and systematic intensification of them, it outstrips anything we have yet seen (or are likely to see). There are critics, Empson observed, 'who merely relieve themselves against the flower of beauty, and those' (among whom he counted himself) 'who afterwards scratch it up'; and another of the latter (Humphrey, 122) has drawn the reasonable inference that since the roots of that flower go deep, 'if we are to expose them undamaged we should start scratching at some distance from the stem'. I shall therefore start scratching at what I hope is a safe distance of about three hundred years from Lǐ's quatrain, by first briefly examining its roots in an earlier one by the fifth-century poet Xiè Tiào:

> Evening [in the] palace; [she] lowers [the] pearl screen.
> Drifting fireflies dart here [and] there.
> Far [into the] night [she] sews silk clothes,
> thinks [of her] lord: when [will] this end?[7]

Here, then, we find a lady (in this case only too literally a lady-in-waiting) of the imperial Court, who in a vain attempt to take her mind

---

[7] Original in Liu 1982: 35 (with modern phonetic transcription), and Lin, 316 f. (with commentary).

off her lover's interminable absence spends her sleepless nights
sewing rich garments for herself or her absent 'lord'. In the light of
the poems we have already seen, what is striking in this one is that
her restlessness is suggested in so much the same way as that of the
gazelles in the robā'i or the kharjas: by kinetic images of to-and-fro
movement, in this case the swift darting of the fireflies in their flight
and the monotonous rise and fall of her needle.

Lǐ himself warmly admired his predecessor of three centuries
earlier, of whose work a notable contemporary poet had exclaimed
with generous enthusiasm 'we haven't seen poetry like this for two
hundred years!' As half a millennium of poetic evolution is thus
directly concentrated in Lǐ's twenty syllables, let us now see what
he made of the earlier poet's certainly very competent if (at least
compared with his own) relatively unremarkable quatrain:

玉階生白露
夜久侵羅襪
卻下水精簾
玲瓏望秋月

Ngyok kǎi srǎng bǎk lo,
ya kyou ts'yěm la mywǎt.
K'yak gha shwi tsyeng lyem,
leng lyong mywang ts'you ngywǎt.[8]

[Her] jade stairs grow white [with] dew;
[in the] night [it] already invades [her] silk stockings.
[She] turns away, lets fall [the] crystal screen,
gazes [through] lattice [at the] autumn moon.

---

[8] *Táng shi sanbái shǒu* (Shanghai, 1932), 6. 1. 56: I transcribe the text according to
Karlgren's conjectural reconstruction of Táng Chinese as modified by Schafer (1967:
267 f.; *mwyǎt, mywang*, and *ngywǎt* are monosyllables). For modern transcriptions see
Cheng 1977: 132 or Liu 1982: 36; for commentaries, Cheng 1977: 97–101; Liu
1982: 35 f.; and Yu 1987: 190 f.

The bracketed words in my versions of these two poems have no equivalents in the originals. The translation of Classical Chinese verbs presents special problems due to the habitual omission of the grammatical subject: 'Qui parle,' asks François Cheng (1977: 98) in an illuminating analysis of this quatrain: 'une "elle" ou un "je"?'

The same question could be asked about Xiè Tiào's poem, in which the *she*s might equally well be *I*s, and [*her*] *lord* simply *you* (which is in fact how both Lin Shuen-fu and James Liu have rendered them in English). But the translator's problem, conversely, is the poet's opportunity: as Cheng remarks elsewhere (1986: 40), the result is often 'a language of two simultaneously present dimensions, one in which the poet describes the external world, and the other in which he evokes his interior world'. Any translator who cannot bring himself to falsify the polysemic nature of the original must opt, like Cheng himself ('nous ne proposons pas de traduction interprétée'), for telegraphese:

> Perron de jade naître rosée blanche
> Tard dans la nuit pénétrer bas de soie
> Cependant baisser store de cristal
> Par transparence regarder lune d'automne.

The contrary option forces the translator to give an arbitrarily univocal interpretation of the poet's calculated ambivalences, as in the version of Tchou Kia-kien and Armand Gaudon:

> Sur le perron de jade se forme une rosée blanche.
> Que la nuit est longue! Elle a la soie de ses bas traversée ...
> À la fin, elle abaisse le rideau de perles de cristal de roche
> Et contemple, par les fentes entre les pierreries, la lune d'automne.

If we look up the first character in the poem, *ngyok* ('jade'), in a Chinese dictionary, we find that it not only has the generic connotation 'whiteness' but is a component of no fewer than half a dozen compound words for 'moon' or 'full moon' and of two others meaning 'dew' and 'autumn dew' (*băk lo*, 'white dew', is itself a meteorological term for the fortnight immediately preceding the autumnal equinox). The second character, 'stair', includes in its lower right-hand corner the fourth, 'white', as a visual 'microsignifier'. By this neologism I mean the submorphemic elements, usually acoustic (tonic or metrical accents, vowel colour, smooth or harsh consonants, etc.), capable of evoking onomatopoeic, synaesthetic, or purely conventional associations with the signified. Their visual equivalents in alphabetic scripts are written accents, diacritics, punctuation, letter shapes, spaces (as in Mallarmé or Apollinaire): in short, whatever can suggest either apparently gratuitous subliminal impressions or vestigial etymologies. In the ideographic Sino-Japanese script, the former obviously belong to the domain of calligraphy (whose artistic and philosophical importance in Eastern culture it would hardly be possible to exaggerate); the latter, on the other hand, correspond to the individual character-components which, though sublexical, are (as Lǐ Bó's text shows) fully morphemic.[9]

In this close-knit web of subliminal visual associations Lǐ Bó has not been content merely to interweave the first two words of his poem with the last two of lines 1 and 3 (respectively 'white dew' and 'autumn moon'): what in fact happens is that those first two words, as well as conveying their primary meanings, constitute nothing less than a syllable-by-syllable anticipation of the entire last line. First, the compound noun *leng-lyong* ('lattice'), with which this line begins, is a disyllabic *Gestalt*-word made up of two independent characters, each meaning in isolation 'precious stone', and including, on its left

[9] The foregoing will rightly be taken as coat-trailing by Sinologists for whom it is axiomatic that Pound and his mentor Fenollosa—in 'The Chinese Written Character as a Medium for Poetry'—were talking pure nonsense (I stress the adjective). For cogent expositions of the orthodox view see Liu 1988: ch. 1, or Hawkes 1988 (for whom the Fenollosa–Pound thesis is 'tommyrot'). Another present-day scholar speaks more demurely of 'what is certainly a peculiar reading of Chinese ideograms', later emending this to 'a powerful and creative misreading' (Zhang 1985: 388; 1989: 214). A celebrated earlier critic, however, writing six years after Fenollosa's essay, and in ignorance of it, stressed the importance of the visual aspects of written Chinese, since 'when we read ... at least half of the impressions we receive are ... visual', whereas European literatures 'lack the ability to present concrete visual images. Our written language can evoke such impressions, and it would be ... sad ... if we did not exploit this potential' (Wen I-to, 'Form in Poetry' (1926), tr. R. Trumbull, in S. C. Soong (ed.), *A Brotherhood in Song* (Hong Kong, 1985), 131). What I am suggesting is not that Lǐ deliberately set out to find as many characters as possible with *jade* or *white* or *moon* cunningly concealed somewhere in them, or that his readers were consciously aware of such elements: they are accidentals, like the unnoticed individual brush-strokes in a painting or the unheard note from the back of the string section, which none the less play their part in the total effect. On the range of intentionality in such 'cryptomorphs', from pure chance in Nature to conscious design in the visual arts, and on their history in theory and practice from Aristotle (via Pliny, Lucretius, Philostratus, Alberti, Leonardo, Mantegna, and various Baroque painters) to Braque, Picasso, and Rohrschach, see H. W. Janson; 'Chance Images', in *A Dictionary of the History of Ideas* (New York, 1973–4), i. 340–53; for a full analysis, Sydney Geist, *Interpreting Cézanne* (Cambridge, Mass., 1989) (cf. Richard Wollheim's review, 'Brushes with Meaning', *TLS* 4–10 Aug. 1989, 839 f., and Geist's reply, *TLS* 29 Sept.–5 Oct. 1989, 1061).

side, the graphic morpheme 'jade' in its abbreviated form: 王 —while
the second character also includes once again, at the bottom centre,
'moon'.

The third character, *mywang* ('look anxiously for' or 'gaze fixedly
at'), is a homograph of still another word for 'full moon', and is
composed of three visual morphemes or microsignifiers: at the upper
left-hand corner, 'absence' (it is a mark of Lǐ Bó's subtlety that his
only explicit reference to the real subject of his poem is an almost
hidden and purely visual hint); on the upper right, for the third time,
'moon'; and at the bottom, 'jade'[10] once again:

GAZE　　　　ABSENCE　　　　MOON　　　　JADE

A shimmering moonlit whiteness floods the poem from beginning
to end: a luminosity that seems in fact to wax along with the character
'moon', which grows in size on each of its three recurrences in the
last line until it becomes autonomous in the final syllable as a full
lexeme:

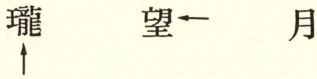

Moreover, every surface and texture, bathed in this same pervading
white light, reflects it in its own characteristic way. 'Lattice', whose
etymology relates it to precious stones, echoes both 'jade' and
'crystal' (the latter itself a disyllabic compound made up of the
individual characters 'water' and 'brilliant') to give a hard glitter that
counterbalances the softness of moonlight on silk and dew.[11]

---

[10] In fact, a false (though not in this case a *Volks-*) etymology. When included in
another character, 'jade' loses the dot on the right that distinguishes it from two similar
ideograms, for one of which it is often improperly used (as here) in the character
'gaze'. Its legitimate occurrence in the two immediately preceding characters (and as
an autonomous word in the *incipit*) may account for its use here. Curiously, the graphic
morpheme 'white', in 'stairs', is the result of an early 'misspelling' of the same kind,
later officially sanctioned by lexicographical authority.

[11] Lǐ Bó's characteristic brittle clarity troubled a fine translator (Robert Payne, *The
White Pony* (London, 1949), 160 f.), to whom he too seemed often to interpose a crystal
screen between himself and the reader. Whiteness is equally typical of the poet, whose
given name comes from his mother's dream of the 'Great White Star' or *Tài Bó Xing*

The jade most prized in ancient China was not green, but a white nephrite found in the White Jade River in far Central Asia, reputedly in places where the riverbed reflected the moon with exceptional brilliance through the clear water. It was itself often said to be crystallized moonlight, and its name was a stock epithet of perfection: 'especially of clear, translucent white, of ultimate purity'.[12]

This association accounts for the frequent appearance of jade in honorific hyperbole: in cold fact the stairs would not have been of jade but of marble, nor the screen of rock crystal but of plain glass beads; to ennoble such materials by hyperbole was to hint in elegantly elliptical language that the stairs and screen were those of the emperor's palace. For a Western counterpart we need only recall, in the sumptuary tropology of the Peninsular *romancero*, the Castle of Rocafrida with its golden battlements and silver walls; or that of Gil Vicente's prince Duardos of Huxonia (*vulgo* Edward, prince of Oxford), likewise made of silver, with its tapestries all of emerald and jacinth and its chambers paved with finest gold from Turkey:

> de esmeraldas y jacintos
> toda la tapecería,
> las cámaras ladrilladas
> d'oro fino de Turquía.[13]

But jade meant also carnal perfection like that of Horace's Glycera, with her 'nitor splendentis Pario marmore purius'; and something of this association clings to the sad imperial concubine, remote and marmoreal behind her screen.

If a tear glistens on her pale cheek for the fickleness of her

---

(Venus) on the eve of his birth (Obata Shigeyoshi, *The Works of Li Po* (Tokyo, 1935; repr. New York, 1965), 9); *bó* (alternatively *bái*) is the modern pronunciation of the early *băk*: 'white'. The 9th-c. poet, painter, calligrapher, and Buddhist monk Guàn Xiu (on whom see below, Ch. 5, n. 32 and corresponding text), himself keenly aware of the spirituality of whiteness—the shamanist colour *par excellence*—found a singular appropriateness in his great predecessor's name (Schafer 1963*b*: 89 f.; 97).

[12] Schafer 1963*a*: 224; 1963*b*: 96. Green jade was for princes, white for the emperor only; its legendary source is recorded in the Táng dynasty Annals (Laufer, 196; 292 n.).

[13] *Don Duardos*, texts A/B, 11. 39–42/41–4 (ed. Reckert 1977: 454 f.). The bilingual playwright and poet Gil Vicente (1465/70?–1536?)—the greatest dramatist of Portugal, and in his day the most important yet to have emerged in post-Classical Europe—was also unrivalled as a lyric poet in Portuguese between King Dinis in the 13th c. and Camões in the 16th, or in Castilian (unless by the Marquess of Santillana) before Garcilaso (1501–36). His masterpiece (to which *The Tempest* is hardly inferior) is the Castilian play *Don Duardos* (1523?).

sovereign's favour,[14] the poet discreetly refrains from calling attention to it. Nor does he need to: the dewdrops on the smooth surface of her jade staircase and the beads of her crystal screen are enough to suggest it, just as her silk stockings wet with the same dew suffice as a fleeting reminder of the classical metonym for sadness in Chinese poetry: silk sleeves wet with tears. Indeed, the word 'stockings' itself (*mywăt*) has the secondary meaning 'silk': a word with which it shares the graphic morpheme 'net' or 'web':

WEB   SILK   STOCKING

Thus 'silk', too, is reduplicated by the same process of impressionistic allusiveness as 'jade', 'white', 'dew', 'moon', and 'autumn'.

Finally, it is impossible to overlook the play of symmetry in the way silk and jade serve as paradigms of soft and hard sumptuousness respectively, or the dew filters through the interstices of the silk just as the moonlight does through those of the screen. François Cheng notes with cryptic delicacy, '*Bas de soie*: corps de femme', and '*Rosée blanche* . . . : nuance érotique', and chooses *pénétrer* as the *mot juste* to express the relation between the two, adding that *store de cristal* means 'intérieur de gynécée'. In fact, a poetic convention dating from the fifth century already identified 'jade stairs' as a standard metaphor for those leading to the private apartments of a court lady; and a covering of dew or frost on the steps would give away the presence or absence of footprints: an image which, as well as being a tacitly narrative element, is no doubt also related to the foot as an erotic object (cf. *JT* 327).

No reasonably mature literary tradition can fail to have accumulated in the course of time a fund of allusions, such as the jade stairs or the gazelle, that belong to the common domain and constitute a highly condensed poetic language: a kind of rhetorical shorthand. What gives Chinese literature as a whole—and Chinese poetry in particular —an unsurpassed capacity for concentration, is the possession of a

---

[14] The promotion of Xiè Tiào's court lady to imperial concubine may have been suggested by the earlier poet's conventional use of 'lord' or 'prince' to mean simply a lover.

script that is not merely ideographic but ideo-*etymographic*, coexisting with a potentially two-way syntax the actual direction of which at any given moment is determined by semantic context. And by a semantics, moreover, with an intrinsic tendency of its own to ambiguity which is perhaps the consequence and perhaps the source (or both, in a cyclical infinite regress) of a tradition—philosophical as well as rhetorical—based on the principle of the *coincidentia oppositorum*.

Thus it is up to the reader to decide whether the voice he hears is that of the poet as observer of the scene, or that of the protagonist herself (a decision, however, that to the Chinese reader would seem not merely unnecessary but in some cases even counterproductive). Similarly, the verb I have translated as 'she turns away' contains a hint of 'she has been turned away'; and underlying the primary meaning 'in the night the dew already invades' are two evanescent but no less literal ones, 'night has long since fallen' and 'darkness at length encroaches' (on her spirit), which are only partly cancelled out when the direct object, 'stockings', appears at the end of the line. The first two meanings imply that she has been waiting for a long time, unmindful of the dampness and the gathering dusk; the third tells us her waiting has been in vain.

Along with her, we have gradually become aware of the bitter parallelism of antithesis, barely hinted at, between past fulfilment and an empty future of absence. The moment when she turns away is the focal point of the poem: the present instant, falling like her screen itself between that past and a future of gazing blankly out[15] while autumn turns to winter and one featureless year merges into the next. And the cold that slowly insinuates itself into her body and her thoughts, along with the darkness—a cold always present but never directly referred to—is signalled indirectly, line by line, in the condensation of the dew, the coming on of night, the drawing of the curtain, and the advance of autumn.

The twenty syllables of Li's micropoem constitute, in short (and 'in short' is surely the way to put it), a structure at once so complex and so compact that it not only defies translation but offers hardly a chink where the scalpel of analysis might penetrate its glittering surface. Once again we can answer our initial question with a clear Yes: the

---

[15] Even here, as Cheng observes, the syntax 'permet une double interprétation: la femme qui regarde la lune et la lune qui éclaire le visage de la femme'.

jué jù works. *How* it works (to come to our second question) is by
the repeated superimposition of one visual or conceptual image on
another, creating an ever greater density of plural meanings.

On metrical evidence as well as that of its name (which means
'truncated verse'), the jué jù form has itself traditionally been supposed to be already the end product of a process of drastic condensation, and not structurally a true quatrain at all but rather half (most
often the second half) of a fissiparous classical octave. This view has
recently been persuasively contested;[16] but in any case, genuine
pentasyllabic folk quatrains, pared down from the heptasyllabic ones
that had already been current there for more than seven hundred
years, are recorded in South China as early as the beginning of the
third century, and conform to a simpler and more familiar pattern:

> My love's like the North Star,
> a thousand years the same;
> yours is like the bright sun:
> East at dawn, West by dusk.

ICL 67

Arthur Waley—along with 'the other Arthur' (Cooper) one of the
finest translators of Chinese the English language has had—once
told me he began his career translating *coplas* in Seville. His eyes
must have opened wide when he first read that fourth-century Chinese
quatrain and remembered this—precisely from Seville, and almost
from yesterday:

> Es tu queré como er toro,   Your love is like a bull:
> qu'adonde lo yaman, ba,   where it's called, it goes;
> y er mío como la piera: and mine is like a stone:
> donde la ponen s'está.   where it's put, it stays.

CPE 3819

Quatrains like these, with their elementary parallelism of contrast,
must be among the most universal of all poetic forms: one has only to
leaf through C. M. Bowra's *Primitive Song*, or the two volumes of
Willard Trask's anthology *The Unwritten Song* (London, 1969), to
find specimens from places as far apart as Greenland, the Philippines,
and Tierra del Fuego. A change to an odd number of lines—for

---

[16] By Lin (among others), whose concise 'revisionist' history of the genre includes
an account of the controversy over its origins; cf. also Wang 1986: 231 f. and n. 20.

example, by reduction of the four-line seguidilla to a tercet, as in the popular *soleá* or 'solitude' of Andalusia—may weaken the parallelistic effect:

> Es tu queré como er viento,
> y er mío como la piera,
> que no tiene movimiento.
>
> CPE 3820

In this next 'solitude', parallelism indeed dissolves completely under the pressure of scorn, as a spirited *sevillana* reacts to the same eternal macho inconstancy with disdainful (even if possibly feigned) indifference:

> A mí se m'importa poco   What's it to me
> qu'er pájaro 'n l'alamea   if a bird in the poplar grove[17]
> se múe d'un arbo a otro.   flits from one tree to another?
>
> CPE 4881

Even the meaning of the symbol itself may be modified: the bird rises to more philosophical heights in a Persian couplet (Bausani, 543) written by the eleventh-century Sufi mystic Abū Saʿīd ibn Abi 'l-Khair on his deathbed:

> The bird that lands on a peak and then takes flight
> adds to it nothing, nothing takes away.

The technique used in these last two examples is once again simple replacement: the bird in the soleá is an unfaithful lover; the one in Abū Saʿīd's couplet is the poet himself, who is modestly taking leave of his fellow mortals while at the same time reminding them of the vanity and transitoriness of Man's life in the world.

But not even total identity of ,form, theme, and technique alike, when all three are so universal and spontaneous, would be enough to justify assuming a common origin, however remote, for poems at

---

[17] To Spaniards, girls we (and the Slavs) would call willowy are like poplars: cf. the young man (*LTT* 96) who tells his mother he has been watching how they sway in the wind: 'De los álamos vengo, madre, / de ver cómo los menea el aire'; a variant has *tálamos* ('bridal beds'), perhaps a printer's Freudian error. The 19th-c. scholar Potebnja (cit. Jakobson 1960: 370) cites analogous examples from Slavonic folk poetry of a girl under a willow tree that is at the same time her image: 'the tree and the girl are both copresent in the same verbal simulacrum of the willow'; cf. Buson's pear-tree haiku quoted below, and n. 37.

once so diminutive and so widely separated in space and time. The really significant common factor in these two poems is rather that both have arrived at condensation of sense through abbreviation of form. Metrically, a Persian couplet is half a classical robā'i, and a soleá the last three lines of a seguidilla, just as the classical jué jù has traditionally and naturally been thought of as the last four of an octave.

NE PLUS ULTRA: TANKA TO HAIKU

Both the octave itself and its presumptive emancipated half were fairly short-lived as verse forms go in China. The laboratory in which minimalist poetics has for the past thirteen centuries been under most thorough and continuous study, for most of that time practically to the exclusion of all other kinds of verse, is Japan.

The norm of Japanese poetry during its first thousand years was the *tanka* or 'short song', a five-line poem of thirty-one syllables: 5—7—5—7—7. Instead of finding this form constricting, as one might have expected, Japanese poets apparently decided after a millennium of putting quarts into pint pots that it would be more of a challenge to try putting them into thimbles, and turned their attention to the haiku—which is merely a 'short song' made even shorter by the lopping off of the last fourteen of its thirty-one syllables. For neither the first nor the last time, the Eastern view seems to have been that the way to perfection is by a process of deletion;[18] and it was only to be expected that the Japanese should have accumulated along this way a larger store of theoretical doctrine and practical experience than any other people.

The problem—far more acute in an agglutinative language such as Japanese than with the monosyllables of Classical Chinese—is how

---

[18] The earliest recorded form of the Sino-Japanese character for 'perfect' or 'auspicious' (Chin. *jí*; Jap. *kitsu*) represented an amphora inverted over a basin, and originally meant 'to empty, drain' (Cooper, forthcoming: no. 393). The Taoist ideal of emptiness has been studied with reference to the arts by François Cheng, who finds it exemplified in painting by the blank space that 'dans certains tableaux des Sung ... occupe jusqu'aux deux tiers de la toile'; in music by silence (cf. Japanese influence on John Cage); and in poetry by parallelism (Cheng 1979: 22). On the latter two see below, n. 35, and Part III: 'The Horizons of Silence'; on painting, Ch. 4, n. 29. The emphasis on 'constraints' by the experimental *Ouvroir de Littérature Potentielle* reflects the East Asian concerns of such *oulipiens* as Jacques Roubaud and Italo Calvino (see below, n. 28).

to offset lack of volume by a correspondingly greater density. Not all the methods and devices adopted by tanka and haiku poets to this end are peculiarly or even originally Japanese; but it was unquestionably in Japan that they were codified with greatest rigour and nicety of distinction and used with fullest awareness. They range from the simplest of simple replacement, as with the bird in the soleá or the Persian couplet, to the most complex kind of superimposition, as in Li Bó's 'Jade Stairs'.

Symbolic equivalence, especially when accompanied by simple replacement, is a favourite resource of the haiku. The narrow compass of three lines and seventeen syllables leaves no room for simile: imagery, if it is to be used at all, has to keep its literal meaning at the same time as it expresses a figurative one. This is hardly less true of the tanka: the oldest and greatest of all tanka anthologies, the monumental eighth-century 'Book of Ten Thousand Leaves' or *Man'yōshū*, anticipates William Carlos Williams's 'no ideas but in things' by describing some of its poems as 'meditating on ideas by referring to things'.

A poetic vocabulary in which most substantives name phenomena perceptible by the senses, and hence readily convertible into symbols, gives the noun a special connotative potential. In Japanese even place-names, for example, are so concrete as to yield imagery of a natural suggestive power and with a frequency unknown in the West (cf. *JCP* 6), which can hardly find any use for them beyond such self-consciously bookish allusions as those to 'Pasárgada' in Brazilian poetry since Manuel Bandeira[19]—though Brazil also provides two of the three exceptions that occur to me: Carlos Drummond's *Brejo das Almas*, João Cabral's *Pedra do Sono*, and *Ilha do Desterro*, by the Portuguese poet Pinheiro Torres (respectively 'Souls' Heath', 'Sleepstone', and 'Isle of Exile': the first two the names of towns in the states of Minas Gerais and Pernambuco, and the last—in which *ilha* is the Roman *insula* or tenement block—the fishermen's quarter in a northern Portuguese town).

In this way the individual words of the poem, independent of their syntactical function, acquire an expanded and extraordinarily effective

---

[19] Cyrus the Great's capital, as an equivalent of Shangri-La or the 'là-bas' of 'L'invitation au voyage', has become a standard allusion in Portuguese since it was used by the 'John the Baptist of Brazilian Modernism'. For a bilingual selection of Bandeira's work see *This Earth, That Sky*, ed. and tr. Candace Slater (Berkeley, Calif., 1990).

and economical *semantic* functionality, denotative and connotative at the same time, and the poem itself gains extra density and depth. Nor is this the only way: such words, once used, may in the course of time develop into traditional and freely transferable symbols, like 'gazelle' in the Islamic tradition; or take on special qualities of tone and atmosphere—like the archaic stock epithets *velida* and *louçana* ('fair', 'comely') in Portuguese—which are then communicated automatically to any new poem in which they appear. This is precisely the function of the celebrated *makura kotoba* or 'pillow word' in Japanese poetic diction.

A typical Japanese device that does not fit into any recognized Western rhetorical category, on the other hand, is the *kake kotoba*— the 'pivot word'—which began to replace parallelism at about the beginning of the ninth century as a conspicuous stylistic element in Japanese poetry (*JCP* 215). Neither quite a zeugma nor quite a pun (for Japanese naturally possesses both of these) the pivot is rather a word or phrase with two different but equally intended meanings depending on how it is parsed. The effect is to allow the poet, by a kind of telescoping or overlapping of syntax, to save as many syllables as there are in the pivot, thus creating a syntactical equivalent of the superimposition of images we found in Lǐ Bó. Yĕhuda ha-Levi's use of the single word *corachón* as the simultaneous subject of two different verbs, with the metaphorical meaning 'lover' in the first two lines of his kharja and the literal one, 'heart', in the last two, is the only comparable thing we have yet seen; but in a Japanese poem both meanings of the pivot word would be perfectly literal.

The ambivalence of the *kake kotoba* is as effective a way as symbolism of packing meanings into a verbally and metaphorically stripped-down form, but has the further advantage that it applies not only to vocabulary but even more to syntax. This can be still more radically compressed by the elimination of logical connections and reliance on the reader's skill in intuitively following the train not so much of thought as of feeling. In Japanese this process was to make the haiku the ideal vehicle for Zen Buddhism, with its flashes of transrational enlightenment or *satori*, analogous to the *zarb* or 'impact' of the Sufis (here, perhaps, rather than in the poetry of Táng China, might be the place to look for Central Asian influence).

The symbolic equation is of course no more than a special application of the same technique, though in the haiku and tanka, with their three and five lines respectively, the equation is almost always asymmetrical.[20] Here is how the second of the recognized masters of the haiku, Buson (1715–83), uses it:

Nashi no hana.	Pear blossom.
tsuki ni fumi yomu	In the moonlight, reading a letter,
onna nari.	there is a woman.

Hk ii. 323

On one level, the scene is of a woman reading a letter by moonlight under a pear tree in bloom. On another level, the pear tree (like the willow in the Slavonic poems mentioned above in n. 17) *is* the *jeune fille en fleurs* herself. Both levels are intended.

More than four centuries before Buson and the great vogue of haiku, the tanka poets, rather than making use of the moon to create effects of distance and vastness, were already deliberately reducing its scope, filtering its rays through the foliage of trees or refracting them on dewdrops (*JCP* 383; 398) until, as in Lorca's ballad, the night became 'íntima como una pequeña plaza'. Buson himself, as heir not only to almost five hundred years of traditional Japanese poetic imagery but to a Chinese thematic motif at least twice as old, has recaptured all the pale glimmer of Lǐ Bó's jade staircase, but with only a third as many words, and none of the brittleness. Now every surface and texture—the pear blossom, the woman's petal skin, the filmy dress or *usumono* which, like another woman he tells of elsewhere, she must surely be wearing;[21] even the rice-paper of her letter—everything the moonlight touches is soft.

The fact that we need not ask who sent the letter, or whether he will ever come, illustrates yet another way of economizing on syllables: the integration of a poem in an extrinsic context. By the early thirteenth century a single loaded word such as 'moonlight' or 'waiting' was already enough to establish that a tanka was concerned with a love affair, and to pinpoint exactly the stage of the *cursus amoris*

---

[20] Active distaste for symmetry and regularity (including parallelism) as embarrassingly obtrusive and unsubtle is held by a Western authority (Keene, 10–13) to be one of the permanent bases of Japanese aesthetics.

[21] *Hk* i. 340. To be as indiscreetly precise as the poet himself, the other is no longer wearing it: '[Thrown] over the gold screen, / whose silk gauze dress? / (The autumn wind . . .)'. The character for 'silk gauze' (the same used by Xiè Tiào and Lǐ Bó) was *de rigueur* whenever a Chinese poem referred to feminine clothing, as in the 6th-c. Xiao Lín's more overtly erotic jué jù (*JT* 293) about an ardent young woman's half-open underskirt of shimmering white and gold silk gauze (for this topos see below, n. 44 and text).

it had reached. Such depth and intensity as a tanka might possess
ultimately depended, of course—like those of any other poem—on
its own inner resources; the external context provided by a pre-
existing poetic canon, on the other hand, gave it a virtual breadth that
transcended its reduced physical dimensions.[22]

The ultimate refinement of this form of intertextuality, involving
the superimposition not of images but of themes, is the technique of
hon-kadori or allusive variation (*JCP* 506), defined as the echoing of
the words or situations of a well-known earlier work in such a way
that they are incorporated into a new meaning, but one in which
that of the original poem is also still present and recognizable. An
example is this twelfth-century tanka by Fujiwara Teika:

Samushiro ya	As bedding,	1
matsu yo no aki no	when autumn winds grow late	3
kaze fukete	in the waiting night,	2
tsuki o katashiku	the lady of Uji Bridge	5
Uji no hashihime.	spreads out moonlight.	4

JCP 454

The point here is not so much the almost surrealistic transpositions—the spreading out of moonlight instead of more conventional bedclothes; the fact that it is the night that waits rather than
the lady, or the wind and not the night that grows late (the reader is
momentarily thrown still further off balance by *fukete*—'grow late'—
because the expected word, 'blow', would be *fukite*[23]): more significant even than these transpositions is what makes them possible.
Teika, the historians of court poetry point out, is standing on the
shoulders not just of one but of two predecessors: he alludes
simultaneously to an anonymous ninth-century poem from the Court
song-book *Kokinshū* in which the legendary lady of Uji's lover fondly
imagines her spreading out her cloak as she waits for his visit, and
also to the final chapters of the supreme masterpiece of Japanese
prose, Lady Murasaki's early eleventh-century novel *Genji Monogatari*,

---

[22] *JCP* 393; 403. For a unique 'experiment in semantic concentration'—a one- or
two-line Somali poem which a traditional tendency to cryptic symbolism enabled to
flourish *c.*1944–55, but which proved too short to survive the loss of its extrinsic
context—see B. W. Andrzejewski, 'The Art of the Miniature in Somali Poetry', *African
Language Review* (1967), and cf. Ruth Finnegan, *Oral Poetry* (Cambridge, 1977), index,
s.v. *balwo*.

[23] I am glad to see this observation of mine (Reckert 1970: 52) adopted by Prof.
Miner (1990: 91), to whose earlier work I owe my introduction to the poem.

which take place in the region of Uji and are pervaded by a mysterious diffuse melancholy (the very name Uji, a typical example of the concretely meaningful Japanese toponym, means 'sadness') and interspersed with allusions to the famous bridge and the old poem.[24] The later of Teika's two models suggests an appropriate mood and atmosphere, which he is able to heighten by providing it with a specific justification (this lady, we know, will wait in vain); his earlier one relieves him of the necessity for a straightforward presentation of the details, allowing him to describe them in terms of impressionistic synaesthesia.

Since contemporary poetic theory in the Golden Age of tanka required its practitioners to treat a precise and narrowly delimited topic (*dai*), striving by sheer concentration of attention to capture its ultimate essence, the little bit of extra room for manœuvre gained by exploiting a pre-existent context could be of disproportionate value. It is instructive to see what Teika has made of this opportunity to accumulate meanings while saving syllables.

His *dai*, we are told, is not, as one might think, the lady but 'autumn moon'. What has apparently escaped notice, however, is that in order to distil the essence of this topic he has resorted not only to allusive variation but to another rhetorical device, which so far as I know does not belong to the recognized repertoire. That we are ourselves in a position to notice it is directly due to our having so recently devoted so much attention to Lǐ Bó's cold white quatrain of the jade stairs.

While the literal meaning of Teika's first line is simply 'bedding' (with the exclamatory particle *ya* to convey surprise at its nature), we can be almost sure that his choice of the particular word *samushiro* instead of the more obvious *mushiro*, or a synonym such as *ina-mushiro* (either one of which could without difficulty have been worked into the metre) is a motivated and perhaps even a consciously motivated one; for the roots *samu* and *shiro*—etymologically unrelated

---

[24] Cf. *Genji*, 6 ('The Bridge of Dreams'), chs. 11–13, esp. 1015 f.: 'He took her to the window to watch the new moon rise. . . . The bridge lay shimmering in the mist, looking a long way off. . . . "A strange, a haunting place—this Uji", [he] thought. . . . What lines were those [he] was murmuring to himself . . . ?: "Tonight too, her cloak half-spread upon her mat, will she be waiting for me, the maiden of Uji Bridge?"' An even older poem from the 8th-c. *Man'yōshū* sounds like an echo of Sappho's 'The moon has set, / and the Pleiades: mid-/ night, and time is passing, / but I lie alone'; cf. *MYS* 950: 'While with my sleeve / I brush my bed, / and sit up / waiting for you, / the moon has set.'

to *sa-mushiro*—mean respectively 'cold' and 'white'. The first word of this tanka, like that of the Chinese quatrain four centuries earlier, foreshadows and reinforces by a kind of subliminal punning both the unexpressed but implicit whiteness of the moon and the no less implicit chill in the air, deducible from the lateness of the hour and the autumn season (again as in Lǐ Bó); from the wind; and from the lady's finding no warmer covering than the moonlight.

SYSTOLE AND DIASTOLE

By the time the Portuguese troubadour-king Dinis—born exactly a century after Teika—began his forty-six years on the throne in 1279, the poets of Japan, in pursuit of a poetic ideal they expressed as 'coolness and slenderness', had already been probing the frontiers of emotional knowledge for a century or more with a microscope that had only to go on narrowing its focus and increasing its magnification until the scene and the action of a poem were as austerely compressed in space and time as the poem itself was in length.

We order these matters differently in the West, and always have done, even when the civilized West consisted mainly of Moslem Iberia. As early as the eleventh century, when the courtly lovers in the *Tale of Genji* were flirtatiously exchanging amorous tankas,[25] and the earliest extant kharjas were written down, there was already a feeling in Al-Andalus that these were altogether too cool and slender to stand on their own. It was not so much a question, as I put it at first, of finding a way to make them work: it was rather that the better they did work—the more piercingly beautiful they were[26]—the more urgently they seemed to demand both expansion and interpretation. These single stanzas of from two to six lines and twelve to thirty-two syllables—poems that seem to be over almost before they have begun—were thought of as precious stones requiring a setting, as much, perhaps, to display as to preserve them.

In later centuries an analogous feeling is detectable in such ele-

---

[25] Brower and Miner (*JCP* 225) understandably wonder 'what a Western reviewer would make of a psychological novel with a third as many lines of verse as *Paradise Lost*'.

[26] 'Piercing' is indeed the word as much for them as for their remote descendants, the haunting *saetas* or 'arrows' still fired off from the balconies of Seville as the Holy Week procession passes, which prompted Lorca (GL 181) to say 'Sevilla es una torre / llena de arqueros finos'.

mentary methods of expansion as the prolonged *¡ayyyyy!* and the fioritura on final syllables in *cante jondo*[27] and Lisbon *fado*, or the three extra lines that turn a plain seguidilla into a *seguidilla sevillana*:

Desde que te ausentastes,	Since you have gone away,
sol de los soles,	my sun of suns,
ni los pájaros cantan,	birds do not sing
ni el río corre.	nor does the river flow.
¡Ay, amor mío!	Alas, my love!
Ni los pájaros cantan,	birds do not sing,
ni corre el río.	the river flows no more.

Brenan, 366

The linking together of two or more seguidillas, another frequent means to the same end, has a parallel in Portugal in sequences of linked quatrains in which the last line of one is repeated as the first line of the next.[28] But the exceptional value the poets of Al-Andalus attached to the kharjas is evident from the much more complicated kind of setting they devised for them: a relatively long and elaborately rhetorical panegyric or love poem in Hebrew or Classical Arabic known as a *muwaššaḥa*, the last stanza of which had to be manœuvred into forming a transition, often obviously and even deliberately forced, between the erudite poem and the appended popular or pseudo-popular kharja. The shock effect is all the more powerful for being both delayed and unexpected: the incense of Oriental praise and the indoor perfume of Oriental eroticism evaporate as the little window is thrown open at the end of the poem to let in the fresh air, and suddenly 'the thyme on the hillsides gives off its every scent'.[29]

[27] A feature of the Gypsy *siguiriya* or *playera* well enough known a century and a half ago to provoke irony at the expense of a *cantaora* who 'would launch out on a weary *¡ay!* that lasted a quarter of an hour' ('por un cuarto de hora lanzaba un ¡ay! con fatiga': *Actas de la Reunión Internacional de Estudios sobre los Orígenes del Flamenco, 1969* (Madrid, 1970), 22). The two constants of *cante*, according to a specialist (Luque Navas, ibid. 54), are precisely 'el melisma y el quejío' ('the *moan*').

[28] Similar 'linked verses' or *lién jù* exist in China (and in Japan as *renga, rengu*, or *renku*, the last two written with the same characters as *lién jù, jù* being the *-ku* of *haiku*). For China see Owen 1975: ch. 7, and Lin, 299 f.; for the much more evolved Japanese forms, Miner 1979: *passim*. The peculiarity of renga, anticipating the Surrealist *cadavre exquis*, is that each poem is normally by a different poet. The form was introduced to the West in the quadrilingual *Renga* (Paris, 1971) of Octavio Paz, Jacques Roubaud, Edoardo Sanguineti, and Charles Tomlinson. Like renga, haiku is known in the West by a confusing (and confused) trio of names, *hokku* being the usual form until the last century, and *haikai* now properly a humorous poem in haiku form.

[29] 'El tomillo por los montes / huele de dos mil maneras' (Gil Vicente, *Os Quatro Tempos, Cop* 17c).

Stylistically refined and classical in language though they were, the form of these poems that served as settings for the kharjas was neither Classical Arabic, nor even Arabic at all, but indigenous: as we know, Arabic poetry everywhere outside the Iberian Peninsula was almost exclusively non-strophic. When the *muwaššaḥa* ceased to be written at about the beginning of the fourteenth century, the form itself went underground for more than a hundred years, only surfacing again in the song-books of the Court *vihuela* composers as one among the proliferating varieties of the general European virelay, rondeau, or carol.

In Spain such songs were and still are loosely called *villancicos*, though this word properly applies rather to the *cabeza* or *mote*: the traditional-style couplet, tercet, or quatrain which is their real *raison d'être* and for which they serve as a framework or support. By the time they were taken up by the Court lutenists they had already evolved a wide spectrum of mutant forms; but one feature common to all these is that instead of sidling up to the point and then abruptly whipping aside a curtain to reveal it, as happens in the kharja, the villancico sets down its theme (or *dai*, as the Japanese would call it) squarely at the beginning and devotes the remaining stanzas (the *glosa*) to commenting and elaborating on it, explaining its symbolism if any, and restating or repeating it wholly or in part.

It would be easy to ascribe this difference to plain-spoken Castilian forthrightness as opposed to the devious subtlety of the East, typified by the shock tactics of Zen *satori* or Sufi *zarb*. The real reason is probably the simpler one that music was continuing to assert its primal ascendancy over poetry: that of the sung word over the spoken. Certainly no one would be likely to regard the true Lisbon *fado* as a typical example of Castilian bluntness (or anything else Castilian); but for all the apparent Orientalism or Africanism of its plangent vibrati, it is constructed on much the same pattern as a villancico, with a theme stanza in quatrain form developed by six or more lines expanding on this nucleus.

In any case, the villancico itself, far from being a monopoly of Castile, was no less popular in Portugal under the name of *vilancete*. Gil Vicente himself used one in 1532 to treat the same theme as our first twelfth-century kharja, 'Vai-se meu corachón de mib'; the thematic nucleus or *mote*, either taken from oral tradition or composed in imitation of traditional style, is

Vanse mis amores, madre,	My love is going away, mother,
luengas tierras van morar;	to dwell in far-off lands;
yo no los puedo olvidar.	I cannot forget him.
¿Quién me los hará tornar?	Who will bring him back to me?
¿Quién me los hará tornar?	Who will bring him back to me?

Though written in Castilian, this villancico is from a play called the *Farce of Lusitania*;[30] and in mood, with its mysterious far islands and prophetic dreams, it is numinously Portuguese. The master stroke, reminiscent of the double question ('si se me tornarad?'; 'quand sanarad?') of the gazelle in the kharja, is undoubtedly the repetition of the last line of the theme stanza. Vicente's poem continues:

Yo soñara, madre, un sueño	I dreamt a dream, mother,
que me dio en el coraçón:	that struck me to the heart:
que se yvan los mis amores	that my love was going away
a las islas de la mar.	to the islands of the sea.
Yo no los puedo olvidar.	I cannot forget him.
¿Quién me los hará tornar?	Who will bring him back to me?
¿Quién me los hará tornar?	Who will bring him back to me?
Yo soñara, madre, un sueño	I dreamt a dream, mother,
que me dio en el coraçón:	that struck mc to the heart:
que se yvan los mis amores	that my love was going away
a las tierras d'Aragón.	to the land of Aragon.
Allá se van a morar:	It is there he goes to dwell:
yo no los puedo olvidar.	I cannot forget him.
¿Quién me los hará tornar?	Who will bring him back to me?
¿Quién me los hará tornar?	Who will bring him back to me?

Cop 245ᵛ

Vicente's full development of this theme might be compared with the following even more mysterious five-line gloss by an anonymous Spanish contemporary on a two-line theme which, as is evident from a vilancete by the Portuguese poet Andrade Caminha based on the head-stanza 'Não podem dormir meus olhos, / não podem dormir' (Torner, 349), was also current in Portugal at the same time:

---

[30] Those of Vicente's later plays (including the *Lusitania*) classified by his son and incompetent posthumous editor as 'farces' are in fact indistinguishable from his romantic allegorical comedies; the pretentious designation of some of his other comedies as 'tragicomedias' very likely derives from the same source.

No pueden dormir mis ojos,   My eyes cannot sleep,
no pueden dormir.   they cannot sleep.

Y soñara yo, mi madre,   And I dreamt, mother,
dos horas antes del día,   two hours before daybreak,
que me floreçía la rosa: that the rose bloomed for me:
ell vino so ell agua frida: wine under cold water:
no pueden dormir.   they cannot sleep.

Alín, 83

The symbolism of rose, wine,[31] and water is partly elucidated by the strange and beautiful thirteenth-century 'Razón de amor' (see Ch. 2, n. 25), and the sixteenth-century Castilian poet Antonio de Villegas explains away the paradox of insomnia alternating with Freudian dreams, reasonably enough, as a matter of fitful dozing between reveries of love:

La niña, que amor había,

.   .   .   .   .

con su amigo se soñaba:
soñaba, mas no dormía;
que la dama enamorada

.   .   .   .   .

no duerme, si amores sueña.

Torner, 349

Or as a tercet recorded in Galicia a few years ago affirms, calling the morning star as witness, no one in love can ever sleep through till dawn:

Estreliña do luceiro,
quen ten amores non durme
sinón o sono primeiro.

Torner, 347

---

[31] The MS seems to read *yino* (which is meaningless), or possibly *pino*. Despite ingenious attempts to make sense of these readings, the analogy with the 'Razón de amor' favours *vino*. Frenk (302) proposes *lyino* as Aragonese for *lino* ('linen'), pointing out that *ell* is only found before vowels; but the graphic distinction *v/u* was erratic, and the *v* of *vino* might have qualified orthographically as a vowel. John Gornall (*La Corónica*, 16 (1987–8)) examines the alternatives *pino/vino* and finds tentatively for the latter.

Just as folk-song in Portugal means above all the quatrain, in Galicia, Portugal's sister land to the north—'held in the long embrace of the same sea'[32]—it means the tercet. Ayras Núñez, a remarkable poet and a priest 'in Galice at Seint Jame' a century before the Wife of Bath made her pilgrimage there, managed to cram five of them into a single four-stanza *pastorela* by the ingenious method of inventing a narrative about a tearful shepherdess who, after singing three tercets in succession, ends with a pair of linked ones that reproduce the same scheme in miniature: the narrator, that is to say, hears the shepherdess sing a fourth tercet about another sleepless lovelorn maiden, who in turn is singing a fifth one about herself:

Oý og' eu ũa pastor cantar,
du cavalgava per ũa ribeyra;
e a pastor estava senlheyra;
e ascondi-me pola ascuytar;
e dizia muy ben este cantar:

'So-lo ramo verde frolido
vodas fazen a meu amigo:
choran olhos d'amor.'

E a pastor pareçia muy ben,
e chorava, e estava cantando;
e eu muy passo fuy-mh' achegando
pola oyr, e sol non faley ren;
e dizia este cantar muy ben:

'Ay estorninho do avelanedo,
cantades vós, e moyr' eu e pen',
e d'amores ey mal.'

E eu oý-a sospirar enton,
e queyxava-se estando con amores,
e fazia guirlanda de flores.
Des ý chorava muy de coraçon,
e dizia este cantar enton:

'Que coita ey tan grande de sofrer:
amar amig', e non ousar veer!
e pousarey so-lo avelanal.'

---

[32] 'Galiza, terra irmã de Portugal, / que o mesmo Oceano abraça longamente' (T. de Pascoaes, *Marânus* (2nd edn., Oporto, 1920)).

Poys que a guirlanda fez a pastor,
foy-se cantand', indo-s'én manselinho;
e torney-m' eu logo a meu camynho,
ca de a nojar non ouve sabor.
E dizia este cantar ben a pastor:

> 'Pela ribeyra do ryo
> cantando ýa la virgo
> d'amor:

>> "Quen amores a,
>> como dormirá?
>> Ay, bela frol!" '[33]

Today I heard a singing shepherdess
as I was riding by a riverbank;
and since this shepherdess was quite alone,
I hid myself that I might hear her sing.
This was the song that she most sweetly sang:

> 'Under the flowering greenwood tree
> my friend is wed today:
> eyes weep for love.'

The shepherdess was fair of countenance,
and she was weeping all the while she sang;
so I, as softly as I could, drew near
to hear her sing, but did not say a word;
and she most sweetly sang this second song:

> 'Starling in the hazel tree,
> you sing, I die of pain
> from pangs of love.'

And then I heard her sigh all grievously;
and she made moan as she was deep in love,
and set about to weave a wreath of flowers.
Anon she wept again with all her heart;
and the next song that she did sing was this:

> 'How great a pain it is I have to bear:
> to love my friend, and not dare see him more!
> I will lie down under the hazel tree.'

---

[33] *CBN* 868 ff./*CV* fo. 72ᵛ. I adopt J. J. Nunes's emendation of *CBN dormoiay / CV dormoray* in the last two lines. Variants of the 4th tercet appear in *CBN* 1155, Vicente's *Four Seasons* play, and a Spanish *vihuela* song; of the 3rd, in *CBN* 644: cf. Ch. 2, n. 30 (on the 5th see immediately below).

> After the shepherdess had made her wreath,
> still singing, she stole quietly away;
> while I, having no wish to trouble her,
> returned again to my own way as well;
> and sweetly the shepherdess then sang this song:
>> 'Along the riverbank
>> singing the maiden went
>> a song of love:
>>> "Whoever loves,
>>> how shall she sleep?
>>> Alas, fair flower!" '

This Chinese-box effect of poem-within-poem-within-poem is surely the most resourceful of the merely mechanical ways of setting a lyric nucleus. In the less elaborate form Eugenio Asensio has called a 'cantiga de cantigas'—a miniature anthology of borrowed theme-stanzas set in a lyric-narrative matrix—it was not only to become the vogue among later Portuguese and Galician troubadours but to produce two small masterpieces of Iberian poetry: the garden scene in Gil Vicente's romantic comedy *Don Duardos*, and the so-called 'villancico to his three daughters' sometimes attributed to the fifteenth-century Marquess of Santillana, which even brings in a Castilian variant of Núñez's final tercet:

> La niña que amores ha,
> sola, ¿cómo dormirá?[34]

But the Portuguese and Galician troubadours had another card in reserve, and one that was to be even more significant in the long run for the future evolution of Iberian poetry. Instead of a more or less mechanically constructed setting, as in the *muwaššaḥa* or the villancico, they hit on a formula that made possible an organic development of the theme.

Their way of doing this was to take one of the oldest and most universal devices of folk poetry—parallelism—and by exploiting its expressive potentialities with a thoroughness and a sensitivity no other poetic tradition (not even that of China, where for some

---

[34] *LTT* 333; the alternative attribution to Santillana's obscure contemporary Suero de Ribera is now generally accepted. The topos itself is at least as old as Sappho, and also occurs, as we saw above (n. 24) in Japan. For examples from all parts of the Iberian Peninsula see *LTT* 502 and Torner, 108; 347–51. Asensio's 'cantiga de cantigas' (69) corresponds to the 'canzone a citazioni' of Petrarchan tradition.

hundreds of years it was actually obligatory in certain poetic genres) has ever felt it deserved,[35] to make of it a means of expansion comparable in subtlety to the condensation that in China and Japan had only been achieved after centuries of a mature and sophisticated literary culture (and in Japan, at least, of almost exclusive attention to a single verse form, the tanka).

The first three tercets set into Ayras Núnez's poem link our universal theme with this peculiarly Galician and Portuguese treatment of it. All three, moreover, associate *chagrin d'amour* not with moonlight or insomnia but with trees, which indeed—whether as mute confidantes in unhappiness, as symbols of it, or as an impassive and ironically beautiful background to it—are a no less widely accepted referent or objective correlative for unrequited love.

To discover the sources of this instinctive association one would probably need to dig far down into the subconscious, if Borges was right in saying that the three truly mysterious things in the world are woman, the sea, and trees—all, as it happens, conspicuously present in the *cantigas de amigo* of medieval north-western Iberia.[36] In any case it comes as no great surprise to find that Ayras Núnez's thirteenth-century Galician shepherdess, weeping 'so-lo ramo verde frolido', is sister under the skin to the Lady Heguri who, five hundred years earlier at the Court of Nara, wrote this:

Matsu no hana,	Pine-blossom
hanakazu ni shimo	(though among so many other blooms
waga seko ga	you may not notice it)

---

[35] Cheng (1977: ch. 1 and *passim*) relates it to ellipsis of *mots vides*, such as particles and auxiliaries (or their substitution for 'full' words), as a way of seeking 'emptiness' (see above, n. 18); Arthur Cooper clarifies the relation: parallelism is basic to Chinese, which 'lacks the Indo-European device of *nexus*; in place of *syntaxis* it has *parataxis*: ideas are juxtaposed with ideas, not drawn along by them. Nouns stand for generalized concepts; verbs are active, passive, causative, past, present, or future, without distinction; and the most admired style avoids the need for distinction and favours the laconic over the extensive' (personal communication); cf. the discussion of Lǐ Bó's 'Jade Stairs', above. On the relevance of parallelism to Chinese concepts of time see Chang (1986a: 109 ff., 123 f.; 1986b: 64–9); on its role in ancient Chinese divination, cosmology, mathematics, and dualistic philosophy, as well as poetry: *Extrême-Orient–Extrême-Occident*, cahier 11 (1989). For its use in other poetic traditions cf. Asensio, ch. 3; Bowra, *passim*; Jakobson 1973: *passim*; Reckert 1980: 12 f.

[36] The interrelation (see below, Ch. 5) of the Magna Mater, the Tree of Life (both avatars of the *axis mundi*), and water (the primordial symbol of life and fertility), justifies Borges's *obiter dictum*.

| omoeranaku ni, | is flowering now— |
| moto na sakitsutsu. | in vain. |

MYS 353

With a little hindsight we can now recognize in the lady of Nara's poem the same motif which, a millennium later, was to surface again in her compatriot Buson's haiku about the woman under a pear tree. In the following popular quadra, heard in the Estrela mountains of Portugal in 1967, it is equally unmistakable:

Encostei-me ao pinho verde	I leant against the green pine tree
por ver se me consolava;	to see if 'twould console me;
o pinho, como era verde,	and the pine tree, being green,
ao ver-me chorar, chorava.	wept to see me weeping.

Between these chronological extremes, examples multiply. The musicologist Torner (83 ff.) quotes Portuguese, Galician, Castilian, and South American variants of the same quadra; Asensio (39 f.) adds a Castilian *incipit*, 'Ay pino, pino, pino florido', and cites, besides Ayras Núnez's cantiga, others by Pero Gonçálvez Portocarreiro and King Dinis. It was in fact the king, Núnez's considerably younger contemporary, who first thought of spinning the motif out in parallelistic form, starting from the basic tercet

> Ay flores, ay flores do verde pyno,
> se sabedes novas do meu amigo,
> aquel que mentiu do que pos commigo?

and adding the obsessive refrain 'Ay Deos, e u é?' before proceeding to expand it:

> Ay flores, ay flores do verde pyno,
> se sabedes novas do meu amigo?
>   Ay Deos, e u é?
> Ay flores, ay flores do verde ramo,
> se sabedes novas do meu amado?
>   Ay Deos, e u é?
> Se sabedes novas do meu amigo,
> aquel que mentiu do que pos commigo?
>   Ay Deos, e u é?
> Se sabedes novas do meu amado,
> aquel que mentiu do que mh'á jurado?
>   Ay Deos, e u é? ...

Ah flowers, flowers of the green pine (*branch*),
have you news of my friend (*love*)?
Ah God, and where is he?

Have you news of my friend (*love*),
of him who lied about what he promised (*swore to*) me?
Ah God, and where is he?[37]

This is one of the best known of all poems in Old Portuguese, and deservedly so; it would be superfluous to elaborate on its structure, with the predictable alternation of parallel synonyms *pyno/ramo*, *amigo/amado*, and *pos commigo/mh'á jurado*. It is perhaps fair to say, all the same, that on this occasion at least, Dom Dinis (though an 'hombre de invenciones sutiles', in the Marquess of Santillana's view) did himself less than justice when he added a further tercet (here omitted) in which the pines considerately reassure the speaker that her *amigo* is safe and sound and already on his way to rejoin her, and then dutifully rang the statutory parallelistic changes on that as well.

What this admirable if flawed cantiga does demonstrate, despite not having known when to stop, is the way the insistent repetitions of rigid verbal parallelism (as opposed to the purely semantic kind or the freer and more irregular parallelistic schemes of Gil Vicente) concentrate the attention on a single frozen moment of time and an irreducibly small-scale scene. Paradoxically, this form of expansion (which naturally involves additional repetitions of the obsessive refrain as well) serves not to destroy but actually to enhance the compactness of the nucleus, compressing its internal space and time even further. The effect, despite the radical difference in the means employed, is not dissimilar to the kind of condensation achieved by the kharjas or even by the miniature Japanese verse forms.

That this analogy is not fanciful is clear from a tanka by Saionji Sanekane, a powerful magnate with one foot in the imperial Heian Court of Kyoto and the other in the shogun's *de facto* military capital at Kamakura, who was also, as it happens, an exact contemporary of King Dinis:

---

[37] For various trees evoked in similar contexts or with symbolic meanings see the next chapter, and cf. *CPBA* i. 901, and the English and Polish folk quatrains quoted in Waley's introduction to the *Shi Jing*. Past happiness is naturally associated with the *locus amoenus* where it was felt, and which, revisited in altered circumstances, increases present pain ('nessun maggior dolore . . .'): cf. Reckert 1977: 414–17; 448 f. (= *Don Duardos*, ll. 1615–58/1527–50; 1884–94); and Reckert 1980: 196 f.; and 1993.

Koishisa wa	Loneliness	1
nagame no sue ni	takes on a shape:	3
katachi shite	green pines on the far mountain	5
namida ni ukabu	that closes off my view,	2
tōyama no matsu[38]	floating in a blur of tears.	4

In this micropoem by Sanekane, distant objects are mentioned only so that the distance may be cancelled out: the far is brought near; the mountain and its pine forest are reduced to the size of the eye that sees them suspended in its own teardrops.

Two other features in Sanekane's poem lead us back again to Dom Dinis. One is the use of the pivot word *nagame*, in the second line, which makes 'the far mountain / that closes off my view' mean at the same time 'the far mountain / *after long rain*'. This word, which if derived from *nagameru* ('to gaze') means 'view' or 'vision' (including the sense of 'daydream'), but which can equally well be understood as a compound of *nagai* ('long') and *ame* ('rain'), gives rise in turn to two of the poem's three examples of another device—known as *engo*, or verbal analogy—also used (as we shall see) by the king. In the present case, 'long' (extent in time) foreshadows *tō*, 'far' (extent in space), in the last line, while 'rain' similarly anticipates and emphasizes 'tears' (*namida*) in the next to last. Like the dim curtain of endlessly falling rain before, a veil of tears now blurs the speaker's vision. Finally, 'pines', the last word of the poem in Japanese, is (like 'to pine', in English) a homophone of 'waiting', and thus echoes the first, 'loneliness'.

If the equating of rain with tears in this tanka by Sanekane reminds us of the association of tears with dew in Lĭ Bó's quatrain, the Japanese poet's miniaturizing and interiorizing of landscape exemplifies the close affinity between poetry and painting—linked by the common base of calligraphic art—in the two great civilizations of East Asia. At the same time, this propensity for looking through the wrong end of the telescope can perhaps be seen as a manifestation, in the sphere of art, of the inveterate and specifically Japanese compulsion to reduce and compress, which, if possibly traceable to the more than Franciscan austerity of certain forms of esoteric Buddhism, was to lead, paradoxically, to the technology of the transistor and the microchip.

---

[38] *Gyokuyōshū* (the most voluminous of the twenty 'Imperial Song-books', completed in 1314), xi, no. 1569 (*JCP* 381).

WIND AND WATER

The sixth king of Portugal would have been surprised to learn that he was using some of the most characteristic rhetorical devices then current in the legendary Isles of Zipangu, whose very existence had only lately been vouched for (with minimal details, none literary) by Marco Polo. To be able to write competently 'en maneyra de proençal' was for Dom Dinis the ultimate in poetic refinement.

It is nevertheless a fact that one of the most delightful of the prolific royal poet's hundred and thirty-eight extant cantigas employs not only the technique of the *kake kotoba* but also *engo*, and even that other quintessentially Japanese artifice *hon-kadori*, or allusive variation. After cavilling at his pine-tree poem, it is pleasant to be able to quote one that is wholly successful. Conceptually, it means nothing more than 'the fair maid rose at dawn and went to wash her clothes on the hillside; the wind blew them about and she was vexed'. Poetically, on the other hand, it means nothing less than

> Levantou-s' a velida,
> levantou-s' âlva,
> e vay lavar camisas
> en o alto:
> vay-las lavar âlva.
>
> Levantou-s' a louçana,
> levantou-s' âlva,
> e vay lavar delgadas
> en o alto:
> vay-las lavar âlva.
>
> Vay lavar camisas
> (levantou-s' âlva);
> o vento lhas desvia
> en o alto:
> vay-las lavar âlva.
>
> E vay lavar delgadas
> (levantou-s' âlva);
> o vento lhas levava
> en o alto:
> vay-las lavar âlva.
>
> O vento lhas desvia
> (levantou-s' âlva);
> meteu-s' âlva en ira
> en o alto.
> Vay-las lavar âlva.

O vento lhas levava
(levantou-s' âlva);
meteu-s' âlva en sanha
en o alto.
Vay-las lavar âlva.

CBN 569/CV fo. 23^{r-v}

If all that is rather dizzying, the king undoubtedly meant it to be, just as the *roupa branca* or small clothes swirling perversely about her in the breeze were for the girl. It is the word *âlva*, obviously, occurring no less than fourteen times in thirty short lines, that creates this effect. At the same time it provides a further example of pivot syntax, since on each of those fourteen occasions it means simultaneously 'at dawn' (*à alva*) and 'the white-skinned girl' (*a alva*). What extraordinarily enhances the power of intensification of the otherwise quite ordinary parallelistic repetitions is this telescoping of meanings, achieved by the superimposing of three whitenesses that mutually reinforce each other: that of the girl's fair skin, that of her *roupa branca* flapping in the wind, and that of the morning light enveloping and illuminating them both. In terms of Japanese poetics, the pivot word has thus in turn given rise to a case of *engo*, or verbal analogy.

This most un-laundresslike fair maid may well be (like so many improbable 'shepherdesses') the imaginary projection of a young girl of the Court against a backdrop of idealized rural landscape whose elements, being purely symbolic, have none of the harmful effects of real water, sun, and wind, but only those befitting the symbols that they are: that is, to make everything whiter and more luminous (water), with the warmth of life (sun) and an enveloping erotic excitement (wind). An alternative interpretation by Helder Macedo ('Uma cantiga de Dom Dinis', in Reckert 1980: 51–60) is that the girl's fairness shows her to be both a 'dona virgo' (whiteness = purity) and very young, since the skin of even the fairest peasant girl, constantly exposed to the elements, would soon coarsen and darken. In either case (and the two interpretations are not mutually exclusive), the dawn portrayed here is not only that of the day but of life.

Fair skin being equated to youth and, by association, purity, a dark complexion may be felt to require an excuse, as when one of Lope de Vega's heroines explains

Blanca m'era yo   White was I
cuando entré en la siega;   when I went to the reaping;

dióme el sol,   I caught the sun,
y ya soy morena.   and now I am dark.

Alín, 254

By implication, to be dark was to be not only older but consequently
more experienced, and hence supposedly more open to further experience: a positive aspect that to some extent counterbalances the
negative one (a double meaning for 'when I went to the reaping'
cannot be excluded).[39]

In his analysis of the king's poem Macedo examines the way the
insistent repetition, in constantly varying order, of the sounds *a*, *l*,
and *v* (the phonetic components of *alva*) ends by establishing a kind
of imaginary but imaginatively convincing cause-and-effect relation
between the two 'polarizing signifiers' of the poem: *alva* and *vento*.
To this it need only be added that if the vowel *a* can in specific
contexts suggest synaesthetic effects of whiteness (as Dámaso Alonso's
analyses of the poetry of Garcilaso and Góngora, for example, have
shown), the alternation of *v* (or its bilabial variant *b*) with *l* (or its
palatal and vibratory variants *lh* and *r*) universally suggests, at least in
the Indo-European languages, images of gyratory motion like that of
the *louçana*'s swirling clothes. The *v—l* and *v—r* of convolutions,
vortexes, and vertiginous or vacillating movements go back to the
Indo-European root *welw-*: 'revolve', 'involve' (cf. Klein, s.v. *volute*);
in St-John Perse's *Anabase* these combinations are interwoven, in a
context reminiscent of King Dinis, with sibilants suggesting the wind:
'Le vent se lève. Vent de mer. Et la lessive / part . . .'.[40]

It makes a change, after so much moonlight and loneliness, to
emerge into this dazzling sunlit world and find at last a girl who has
not waited in vain. What tells us she has not is the king's third

---

[39] On dark skin = sexual experience see John Gornall, ' "Por el río de amor,
madre": An Aspect of the *morenita*' (*Journal of Hispanic Philology*, 10 (1985–6); on the
theme of the *morena* in traditional verse since the biblical 'Nigra sum, sed formosa',
Aguirre 1965; and cf. Alín, 253–8. King Dinis's *alva* is at the opposite pole from the
Gypsy girl Lorca calls *luz morena* (GL 49), and for whose *cuerpo requemado* he would
'bite the apple' in an olive grove with a tower the colour of her flesh (for apples, olives,
and towers as erotic symbols see below, n. 43, and Ch. 2, nn. 25–6). But the white
skin of a laundress was already enough to wreak havoc even in 10th-c. Japan, where a
celebrated ascete 'lost his magic powers [of flight] after noticing the whiteness of the
legs of a girl who was washing clothes' (Kenkō, ch. 8).

[40] For sparkling whiteness evoked by *a* see Reckert 1977: 10 ff.; for *v/b* in
association with *l/r* in the medieval cantigas, Camões, and Fernando Pessoa: Reckert
1980: 55 ff., 148 f., and 205 f.; 1984: 529 f. and 533; and 1987: 30.

unconsciously Japanese rhetorical artifice: allusive variation. The earlier poem he alludes to (*CBN* 1188/*CV* fos. 124ᵛ–125ʳ) while altering it in a decisive way, is by that most magical and disturbing of all Galician troubadours, Pero Móogo (so unmonastic despite his name 'Peter the Monk'[41]), whose cantigas are without exception filled with the erotic symbolism of troubled fountains, phallic stags, and dresses torn in the dance. It is a parallelistic expansion, in thirty-six lines, of two linked quatrains which we can reconstruct as follows:

Levou-s' a velida:	The fair girl has risen;
vay lavar cabelos	she goes to wash her hair
na fontana fria,	in the cold fountain,
leda dos amores.	joyous for love.
Passou seu amigo	Her friend passed that way
que lhi ben queria:	who loved her dearly:
o cervo do monte	the mountain stag
a augua volvia.	stirred up the water.

Although the poet has inverted the conventional order of the proper and symbolic terms, his second quatrain is easily recognizable as a symbolic equation with simple replacement: 'the mountain stag stirred up the water' is merely a coded repetition of 'her friend passed that way' (though with the further implication that in passing he has left her fresh and limpid sensuality stirred to unsuspected depths).

As Dom Dinis's 'allusive variation' on Peter the Monk's cantiga is not just a later poem but the continuation of the same story at a later stage—a continuation, moreover, that assumes our knowledge of the earlier stage—it may be useful to examine in a broader context the substitutions, additions, and deletions he has made in the older poem that served as his model.[42]

The wind (which comes *do alto*) plays the same part in Dom Dinis's continuation as the stag (*do monte*) in Pero Móogo: as a concrete symbol of the sex drive conceived as a superior force and principle of Nature that is at once alluring and alarming. Poetry has

---

[41] On Móogo (<*Monachu*) vs. Meogo see respectively Picchio 77, and X. L. Méndez Ferrín, *O Cancioneiro de Pero Meogo* (Vigo, 1966), 14–19.

[42] The allusive variation, while not specifically recognized by Western rhetorical theory (or, in effect, by Umberto Eco, who dates the *opera aperta* only from the last century), is already implied by the 'hábito intelectual, nacido al cobijo de las escuelas de gramática', of readiness to complete an existing text and develop elements understood to be implicit in it (Rico, 688).

not yet exhausted the erotic connotations of the wind, and shows no sign of doing so. They are still a constant in Lorca's symbolism, beginning with the first poem in his first book, *Libro de poemas*, and culminating in the *Romancero gitano* when 'el viento que nunca duerme' pursues the terrified Gypsy girl Preciosa with his hot sword and his plea 'Niña, deja que levante / tu vestido para verte'.[43]

The specific motif of impregnation by the wind extends from pre-Classical Greece to the Amerindians and from the North Atlantic isles of Scotland to the atolls of the South Pacific; and there is even a tradition of 'blaming the wind' in which it serves the same purpose as the stags in another of Pero Móogo's songs (*CBN* 1192), where a girl's excuse for coming back late from the spring is that they muddied the water so much she could not do her washing. Here is a fourteenth-century example of the topos from South China:

> Holding my skirt with the sash undone,
> eyebrows not yet made up, I go to the window.
> My silk dress blows about;
> if it opens a bit I'll blame the spring wind.

> *ICL* 67

This silk dress recalls the ones in Buson's haiku and the poems of Xiè Tiào and Lǐ Bó—not to mention the underskirt (also 'open a bit') in that of Xiao Lín quoted above (n. 21). The ultimate source of this quatrain, though, may perhaps be another, likewise a folk-song and from the South, but a thousand years older, in which a girl exclaims: 'How amorous the spring wind is! / It's blowing open my silk gauze skirt'.[44]

In eighth-century Japan, too, a determined girl with her wits about her had an explanation ready to hand if needed:

> Tamadare no osu no sukeki ni   Push through the bamboo blinds
> irikayoikone   and come in to me, my love;

---

[43] GL 396. Cf. the opening lines of the 1921 *Libro de poemas*: 'Viento del Sur, / Moreno, ardiente, / Llegas sobre mi carne'; and, from *Canciones* (1921–4), 'La niña del bello rostro / está cogiendo aceituna. / El viento, galán de torres, / la prende por la cintura' (below, Ch. 3). Robert Graves, three years Lorca's senior, assumes the role of the wind in 'The Hills of May': 'Me, the Wind, she took as lover / . . . / Let me toss her untied hair, / Let me shake her gown'. On medieval and traditional analogues see Deyermond; for 8th–11th-c. China, Owen 1989: 177; 181 f.; for 'impregnation by the wind', Stith Thompson, s.v.

[44] Spring song 10, from 'Tzu-yeh Songs of the Four Seasons' (after J. D. Frodsham, *An Anthology of Chinese Verse* (Oxford, 1967), 101).

| tarachine no haha ga towasaba | if my mother should ask, |
| 'kaze' to mōsan. | I'll say 'it's just the wind'. |

MYS 887

The lover who shakes the blinds and pretends to be the wind is another universal theme of folklore;[45] but to find anything comparable to the charming exasperation of King Dinis's 'alva en ira' we have to go either to sixteenth-century Castile—

Un mal ventecillo	A wicked little breeze
loquillo con mis faldas:	playing the fool with my skirts:
¡tira allá, mal viento!	leave me alone, wicked wind!
¿qué me las alzas?	What are you lifting them for?

Alín, 714

—or else back to Japan again, this time to a seventeenth-century haiku by Buson's contemporary, Gyōdai:

Harukaze ni	(A lovely girl,[46] jostled	2
osaruru bijo ni	by the spring wind:)	1
ikari kana.	'How very *tiresome*!'	3

Hk ii. 99

The playfully amorous wind, the girl washing clothes, dazzling whiteness, and symbolic trees all converge in a folk-song of the last century from the Greek islands, with faint echoes (though not too faint for their uncannily ancient resonance to provoke a mild *frisson*) of the *Odyssey*. As in the parallelistic cantigas of the troubadour king, its forty lines have been generated by expansion from a nucleus which in this case can be reduced approximately to:

> On the beach, a priest's daughter of Chios—
> a young orange tree in bloom—
> was washing and hanging out clothes
> when a shining gold ship sailed by.
> The North wind blew
> and lifted her skirt,
> exposing her ankle to sight;

---

[45] Cf. A. Aarne (with Stith Thompson), *Types of the Folk Tale* (Helsinki, 1928), type 1419.

[46] The stock epithet *bijo* (a Chinese loan-word) has much the same effect as Old Portuguese *velida* or *louçana* in the *cantigas de amigo*.

then the beach shone as well,
and the whole of the universe shone![47]

In the refrain, 'orange tree', νεραντζοῦλα, alternates with 'lemon tree', λεμονίτσα (such citrus metaphors will be the main subject of the next chapter). Variant versions of the ballad clumsily gild the ship's refined gold by tacking on more tercets describing its crew, their conjectures about why "ἔλαμψ' ὅ κόσμος ὅλος", etc.: the opposite process to that of the no less magical Spanish ballad of Count Arnaldos, in which most of the enchantment comes precisely from the suppression of a pedestrian second part explaining away the mystery of the silken-sailed galley that draws near the shore on Midsummer morning to lure the count on board.[48] No topos need be invoked to account for the glamour of a passing ship on the horizon: compare Buson—

Komabune no	The Korean boat
yorade sugiyuku	draws near, then passes by
kasumi ka na	in the mist

Hk ii. 80

—but the Greek song may be related to a general European epic motif which includes not only the ship but a hero and his retainers (in this case the captain and crew), a beach, and a flashing light.[49]

A girl's washing of her hair, in poems like Pero Móogo's, invariably signals and precedes a meeting with her *amigo*. Her washing of his shirts, on the other hand, as in Dom Dinis's allusive variation, ought in principle to connote her magic power over him. But some doubts arise. Are these *camisas* in fact shirts, and his, or are they (as Helder Macedo proposes) 'feminine clothing, much more intimate than the modern word suggests'? Though not a universal archetype like the wind, the theme of a woman washing her own clothes (with obvious implications of an erotic ritual—and the more intimate the clothes, the more obvious the implications) is of more than respectable antiquity, extending from Nausicaa—still not forgotten by her compatriots, even if demoted to a simple παπαδοπούλα or transformed,

---

[47] Abbot, 148–51 (see Textual Appendix for the original).

[48] The magico-erotic elements of this ballad in its Castilian and Catalan versions are studied in Aguirre and Hauf. On the 'liminality' of Midsummer Night see 'Midsummer Mirrors, Bonfires of St John', in Ch. 6, below.

[49] See David K. Crowne, 'The Hero on the Beach: An Example of Composition by Theme in Anglo-Saxon Poetry', *Neuphilologische Mitteilungen* (1960), 362–72.

as in one variant of this song (*CGD* 147), into a Turkish emir's daughter—by way of the three mysterious *mozuelas* in a sixteenth-century villancico who 'en aguas corrientes / lavan sus camisas', down to the present day.[50]

In the world of symbols, however, nothing is unequivocal; which is why parallelism, with its built-in ambivalence, is an ideal way of interpreting that world. And one of the conspicuous characteristics of Galician-Portuguese parallelism is exactly its ability to avoid the monotony of the predictable, inherent in quasi-synonymy, by introducing minor differentiations (whether by gradation or antithesis, and at times even disguised or dissimulated) between the obligatorily parallel words, or even between successive reiterations of the same word, such as *alva* in King Dinis's cantiga of the fair laundress.[51] For a Castilian example of gradation, compare the descending scale of courtliness in this sixteenth-century parallelistic gloss by Cristóbal de Castillejo:

> Madre, un caballero (*escudero*)
> qu'estaba en este corro (*esta baila*),
> a cada vuelta,
> hacíame del ojo (*asíame de la manga*).
> Yo, como era bonita,
> teníaselo en poco (*nada*).
>
> LTT 367
>
> Mother, a gentleman (*squire*)
> who was at this ball (*dance*),
> at every turn
> made eyes at me (*pulled my sleeve*).
> As I was pretty,
> I paid him little (*no*) heed.

Thus it is possible that *camisa* and *delgada*, though synonyms in the sense that they are both articles of clothing, are antonyms in so far as they are men's and women's clothing respectively. This is clearly the case in an anonymous poem from a sixteenth-century Castilian song-book, in which the phallic stag (*cervo*) is disconcertingly metamorphosed into a pretty and inoffensive *cervatica*, or water

---

[50] On the ambiguous word *camisa* and the significance of the garment itself as worn by women in the Sephardic community of the Maghreb see Alvar, 85, 232 f.

[51] For further examples of this technique see my 'A Variação Subliminar na Poética da Cantiga', in Reckert 1980: 7–34.

insect (*Phasgonura viridissima*):[52] not only feminine, but even with a propitiatory diminutive suffix:

Cerbatica, que no me la buelbas,	Don't stir it up, water beetle,
que yo me la bolberé.	I'll stir it up myself.
Cerbatica tan garrida,	Gaily-coloured water beetle,
no enturbies el agua fría,	don't trouble the cold water:
que he de lavar la camisa	I have to wash the shirt
de aquel a quien di mi fe...	of him I pledged myself to.
Cerbatica tan galana,	Gaudy water beetle,
no enturbies el agua clara,	don't trouble the clear water:
que he de lavar la delgada	I have to wash my shift
para quien yo me lavé...	for him I washed myself for...

Frenk, 322

In another poem of the same period the antonymy is even more evident, because in the absence of any parallelistic expansion to distinguish between them, the *camisas* are both his and hers:

A mi puerta nasce una fonte:	At my door a spring gushes out:
¿por dó saliré que no me moje?	how shall I get round it dry?
A mi puerta la garrida	At my bright-coloured door
nasce una fonte frida	a cold spring gushes out
donde lavo la mi camisa	where I wash my own shift
y la de aquel que yo más quería...	and the shirt of him I love best...

Frenk, 321

Often, too, it is specifically men's shirts that are concerned, as in the anonymous Welsh poem, also sixteenth century,[53] in which a girl washes 'the shirt of him I love best' (*crys y mab mwya' a garwn*) under a span of Cardigan bridge; or the contemporary Sephardic wedding song from the Maghreb quoted below at the end of Chapter 3.

In view of the foregoing, the mingling of 'his' *camisas* with 'her' *delgadas* in the king's poem clearly implies an evolution of the relations between them towards a deeper intimacy than in the cantiga King Dinis alludes to in order to vary it. Deeper, certainly—but just

---

[52] Alan Deyermond suggests the alternative interpretation *cerbatica* = diminutive of *cervata* = feminine of *cervato*: a stag less than 6 months old (personal communication). On this reading, the *cerbatica* would be the speaker's rival for the affection of her lover the 'stag'.

[53] Gwyn Williams (ed. and tr.), *The Burning Tree: Poems from the First Thousand Years of Welsh Verse* (London, 1969), 218.

as certainly not (or at least not yet) sanctioned by matrimony. The girl's confused emotions, buffeted like her washing by elemental forces, are for the moment more upsetting in their turbulence, like Pero Móogo's stag-troubled waters, than serenely fulfilled. But in time the troubled waters will surely run clear:

> Turbias van las aguas, madre,
> turbias van;
> mas ellas se aclararán.

LTT 265

What is curious is that, with twenty-three fewer words than its model, King Dinis's allusive variation is in real terms a considerably greater expansion of their common nucleus. The fact is that every one of the most conspicuous and individualizing elements in the king's poem—shirts and shifts, morning light, the girl's fair skin and her perturbed emotions, the sensation of pervading whiteness and dizzying spiral motion—has been added by him.

And that is not all. In manipulating the different meanings or shades of meaning of such words as *alva* and *camisa*, and thus increasing the semantic content of his poem at the same time as he reduces its physical extension, the king is subtly exploiting the inherent potential of parallelism for plural signification: a potential which his predecessor, more interested in taking advantage of the analogous ambiguity of the device of *leixa-pren*,[54] has not put to full use, merely weaving the original micropoem into a simple scheme of *versus transformati*, with 'fontana fria' echoed by 'fria fontana', 'leda dos amores' by 'dos amores leda', and 'a áugua volvia' by 'volvia a áugua'.

WHERE THE TWAIN MEET

The West (in the excessively simplistic generalization I put forward earlier) has a tendency to expansion: whether by laying down a delayed-action fuse to detonate a kharja at the end of a correctly stylish panegyric, or by saying 'vamos por partes' and setting out in a

---

[54] That is, 'leave and take' (*laisse-prend*): the second line of each odd-numbered parallel couplet is repeated as the first line of the next and followed by a new line introduced to rhyme with it. King Dinis's 'Ay flores...' exemplifies the process, which is analogous to that of linked quadras, or of *lién jù* and *renga* (cf. n. 28 above).

no-nonsense Castilian way to demonstrate the truth of an initial premise, or by weaving the convoluted intricacies of Portuguese-style parallelism. Its standards, one suspects, are at least partly quantitative— and it has the defects of its quantities. Its restless dynamism makes for easily distracted attention, to catch and hold which the Western artist is too often tempted to resort to winks and nudges: to stating the obvious and overstating what might be merely stated.

The East, on the other hand, condenses and deepens. Its criteria are qualitative: the aesthetic vices it is prone to are preciosity and sterile academic conservatism; and its virtues, both moral and aesthetic, are patience and concentration. The relevance of such virtues to micropoetics could hardly be better put than in the words of the twelfth-century tanka poet and theorist Chōmei (*JCP* 269):

Only when many meanings are compressed in a single word, when the depths of feeling are exhausted without being expressed . . . , and 'the words are too few' [an ironic quotation of the pejorative expression used by a famous earlier poet-critic], will a poem . . . have the power to move Heaven and Earth in the narrow confines of thirty-one syllables, and soften the hearts of gods and demons.

But the further one pushes this antithesis, the more evident its superficiality becomes. It is even momentarily tempting to explain the whole thing away by hazarding a guess that the orientation of poetry towards music favours its expansion, while a purely literary evolution might encourage it to contract. Yet that will hardly do either; for the East, which invented those ultimate distillates the tanka and the haiku, has also evolved techniques for linking them together in sequences extending to thousands of lines, with a thematic complexity as formidable as that of the linked tercets of the *Divine Comedy*.[55] And the West itself, for its part, has not abandoned the bare lyric nucleus, but merely relegated it to the limbo of folklore.

To recognize this is in a way to come back to our original antithesis, but differently formulated. 'The East' is not so much a geographical region as a state of mind: that of the traditional rural society as opposed to the urban technological one that was born in the West and first developed there. Until perhaps the sixteenth century, that state of mind was the norm in all societies then existing or known to have existed. Though it has since largely withdrawn behind the

[55] See above, n. 28, and cf. *JCP* 319–29, 403–20, and 491.

frontiers of what we now call the Afro-Asian world, however, there still remain in the West not inconsiderable vestiges—for the most part rural, at least in origin—of an internal Third World of its own. And if with the spread of Western-style technology from Japan to the rest of the Pacific rim it has become more frequent in a socio-economic context to speak of a North–South axis instead of the classical East–West divide, it was the indisputably Eastern Chairman Máo who called the West 'the cities' and the Third World 'the countryside'.

It was in the countryside that the minimal lyric was born, and it is in the countryside that it has taken refuge again, among the most 'Eastern', in the cultural and sometimes even the ethnic sense, of Western populations: among the Gypsies and still partly-Arabized *labradores* of Lower Andalusia, for example, or the traditional peasantry of Galicia and the North-East of Portugal—or the *jangada* fishermen of the Brazilian North-East, where even today (though some of the words may be in Yoruba or Nagô, just as nine centuries earlier in Al-Andalus they were in Arabic),

> Quando a gente é criancinha,   When we're kids
> canta quadras pra brincar;   we sing quadras for fun;
> quando fica gente grande,   once you grow up
> ouve quadras a chorar.[56]   they'll make you cry.

[56] Dorival Caymmi, *Cancioneiro da Bahia* (4th edn., São Paulo, n.d.), 95.

2

GOLDEN LAMPS IN A GREEN NIGHT

Em cada fruto a morte amadurece,
deixando inteira, por legado,
uma semente virgem que estremece
logo que o vento a tenha desnudado.

In every fruit death ripens,
leaving whole as legacy
a virgin seed that shivers
once the wind has stripped her bare.

Eugénio de Andrade

THE *jangadeiros* of Bahia—well named 'Bay of All Saints'—light
votive fires on the beaches to Yemanjá, the Yoruba goddess of the
sea, before they set sail for the night's fishing on their fragile rafts.
But pre-technological attitudes and practices are not peculiar to the
Third World, as the Midsummer Night bonfires[1] along the banks of
the Galician *rías* and on the rocky hillsides of Trás-os-Montes bear
witness; even in our own century a substantial part of the population
of north-western Iberia has continued to inhabit in imagination
'a region of fiery dragons and apples of gold' (as a historian of
Portuguese literature called it) hardly less syncretic, if more discreetly
camouflaged, than anything in north-eastern Brazil. And the corresponding part of the population of Andalusia, with its Gypsy and
Moorish leavening, shares the same mythic or symbolic mode of
apprehending and interpreting the natural world.

To provide continuity for the analysis of the various forms taken by
lyra minima, I made use in the previous chapter of the single theme of
a woman waiting—consciously or unconsciously, with or without
hope—for the arrival or return of the beloved. For the examination
of the role of symbolism in traditional verse that follows, this single

---

[1] To be discussed below in Ch. 6.

theme will be replaced by a pair of concrete symbols: the 'apple of gold'—more prosaically *Citrus aurantium*—and its first cousin *Citrus limon*; and while the micropoem will continue to be the centre of our attention, the nuclei of the poems studied in the present chapter will not infrequently exceed the previous limit of thirty-two syllables.

Although our earliest record of this Castilian folk-song (with a Portuguese setting) is in an anonymous interlude of 1655, it has been heard within the past few years in the provinces of Ávila and Cáceres:

Que arrojóme la portuguesilla	The Portuguese girl threw me oranges:
narangitas de su naranjal;	little ones from her orange grove;
que arrojómelas y arrojéselas	she threw them and I threw them
y bolviómelas a arrojar.	and she threw them back again.

Frenk, 1622B

Such verses as these belong, we have seen, to the common domain, and are available for expansion, paraphrase, and interpretation by any poet who cares to take them up. Indeed, we could well say of the traditional lyric, as Menéndez Pidal did of the *romancero*, that it is 'una poesía que vive en variantes'. An even earlier variant of this quatrain in a sixteenth-century manuscript introduces orange blossoms—*azahar*—as well as the oranges themselves, but in the process leaves itself no room to say who is throwing them:

Arrojóme las naranjicas
con los ramos del blanco azahar;
arrojómelas y arrojéselas
y volviómelas a arrojar.

The anonymous poet who glossed these lines, faced with the problem of explaining who the thrower was, decided to leave her anonymous as well and identify her as just 'the girl': *la niña*:

De sus manos hizo un día	With her hands one day
la niña tiro de amores,	*la niña* fired shots of love,
y de naranjas y flores	with oranges and flowers
balas de su artillería...	for her artillery...

LTT 236

'LA NIÑA'

This archetypal *niña*, found everywhere from Santillana's (or Suero de Ribera's) 'niña que amores ha' to the 'niñas de España de...

temblorosas faldas' of Lorca, may perhaps be taken as an illustration
of Gerald Brenan's remark (370) that the Spanish *copla* is never
personal, but expresses 'the idiosyncracy of a situation rather than of
a character'.

Lope de Vega shifts the scene all the way across the Peninsula
from a Portuguese orange grove to a window in far-off Valencia.
Lope must surely have known the anonymous version, for he has kept
both the orange blossom and the *niña*, while at the same time making
explicit both the earlier poet's suggestion of a festival atmosphere and
his assumption that the ultimate significance of all these *juegos florales*
and *frutales* is flirtatious:

Naranjitas me tira la niña	Oranges, *la niña* throws me
en Valencia, por Navidad;	in Valencia, at Christmas time;
pues a fe que si se las tiro	well, I swear if I throw them back
que se le han de volver azâr.	they'll turn to orange blossom.
A una máscara salí	I went out to a masked ball
y paréme a su ventana;	and stopped under her window;
amaneció su mañana,	her morning dawned
y el sol en sus ojos vi.	and I saw the sun in her eyes.
Naranjitas desde allí	Oranges, from above,
me tiró para favor:	she threw me as a favour:
como no sabe de amor,	since she knows nothing of love,
piensa que todo es burlar.	she thinks everything's a game.
Pues a fe que si se las tiro	Well, I swear if I throw them back
que se le han de volver azâr.[2]	they'll turn to orange blossom.

Lope's unerring instinct for dramatic relevance has enabled him
to give, without any discursiveness, a complete account of the circumstances: time, place, probable denouement, and even motivation:
the *niña* is naïvely throwing oranges 'para favor'—as a mere game—
all unaware that if the 'favour' is reciprocated she will be committed
by the symbolic exchange of love-tokens to more than she bargained
for. Moreover, the apocopated form *azâr* (for *azahar*), at the same
time as it means orange blossom, is a pun hinting that the innocent
game has become instead a perilous game of chance: a *juego de azar*.

Back in Portugal again, and in the present day, girls in the Lower
Alentejo sing:

---

[2] *El bobo del colegio*, II.x. See Alín, 519 for other variants, some also by Lope.

Tenho uma laranja d'oiro	I have a golden orange
no canto do meu baú	in the corner of my trunk
para dar ao meu amor:	to give to my love:
prouvera a Deus sejas tu.	please God he may be you.

CPBA ii. 40

And an Alentejan lover who is out of sorts is given a loaf of bread and an orange cut in two to signify true love:

> Quem me dera um pão mole
> e uma laranja partida
> para dar ao meu amor,
> que anda de tromba caída!

CPBA i. 1296

The Sephardic Jews of Tetuan, in Morocco, until recently kept up a similar custom (*CRHJ* 35/71):

> Un amor que yo tenía,
> manzanitas de oro él me envía (*daba*),
> cuatro y cinco en una espiga (*rama*):
> 'La mejorcita (*más chiquita*) de ellas para mi amiga (*amada*)!'

> A lover that I had
> sends (*used to give*) me golden apples:
> four and five on a single stem (*branch*):
> 'The best (*smallest*) of all for my friend (*beloved*)!'

Once we piece together the clues in these three poems—the *laranja partida*, the *laranja d'oiro*, and the *manzanitas de oro*—the meaning of Gil Vicente's puzzling song in the *Pastoral Tragicomedy of the Estrela Mountains* ceases to hold any mysteries:

> Um amigo que eu havia
> mançanas d'ouro m'envia,
> garrido amor.

> Um amigo que eu amava
> mançanas d'ouro me manda,
> garrido amor.

> Mançanas d'ouro m'envia:
> a milhor era partida,
> garrido amor.

Cop 174a

Oranges are not necessarily the only appropriate fruit for use as love-tokens: in a villancico recorded in Seville in 1560, a *galán* reproaches his lady:

Entrastes, mi señora,	You came, my lady,
en el huerto ajeno:	into another's orchard:
cogistes tres pericas	you picked three little pears
del peral del medio;	from the pear tree in the middle;
dejárades la prenda	you should have left the token
d'amor verdadero...	of true love...

LTT 125

The mysterious *peral del medio* recalls 'thilke pyrie' where the lovers in *The Merchant's Tale*[3] meet 'an heigh among the fresshe leves' after May has quieted her aged husband's suspicions with the ambiguous explanation that she must have pears, 'Or I moot dye, so soore longeth me / To eten of the smale peres grene' (as for the 'tres pericas', it may be relevant to recall that the number three, as a male symbol, is a cliché of Freudian analysis of the *Traumwerk*).

That the throwing as well as the giving (or unauthorized taking) of fruit with similar implications is a custom of respectable antiquity will be clear from this trio of parallelistic quatrains, with a construction that calls to mind that of some of Vicente's songs:

> She throws me a quince;
> in requital I give her rubies.
> No, not in requital:
> as a pledge that I'll always love her.

> She throws me a greengage;
> in requital I give her jade.
> No, not in requital:
> as a pledge that I'll always love her.

> She throws me a plum;
> in requital I give her jet.
> No, not in requital:
> as a pledge that I'll always love her.[4]

---

[3] *Canterbury Tales*, ed. F. N. Robinson (2nd edn., Boston, 1957).

[4] *Shi Jing*, 72 f. (no. 18). Each quatrain has 18 syllables (5—5—3—5). As is to be expected in such an archaic text, the fruits and jewels mentioned do not correspond exactly to those now designated by the same characters: 'quince', for example (literally 'tree melon') means in modern Cantonese the papaya. I render the name of an unidentified precious stone as 'rubies' to bring out what I take to be a suggestion of

That courtship song from the Chinese 'Canon of Odes', the *Shi Jing*, dates from the seventh century BCE. The different fruits it mentions foreshadow the variety of those later to be used as love-tokens in Western poetry. But for throwing, it seems that nothing but an orange (or, as we shall see, a lemon) will do. In Trás-os-Montes, just as four hundred miles away in Lope's Valencia, the narrow street under a girl's window can become an improvised court for the 'orange game':

> Esta rua é comprida;
> no meio, apertadinha:
> eu hei-de cá jogar nela
> o jogo da laranjinha.

AMRP

The speaker in this quadra is as little inclined as Lope's Valencian *galán* to let the favour go unrequited. Here, moreover, the symbolism is superimposed on a double (or treble) meaning: in ordinary usage the *jogo da laranja* is a fairground sleight-of-hand trick corresponding to our 'shell game'; while *jogar*, in some regions (and in Brazil), means not only 'to play' but 'to throw'.

In the following pair of linked quatrains from the Algarve, on the other hand, the throwing of oranges is no longer either a game of chance or an actual symbolic courtship ritual, even in an attenuated sense as representing the suitor's first timidly hopeful approach, but has become no more than an allegory of the moment when the girl herself breaks free of her mother's apron-strings:

> Joguei a laranja ao ar;
> laranja ao ar, no chão caiu:
> fui falar ao meu amor,
> logo a minha mãe òviu.
>
> Logo a minha mãe òviu;
> logo se pôs a chorar.
> Ò que chore ò que não chore,
> lá vai a laranja ao ar.

> I threw an orange in the air:
> in the air, but down it fell:
> I went to talk with my true love,
> but straight away my mother heard.
>
> Straight away my mother heard,
> and straight away began to cry.
> Whether my mother cries or not,
> here goes the orange, into the air.

CPA 434/7

colour parallelism between the fruits and the respective gems given to the girl in 'requital' (a technical courtship term borrowed from Waley) as adornments for her girdle. On the ancient half-aesthetic, half-ritual custom of wearing tinkling girdle pendants see Laufer, 194 f., 198 f.

The first of these quadras is a particularly neat example of the symbolic equation: not only are its couplets parallel but so are the corresponding lines of each couplet: 'Joguei a laranja ao ar' *means* 'I went to talk with my love'; and 'laranja ao ar, no chão caiu' *means* 'then my mother found out'. In quatrains of this kind, the strongly marked parallelism has the effect of nudging the hearer into recognition of the symbolic equivalence.

Sometimes, though, things work the other way round, and the parallelism is too asymmetrical and inconspicuous to be perceptible unless the equivalence has already been recognized. This is the case in a philosophically resigned tercet from Betanzos, in the Galician province of Corunna:

> Arriba sí, abaixo non:
> onde se dá a laranxa
> tamén se dá o limón.
>
> CPG ii. 62

That is, 'Up for yes and down for no: where there's an orange a lemon may grow'. In this tercet, as in Pero Móogo's mountain-stag poem, the equation is inverted, with the proper terms at the beginning (here both crammed into the two halves of the first line) and the symbolic ones occupying the last two lines. Before we can recognize the parallelism and see that 'arriba sí' is a paraphrase of 'se dá a laranxa', and that 'abaixo non' performs the same explanatory function for 'se dá o limón', we have to muster a certain amount of external evidence, first abstracting from the Algarvian linked quatrains the general proposition that what goes up must come down, and that citrus fruit falling to the ground is a bad sign, and next extrapolating from the earlier poem on the *jogo da laranjinha* the mental picture of a young man hopefully tossing an orange up to an upper-storey window and, to his pained surprise, getting a lemon back.

Even then, however, to grasp the full import of the Galician tercet we must know beforehand what the lemon traditionally means in this context, and why it wrings from three rejected suitors—Algarvian, Argentine, and Spanish—what is in essence the same disconsolate exclamation, as they gaze up at what is in essence the same inaccessible window:

> Daquelas janelas altas   From yonder lofty windows
> me jogaram um limão: someone threw a lemon down;

a casca deu-me no peito	the peel hit me upon the chest;
e o sumo no coração.	the juice went to my heart.

CPA 443

De tu ventana a la mía	From your window to mine
me tirastes un limón:	you threw a lemon down:
el limón cayó en la calle;	the lemon fell into the street;
el zumo en mi corazón.	the juice into my heart.

ACA 1875

El limón que me tirastes	The lemon that you threw me
a mi puerta se paró:	came to rest at my door:
no fue limón, que fue clavo	it was no lemon, but a nail
que me clavó el corazón.	that pierced me to the heart.

Torner, 87

Naturally, this association of the lemon with rebuff or refusal is not exclusively Iberian. The ethnographer Rodríguez Marín (*CPE* 665) mentions that in India it is usual for 'a young man who seeks illicit relations with a young woman to offer her a lemon . . . , which she accepts if she favours his advances or throws to the ground if not'; and Stith Thompson's *Motif-Index* records Indian folk-tales in which a princess indicates her refusal or acceptance of a suitor by throwing him a lemon or an orange (in other culture areas an apple: sometimes, as in Gil Vicente, a golden one).

The affirmative implications of the orange are likewise no monopoly of the Iberian *Kulturkreis*: one of Rilke's *Orpheus* sonnets, for instance, urges a group of girls (in an uncharacteristically popular dance rhythm which my version attempts to suggest) to 'dance the orange':

> Mädchen, ihr warmen, Mädchen, ihr stummen,
> tanzt den Geschmack der erfahrenen Frucht!

> Tanzt die Orange. Wer kann sie vergessen,
> wie sie, ertrinkend in sich, sich wehrt
> wider ihr Süsssein. Ihr habt sie besessen.
> Sie hat sich köstlich zu euch bekehrt . . .[5]

> Maidens ardent, maidens mute,
> dance the taste of the savoured fruit!

> Dance the orange. Who can forget it:
> how, drowning itself in itself, it wards off

---

[5] *Sonette an Orpheus* (Leipzig, 1923), i, Sonnet XV.

all its own sweetness. You have possessed it.
It has deliciously turned into you . . .

In Sonnet XIII Rilke had already evoked other fruits: pear, apple, blackcurrant . . . : 'Alles dieses spricht / Tod und Leben in den Mund . . . Dies kommt von weit . . .'. (It does indeed.)

By an odd coincidence it is another evocation of Orpheus—Marcel Camus's Brazilian film *Orfeu Negro*—that furnishes the most recent example I know of (and one that does not, as it happens, appear in the original play by the Jacques Prévert of Brazil, Vinícius de Moraes[6]) of the *jogo da laranjinha*. In the scene in which the fated and fateful mutual *coup de foudre* takes place, Eurídice begins absent-mindedly playing with an orange, and Orfeu—fearing she is too young for him, and suspecting, like the protagonist of Lope's villancico, that 'since she knows nothing of love, she thinks it is all a game'—takes the fruit from her hand with brusque tenderness and gently puts it back on the table. The French director may have been remembering some lines by Prévert himself (*Paroles* (1949; Paris, 1961), 30) that sound like a distant echo of Buson's haiku about the silk dress thrown casually over a screen:

> Une orange sur la table,
> Ta robe sur le tapis
> Et toi dans mon lit.
> Doux présent du présent,
> Fraîcheur de la nuit,
> Chaleur de la vie.

We are now in possession of almost all the data we shall need for the deciphering of the next Portuguese quadra, which is again from the Algarve (*CPA* 71), and though at first sight the most incoherent, is in reality the most disconcertingly subtle one we have met so far:

Laranjeira de pé d'oiro	Orange tree with golden trunk
que dá laranjas de prata;	and oranges of silver,
ter amores não me custa:	to be in love gives me no pain;
deixá-los é que me mata.	to lose my love's what kills me.

---

[6] *Orfeu da Conceição* (1956). A law graduate and diplomat as well as an irreverent *modernista* poet, Vinícius (by antonomasia) was also active in Brazilian jazz circles and wrote the original lyrics for 'Girl from Ipanema', which first brought *bossa nova* to the attention of the outside world. His eclecticism extended to an interest in folk poetry (as we shall see) and—unusually for a Brazilian—the Portuguese *fado*.

The quatrains quoted so far were all of course chosen to illustrate a point. In practice we shall hardly suppose that everything that happens to have four lines is obliged *ipso facto* to be a symbolic equation; and indeed, the first couplet in the majority of 'folk' quatrains is no more than a bit of euphonious padding: a pair of ready-made formulaic phrases with the right number of syllables, chosen off the peg to provide a rhyme for whatever sententious or amorous statement the improviser feels like making.

That is probably how we shall interpret 'Laranjeira de pé d'oiro / que dá laranjas de prata' if we fail to see the parallel between this couplet and the following one. But this parallel is in turn as effectively concealed as the symbolism itself; and unless we are already pre-disposed to take the first two lines symbolically, we probably *shall* fail to see it behind the smoke-screen laid down by the more obvious and facile parallelism of individual lines and even hemistichs: *oiro/prata*; *ter amores/deixá-los*; *não me custa/me mata*. These are in reality contrapuntal parallelisms of contrast cutting clean across the underlying structure of the quadra, which when seen as a whole turns out to be once again not a contrast but an equation.

Before we can get that equation to come out, though, it will be necessary to anticipate a conclusion that would otherwise only emerge little by little. It is, briefly, that in traditional symbolism there exists a consistent association of oranges and lemons respectively with a whole series of other complementary or antithetical dualities: gold and silver (or the white of purity); sun and moon; ripeness and unripeness; fecundity and sterility; the acceptance and rejection or renunciation of love (as a folk couplet says, 'O limão o fastio; / a laranja o bem querer' (*CPE* 665)); and ultimately even life and death.

This complex of binary associations is one of several thematic constants, such as the motif of the wind, that link the cultivated poet García Lorca (as conscious an artist as he was a cunning artificer) with the popular and traditional substratum in which his only peers in the Iberian languages are the no less cultivated and conscious artists Gil Vicente and Lope de Vega in the sixteenth and seventeenth centuries. The dichotomy solar fruit/lunar fruit (or, as one might say, *yáng* and *yin* fruit) appears implicitly in such verses of Lorca's as 'La luna llorando dice: / Yo quiero ser una naranja' (GL 341), or

Nadie come naranjas	No one eats oranges
bajo la luna llena.	under the full moon.

Es preciso comer	It is required to eat
fruta verde y helada.	green and icy fruit.

GL 339

If acceptance of love is clearly identified with oranges in 'Alma, / ponte color de naranja. / Alma, / ponte color de amor' and 'La mar no tiene naranjas, / ni Sevilla tiene amor',[7] the two terms of the antithesis are in ambiguous equilibrium in

Naranja y limón.	Orange and lemon.
¡Ay de la niña	Alas for the girl
del mal amor!	ill-loved!
Limón y naranja.	Lemon and orange.
¡Ay de la niña,	Alas for the girl,
de la niña blanca!	the girl with white skin!
Limón.	Lemon.
(Cómo brillaba	(How the sun
el sol.)	shone.)
Naranja.	Orange.
(En las chinas	(On the pebbles
del agua.)	in the water.)

GL 335

This conjunction of water and sun reinforces the positive aspect as opposed to the negative one represented by the pale *niña-limón*. Rejection pure and simple, with the lemon once again equated to whiteness (here tacitly the pallor of death), is appropriately registered in one of the *Canciones de luna* (GL 343):

Llevo el No que me diste	I carry the No you gave me
en la palma de la mano,	in the palm of my hand,
como un limón de cera	like a wax lemon,
casi blanco . . .	almost white . . .

The antithesis fruitfulness/barrenness—a constant preoccupation of Lorca's, culminating in his tragedy *Yerma* ('The Barren One')—is inseparable, in the last analysis, from those of life/death and love/

---

[7] 'Soul, / turn orange colour, / Soul, / turn the colour of love' (GL 369); 'There are no oranges in the sea, / nor any love in Seville' (GL 309: a symbolic equation based on the Spanish adynata 'to look for oranges in the sea' or 'ask the elm tree for pears'; cf. our 'blood from a stone').

renunciation. In the last synthesis, so to speak, all three of these negative terms converge, signified in the following two poems not by lemons but either by the absence of oranges or by their anomalous transformation into a symbol not of freedom but of confinement:

La dama	The lady
estaba muerta en la rama.	was dead upon the branch.
La monja	The nun
cantaba dentro de la toronja.[8]	was singing inside the orange.

GL 537

Leñador.	Woodman.
Córtame la sombra.	Cut off my shadow.
Líbrame del suplicio	Free me from the torment
de verme sin toronjas.	of seeing myself with no oranges.

GL 389

But in the end, lemon grove and orange grove are only two faces (and two temporal phases) of a single reality:

Limonar.	Lemon grove.
Naranjal desfallecido,	Withered orange grove,
naranjal moribundo,	dying orange grove,
naranjal sin sangre.	bloodless orange grove.

GL 622

Coming back now to the quadra of the silver oranges, we are at last in a position to recognize that the carefree enjoyment of love ('ter amores não me custa') is being equated to the promise implicit in the orange tree with its golden trunk, and the fatal loss of love ('deixá-los é que me mata') to the disappointing realization that the fruit the tree bears is more of a lemon than an orange. But while in one sense it is true, as a Galician couplet has it, that one can eat any fruit but the green lemon ('Todo-los froitos se comen / sinón o verde limón'[9]), if we suppose that is the whole story we shall be reckoning without two disturbing factors that work to cancel out the negative implications of the lemon. One is the plurivalence (more than ambivalence) of

---

[8] Lorca sometimes uses the regionalism *toronja* (properly a grapefruit) for the Seville orange. This couplet seems like a distillation of 'La monja gitana' (GL 404), with the prison walls of the convent reduced to the peel of one of the 'cinco toronjas' that inspire the nun's daydream of highwaymen galloping through a landscape of hills and clouds, 'with twenty suns in the sky'.

[9] Ramón Cabanillas, *Antífona da Cantiga* (Vigo, 1951), 151.

symbolism itself; the other, the interference, in this specific case, of a
traditional metaphorical current that runs directly counter to the
symbolic one. I shall deal with this second factor first, and briefly:
both because metaphor is not our primary concern at this point and
because of the paradoxical fact that, although it is a more sophisticated
and intellectualized form of comparison than symbolism, it is at the
same time a less complex one.

METAPHOR VERSUS SYMBOL

The particular metaphor concerned is a visual one, which I shall
exemplify by means both of micropoems and of excerpts from longer
ones, ranging from the isles of Greece to the Jewish quarter of
Marrakesh, and from Aragon in the high Renaissance to contemporary
Trás-os-Montes—once again, not surprisingly, by way of Lorca's
Granada:

> Limonar.
>
> Nido
> de senos
> amarillos . . .
>
> GL 622

Lorca's vision of the lemon grove as a nest of yellow breasts is not
unlike that of a Miguel Torga, observing the lemon tree outside his
window and wondering whether it would be permissible to sing of

> . . . as tetas de donzela
> Que daqui da janela
> Vejo no limoeiro . . .[10]

But even the austere and donnish Fray Bartolomé de Argensola,
musing in the sixteenth century about all the citrus fruits that used to
come up to the barren wastes of his Aragonese homeland from the
vega of Valencia (the Valencia of that *niña* who was later to be found
engaged in citric target practice from her own high window), saw no
impropriety in remarking on such an obvious resemblance:

> Desde Valencia dan Pomona y Flora
> la cidra y la naranja a nuestra Pales,

---

[10] *Diário*, iii (Coimbra, 1954), 135.

con las limas que el sol adulza y dora
cuando a breves tetillas virginales
imitan . . .[11]

Not infrequently the vehicle and tenor of the metaphor are inverted, and instead of lemons (or limes) recalling breasts, the latter recall the former, as in these verses from a Sephardic wedding song from Morocco (Alvar, 173), a late vernacular specimen of the ritual epithalamia of which the prototype is the Song of Songs, and which celebrate in minute and enthusiastic detail all the bride's best points from head to toe:[12]

—¿Cómo se llaman los pechos?
—No es 'pechos' que ellos se llaman,
sino limón limonar
(¡ay, mi limón limonar!) . . .

'What are her breasts called?'
'It isn't "breasts" they're called!
It's lemons: lemon grove
(oh my lemons, my lemon grove!) . . .'

With this we could compare the first couplet of a popular Portuguese quadra: 'Teu peito são dois limões, / o teu corpo um limoeiro' (Lima, 150); and much the same metaphor reappears in this song from the Dodecanese:[13]

Τὰ στήθη σ' ἔνε λεμονεὰ	Your bosom is a lemon tree
καὶ τὰ βυζιά σου κλῶνοι,	and your breasts the boughs:
χαρὰ' ς τὸν νέον ποὺ νὰ μπῆ	happy the young man who can
νὰ κόψη τὸ λεμόνι.	come in and pick the lemons!

The other factor that militates against a purely negative connotation for the lemon is inherent in the nature of symbolism. When I called the poem about the golden orange tree that bore silver oranges 'subtle', and its parallelism 'effectively concealed', I was speaking as if

[11] *Rimas*, ed. J. M. Blecua (Saragossa, 1950).
[12] Or rather from toe to head: on the convention of an ascending order in such descriptions in both the Hebrew and the Arabic traditions see Picchio, 72–6.
[13] *CGD* 329. To bring out its symmetry with the typical Portuguese quadra I have transcribed in four verses the form conventionally represented in Greek by a monorhyme couplet with caesura. Another folk distych (Abbot, 126) speaks of a girl 'who has lemon breasts' ("Π' ὤχει τὸ βυζὶ λεϊμόνι") so lovely that whoever sees them is wounded: 'Let me see them and be wounded; / . . . / could I see them, could I touch them, / I'd give everything I own!'

it were the work of a professional poet, full of conscious artifice and addressed (like the *poesía de tipo tradicional* of a Vicente or a Lope or a García Lorca) to a discriminating literary audience. Since it is in fact nothing of the sort, the question arises whether it has not put itself in the false position of being rather too clever to carry out its job of communicating efficiently.

The short (and, I think, the right) answer to this is that such an analytically minded reading public is in practice considerably likelier to be thrown off the scent than is the largely illiterate listening public it *is* addressed to: a public more at home with symbolism—an intuitive and synthetic method of comparison—than with the intellectual and analytical strategies of metaphor, and more with emotional than with logical consistency. Such an audience can take in its stride the fact that one symbol may stand at the same time not only for different concepts but even for contradictory ones.

In Freudian terms this possibility of representing several concepts by a single symbol is the 'condensation principle'. The fusion of contraries is the 'ambivalence principle' (which Nicholas of Cusa, five centuries before Freud, knew as the *coincidentia oppositorum*). Neither principle is compatible with discursive analytical reason: both belong rather to the category of what Suzanne Langer has called 'laws of the imagination', valid only for the creation of such non-discursive constructions as dreams, myth, and poetry (in the broad sense of *poiesis*). And as 'every product of imagination', in Langer's words (241), 'comes as a qualitative direct datum . . . any emotional import conveyed by it is perceived just as directly'. Or as C. S. Lewis once remarked (345), 'the more concrete and vital . . . poetry is, the more hopelessly complicated it will become in analysis; but the imagination receives it as a simple'.

One quadra from the north-eastern Brazilian state of Sergipe synthesizes such a qualitative direct datum or simple, with an ambiguity it is hard not to think deliberate, out of a number of familiar motifs:

Atirei um limão verde	I threw an unripe lemon
lá na Torre de Belém;	up at the Tower of Belém;
deu no ouro, deu na prata,	it hit the gold, the silver,
deu no peito de meu bem.	and my beloved's breast.

CPB ii. 475

This does indeed become complicated in analysis; but perhaps not hopelessly so, at least so long as the analysis is not narrowly logical.

The tentativeness of the suitor's approach is shown by his throwing a lemon (and a green one at that) instead of an orange: he is uncertain of his reception, and the lemon he throws stands for his subconscious anticipation of the one he fears he may get back. The hope of exorcizing or at least minimizing this danger can be deduced from variants of the first line recorded in other parts of the North-East, in which the green lemon has become a *limãozinho* (with a diminutive suffix to sweeten it), or sweet-smelling (*cheiroso*), or quite simply sweet: a *limão doce* (ibid. 495, 516, and 564).

As for the Tower of Belém, this Lisbon landmark's survival of its transatlantic migration (despite making no sense in the new setting of Belém do Pará) is no doubt due to its appropriateness as a symbol not only of haughty inaccessibility, like the window in other quadras we have seen, but also of a woman's body, like the Tower of David in the Song of Songs (4: 4, where the eulogy of the beloved's breasts follows immediately after), or the 'jade tower' that serves in Chinese poetry as a metaphor for the shoulders of a beautiful woman.[14]

Recalling the equation of gold and silver to oranges and lemons, we find the suitor's tentativeness reflected also in 'it hit the gold, it hit the silver': as much as to say 'she loves me, she loves me not'. At the same time the semantically and even phonetically parallel structure of 'deu no ouro, deu na prata, / deu no peito de meu bem' makes it clear that *ouro* and *prata* are both being equated to *peito*, and are to be taken not simply as opposites but also in their most obvious sense as twin paradigms of beauty and value. A Pernambuco version of the same poem, confirming this assumption, reads 'deu no cravo, deu na rosa', with carnation and rose replacing the precious metals (cf. n. 15, below).

The duality not only of the symbols themselves but of what they stand for is emphasized when we consider the metaphorical equation of *limões* and *peitos* in the light of another variant in which the lemon thrown to a girl in her window 'bateu nos peitinhos dela'. But the version with the singular 'deu no peito' nevertheless remains the better one, because it implicitly includes the idea of duality while at the same time allowing for the development of at least three additional planes of meaning:

1. As we saw when another lemon thrown *down* from a high window 'deu-me no peito, e o sumo no coração', *peito* and *coração*, if

---

[14] On the sexual symbolism of the tower cf. 113 below, and Ch. 1, n. 39.

not virtual synonyms, can represent successive stages in a progression; and by these lights 'deu no peito de meu bem' means 'my throw was dead on target': the appeal has gone straight to her heart.

2. In certain cultures, striking a woman's breast with a fruit has specific sexual implications: in Indonesia, for instance, according to Stith Thompson, it is believed to cause pregnancy. The erotic implications of the following *tetrástikhon* (Abbot, 124), less veiled than in any of our analogous Iberian poems, help us to interpret these better:

Νὰ εἶχ' νεράντζι νά' ριχνα	If only I had an orange
στὸ πέρα παραθύρι,	to throw at yonder window
νὰ 'τσάκιζα τὸν μαστραπᾶ	and shatter the vase
πώχει τὸ καρυοφύλλι.	with the carnation[15] in it.

3. Finally, thanks to the association of oranges and lemons with ripeness and unripeness, the equivocal citrus (is it still *verde*? or is it, rather, already *doce* and *cheiroso*?) symbolizes, like the flower in the Greek poem, the girl herself.

CUPIDO IMMITIS UVAE

Just as for some there is a special thrill in the precarious balance of Yes or No, will she or won't she—'aquel si viene o no viene, / aquel si sale o no sale' which, as the sixteenth-century playwright Timoneda said, 'en los amores no tiene / contento que se le iguale'— so there are those who are drawn, like the Marquess of Santillana in his dawn encounters with the barely nubile shepherdesses and cowgirls of the sierra, to the tartness of *fructa temprana*.

Horace, to be sure, already knew only too well this 'cupidinem immitis uvae' (*Od.* 1. 4); and his disciple the worldly-wise Seville Jesuit Francisco de Medrano—perhaps the most notable Horatian poet of the seventeenth century—warned sagely of the perils of an 'apetito ... malseguro / deel ermoso razimo que aun azedo / está'.[16] But the most unusual and even exotic celebration of this suspect appetite is by the contemporary Brazilian poet João Cabral, who, like

---

[15] This καρυοφύλλι is the same as the *cravo* mentioned in the quatrain from Pernambuco, above. On the vase as a feminine symbol see Ch. 4. The obvious words for 'vase' would be βάζο or γλάστρα: has μαστραπᾶ perhaps been used here because of a subconscious association with μαστός: 'breast'?

[16] Alonso and Reckert, 249.

Medrano (and unlike Horace), faces squarely the hint of potential perversity inseparable from it. In a sequence of twenty-eight short stanzas (originally printed as forty-four-syllable micropoems) entitled 'Jogos Frutais', Cabral explores in meticulous and lingering detail, as they successively present themselves to his mind, a series of analogies between a girl poised on the brink of maturity and the precocious and 'almost animal' fruits of the tropical *Nordeste* of Brazil.

These analogies are not metaphorical but quite concrete ones, in which a multiplicity of symbolic fruits are fused one by one with the single object[17] symbolized; for, as the poet tells her:

És uma fruta múltipla,	You are a multiple fruit,
mas simples, lógica;	but simple, logical:
Nada tens de metafísica	nothing about you metaphysical
ou metafórica.	or metaphorical.
Não és O Fruto	You're not The Fruit,
e nem para A Semente	and I can't quite see you either
te vejo muito...	as The Seed...

What she is, rather, is

...fruta de carne acesa,	...a fruit with pungent flesh
sempre em agraz,	for ever unripe,
como araçás, guabirabas,	like guavas, *guabirabas*,
maracujás.	passion fruit.
Também mangaba...	*Mangaba*, too...

Which is why—he explains, with an image that recalls, perhaps by chance (but perhaps not[18]), Rilke's oranges drowning in their own sweetness—

Aumentas a sede como	You increase thirst
fruta màdura	like fruit so ripe
que começa a corromper-se	it's begun to decompose
no seu açúcar.	in its own sugar.
Ácida e verde:	Acid and green:
contudo, a quem te conhece	yet anyone who knows you
só dás mais sede...	you leave thirstier still...

---

[17] To forestall possible misunderstanding: Cabral's whole poetic stance, which allows him to regard even a woman as an 'object' without thereby demeaning her, is predicated on the indeterminacy of subject and object: see 'To Learn from Stone', in Ch. 6, below.

[18] The first of Cabral's 'Estudos para uma bailadora andaluza' (225 f.) seems like a variation on Rilke's 'Spanische Tanzerin', in *Neue Gedichte* (Frankfurt, 1976), 57.

But though we might seem at this point to be on the borders of Nabokov country, this is no mere nymphet:

> Ácida e verde, porém   Acid and green, yet already
> já anuncias   with a foretaste
> o açúcar maduro que   of the ripe sugar
> terás um dia.   you'll have one day.

The conviction—or more often the hope—most frequently expressed is in fact the one hinted at here. It had already been formulated at least as early as the fifteenth century by an anonymous poet who was one of the last to write in Galician of a sort, before its four-century eclipse as a literary language:

> Meu naranjedo no ten fruto,   My orange grove has no fruit,
> mas agora ven.   but it's coming now.
> No me lo toque ninguén!   Let no one touch it!
>
> Meu naranjedo florido,   My orange grove in bloom—
> el fruto no l'es venido,   its fruit has not yet come,
> mas agora ven.   but it's coming now.
> No me lo toque ninguén...   Let no one touch it...
>
> CMP 310

It is of course a hope analogous to the one that can be detected behind propitiatory references to a *limão doce*: if a symbolic golden orange tree can bear lemons, might not a symbolic lemon be persuaded to ripen into an orange? At all events (as one Alentejan 'orange' confesses), even the fruit that is most thoroughly 'mûre pour l'amour savant' had to begin by being green:

> A laranja nasceu verde;   The orange was born green;
> com o tempo amadurou.   in time it grew ripe.
> Meu coração nasceu livre;   My heart was born free;
> esse teu o cativou.   yours took it captive.
>
> CPBA i. 649

The water of life that is relied on to hasten this ripening process and encourage the hoped-for transformation is naturally, as a Greek quatrain (Petropoulos, 127 f.) makes clear, love:

> Γίνου στὸν κάμπο λεμονιά,   Be a lemon tree in the field;
> κι' ἐγὼ στὰ ὄρη χιόνι,   I'll be snow on the mountains,
> νὰ λειώνω νὰ ποτίζωνται   to melt and give you water
> οἱ δροσεροί σου κλῶνοι.   for your cool limbs to drink.

And in a parallelistic 'traditional-type' villancico, that timid hope—
with the aid of some traditional-type Andalusian machismo—has
turned to bold assurance (or possibly mere bravado):

> Me tirastes un limón,
> me distes en la cara;
> todo lo allana el amor;
> l'amor todo lo allana;
> todo lo allana el amor,
> morena resalada.
>
> Me tirastes un limón,
> me distes en la frente;
> todo lo vence el amor,
> l'amor todo lo vence;
> todo lo vence el amor:
> dame la mano y vente.[19]

A Galician quatrain displays equal but even more daringly
outspoken confidence:

Vente comigo, laranxa;	Come away with me, orange,
deixa quedar o limón:	and let the lemon be:
dormirás na miña cama,	you shall sleep in my bed,
depar do meu corazón.	next to my heart.

CPG i. 45

But another from Brazil shows the possible consequences of
appearing too sure of oneself:

Tanta laranja madura,	So many ripe oranges,
tanto limão pelo chão;	so many lemons on the ground;
tanto sangue derramado	so much blood shed
dentro do meu coração!	within my heart!

CPB ii. 486

A European variant (Lima, 105) gives the last two lines as 'tanta
menina bonita, / nenhuma na minha mão', to make sure no one
misses the point that the oranges are the pretty girls themselves, and
that they have thrown the lemons down to the ground in the standard

---

[19] Torner, 87. 'You threw me a lemon, / and hit me in the face (*on the forehead*); /
love simplifies (*conquers*) all: / give me your hand and come' (the give-away is of course
the Virgilian tag). *Morena resalada* defies translation. To call an English-speaker 'you
vivacious brunette' would be unlikely to get one very far; but Andalusian realities are
what they are (Lorca: 'aquí somos otra gente').

gesture of disdain. But the very fact that it has been felt necessary to use a parallelistic equation in such a familiar context begins to seem like an excessive dotting of *i*s and crossing of *t*s. Having absorbed such an amount of citrus symbolism we are perhaps being wise after the event; but the version from the *Nordeste* does seem preferable, if only because by substituting simple replacement for the usual symbolic equation, and leaving something unsaid, it leaves itself room to say something more.

It is a special quality of symbolism, due to the intimate fusion of the symbol with the object symbolized, that the latter's attributes are easily transmitted to others metaphorically or metonymically related to it. Thus, just as orange blossom shares the properties of the orange, so in the Alentejo the tree itself, and even its shade—though it is said the only shade there comes from the sky—take on the symbolic values usually ascribed to its fruit and flowers, and come to stand for the protective aspect of marriage:

Debaixo da laranjeira	Underneath the orange tree
não chove nem faz orvalho;	there's neither rain nor dew;
menina, case comigo,	come on, girl, and marry me;
nã' me dê tanto trabalho.	don't give me such a hard time.

CPBA 842

Even at night, the shade of the orange tree, by an obvious association of ideas, is propitious for a lovers' meeting:

À sombra da laranjeira	The shade of the orange tree
é um regalo amar;	is great for making love:
tem a folha bem juntinha:	the leaves are so close together
não entra lá o luar.[20]	the moonlight can't get in.

The straightforwardness of this quadra contrasts with the puzzling implications of the preceding one: rain and dew, as universal symbols of impregnation, are just what might be expected under the orange tree. Disappointment of the speaker's hopes of Nature as an ally in seduction has perhaps made him resign himself to complying with the norms of society as his only way of getting what he wants.

In the light of these two poems, and the atmosphere of sympathetic magic that pervades Gil Vicente's *Don Duardos*, it is not hard to guess

---

[20] Heard in Vale Formoso (Estrela Mountains) in 1969. Alentejan variants of the last two quadras have *oliveira* for *laranjeira* (*CPBA* i. 846; 769); on the sexual connotations of the olive see below, nn. 25–6.

why, when the infanta Flérida innocently suggests sheltering from the heat in the shade of the orange trees—

> Vamos passar los calores
> debaxo del naranjal—

the hero agrees with such alacrity that this is just the thing to do, for then 'a flower will fall among flowers':

> Señora, ahi es natural:
> caeraa flor en las flores.[21]

The sexual innuendo would naturally be lost on the ingenuous infanta, but not on the audience.

By the same token, one need not look far for the reason why a girl in the fifteenth-century *Cancionero de Palacio* who confesses to her mother that love is troubling her—

> Las mis penas, madre,
> de amores son—

is so promptly and urgently warned (conceivably by the causer of the trouble[22]):

> Salid, mi señora,   Come out, madam,
> de so'l naranjale,   from under the orange trees:
> que sois tan hermosa,   you are so fair
> quemarvos ha el aire: the air will burn you—
> de amores, sí.   yes, with love!
>
> *LTT* 26

As with the golden *laranjeira* that bore silver oranges, it is again an Algarvian *quadra* that resorts to the symbol of the orange tree to explain an antithesis, this time a *coincidentia oppositorum* (to be precise, one of *chiaroscuro*):

> Debaixo da laranjeira   Under the orange tree
> estou à sombra e estou ao sol: I'm in the shade and the sun,
> estou ao pé do meu amor,   for there I'm with my love,
> onde é que melhor estou.   and that's the best place for me.
>
> *CPA* 73

---

[21] Reckert 1977: 374 f.: ll. 1210–15.

[22] Given the courtly provenance of the song, it is also quite possible that the mother herself would address her daughter as 'madam' and remark on her beauty (a matrimonial asset but a potential source of danger).

The gravitational field of such a cluster of symbols as the citrus complex is powerful enough to draw into its orbit even something as remotely connected with it as the herb *toronjil*, purely on the strength of its citric smell and name. Lope de Vega brings it into a wedding song in which the bride is portrayed as a *niña*, wandering here and there amid the orange blossom and lemon balm:

> Por aquí, por aquí, por allí,
> anda la niña en el toronjil;
> por aquí, por allí, por acá,
> anda la niña en el azahar.
>
> *LTT* 451

Lorca, whose own wedding songs often show the strong influence of Lope, must have had these verses in mind when he wrote, in *Blood Wedding* (II. i):

> Por el toronjil
> la novia no puede dormir.
> Por el naranjel
> el novio le ofrece cuchara y mantel.
>
> Amid the lemon balm
> the bride cannot sleep.
> Among the orange trees
> the groom offers her spoon and tablecloth.

An anonymous song recorded in Diego Pisador's *Libro de música de vihuela* of 1552 calls to mind the orange tree so discreet it would not let the moonlight through, or the 'flowers round Espinama' that were the *encubridores*—at once the accomplices and the literal cover-up—in Santillana's encounter with a fair mountain cowgirl; at the same time this villancico provides an example of the simultaneously symbolic and literal use of a single motif: the herb-covered, flower-strewn, and copiously watered mountainside it describes is both a complex semi-metaphorical symbol of the act of love and the literal scene of it:[23]

---

[23] Among the Santals of India, 'places of assignation are . . . "the foot of the mountain"'; unintended pregnancy is 'making a citron fruit fall': and love-making is 'crying for water' (W. G. Archer, *The Hill of Flutes* (London, 1974), 66). In the universal folk-tale made famous by Prokofiev's *Love for Three Oranges*, a prince finds three citrons, from each of which a maiden emerges crying: 'Give me water, or I die'; the first two die of thirst, but on opening the last fruit the prince has water and the spell is broken. More elaborate correspondences between 'fruit' (girl) and 'water' (man

Aquellas sierras, madre,	Those mountains, mother,
altas son de sobir;	are high to climb;
corrían los caños,	the channels flowed, and emptied
daban en un toronjil.	into the lemon balm.
Madre, aquellas sierras	Mother, those mountains,
llenas son de flores;	are covered with flowers;
encima de ellas	there on the heights
tengo mis amores.	I have my love.
Corrían los caños;	The channels flowed, and emptied
daban en un toronjil.	into the lemon balm.

LTT 132

Another version of the *mote*, published twenty-eight years later by Pedro da Padilla (*LIT* 410) with a gloss of his own composition to complete it, reads

La sierra es alta
y áspera de subir;
los caños corren agua
y dan en el toronjil.

In Padilla's continuation the girl expands on her first bare statement that she 'has her love' on the heights, and confides in her mother that she happened one day to see her handsome friend on yonder lofty ridge—'aquel lomo erguido'—and

llaméle con mi toca	I beckoned with my bonnet
y con mis dedos cinco...	and with my fingers five...
Los caños corren agua	The channels flow with water
y dan en el toronjil.	and end in the lemon balm.

DOWN IN THE REEDS BY THE RIVER

The specific references to *agua* in these two villancicos would be enough, if anything more were needed, to remind us that not only is flowing water the universal symbol of life and fertility, but that virtually every item of décor in our last few poems—trees, mountainous rocky landscapes, flower gardens, almost any herb one can

or love) occur in Scott Fitzgerald's 'The Ice Palace', where the 19-year-old protagonist is symbolized, before and after a disastrous visit to the North, by a green apple and a peach; the antithetical dualities are *apple—North—cold—ice—death/peach—South—warmth—water—life*. Apples and peaches as citrus surrogates are discussed in the final section of this chapter; cf. also n. 25, below.

think of—belongs to the most elementary Freudian arsenal of sexual imagery.

The same high peaks, herbs, and flowing water recur in another villancico, this one from the 1556 Uppsala song-book (*LTT* 141); the device used here is again simple replacement, and depends for its efficacy on our being able to supply the missing proper terms from memory and imagination. Once we do, it becomes clear that what the poem is really about (if we must say it is 'about' something) is the same kind of encounter as in the two previous ones:

> Alta estaba la peña,　　High was the peak;
> nace la malva en ella.　on it grows the mallow.
>
> Alta estaba la peña,　　High was the peak
> riberas del río;　　　　by the riverbank;
> nace la malva en ella,　on it grows the mallow
> y el trébol florido.　　and the flowering clover.

Gerald Brenan's suggestion (122) that the mallow stands for a girl[24] looking out of her upstairs window is also admissible, since alternative interpretations of a symbol need not be mutually exclusive (and may even not be alternative, properly speaking, but equally applicable at the same time). Our citrus poems have already made us abundantly familiar with the standard motif of the girl at the window; and it is certainly true that in Spanish traditional verse the *malva* (or *malvica*, *malveta*, or even—less expectedly, but on reflection not surprisingly—*malva morena*) consistently represents a girl.

Support for Brenan's thesis might also be found in

> Manjaricão da janela,　　Sweet basil in the window,
> dá-me a mão para subir:　give me a hand to climb up,
> eu sou muito vergonhoso;　for I'm far too bashful
> pela porta não hei-de ir.　to come in through the door.

> *AMRP*

[24] 'Girls. The very word is like a bell, tinkling us back to a lost world . . . How could we think that a small linguistic shift . . . , imperceptible . . . to all but a few . . . *Guardian* readers, would reflect any . . . significant change?' (Michael Wood, reviewing Kingsley Amis's *Difficulties with Girls*, *TLS* 23–9 Sept. 1988). The constant tinkling of this word in the present chapter may be offensive to some women readers; but the fact is that it is *girls* that the poems studied are mostly about (or addressed to, or spoken by), since in so far as these are or purport to be folk poems, their protagonists—shepherdesses, fruit-pickers, laundresses, reapers—are necessarily peasants, whose time of flowering before they grow thick of waist and coarse of skin (and cease to inspire poems) is all too short (cf. the commentary on Dom Dinis's 'Levantou-s' a velida' in Ch. 1).

But his further conjecture that the flowering clover might be the younger sister of the 'mallow' is unconvincing: the masculine associations of the trefoil in folklore, and of the number three itself in Freudian dream interpretation, are well known (compare the 'tres pericas' in the pear-tree poem quoted earlier).

A peculiar expressive advantage of symbolism is its freedom to slip almost imperceptibly from the symbolic to the literal plane of meaning and back again, sometimes balancing midway between the two. This is especially true when it takes the form of simple replacement, in which a literal fact, scene, or object acquires symbolic meanings through the chance connotations and associations that accumulate in the course of time around certain words in a given culture or literary tradition while their primary meanings remain the obvious and purely literal ones (cf. Brooke-Rose, 288).

Flowers, herbs, groves, gardens, and water are among the commonest of erotic symbols; but quite apart from such inherent or Freudian associations as they may happen to have or to have taken on, a green hillside, an olive grove, an orchard, a rose garden, or a canebrake by the river, are all, in simple fact, eminently suitable places for an actual lovers' meeting. Awareness of this literal 'extrinsic context' will often provide a key to unlock such otherwise enigmatic micropoems as

> En aquella peña, en aquella,
> que no caben en ella,
>
> *LTT* 167

where so many couples have met on the mountain that there is no room for more; or, in Gil Vicente's *Inês Pereira*, this song, with its hyperbolic adynaton (for who has ever seen the cane in bloom—or felt the earth move?),

Canas do amor, canas,	Reeds of love, reeds,
canas do amor.	reeds of love.
Polo longo de um rio	Along the riverbank
canaval vi florido:	I saw the canebrake in bloom:
canas do amor.	reeds of love.

Cop 217^v

The canebrake reappears, together with a pine-wood, in the quasi-synonymous form of a *mimbrera* or osier-bed, apparently as a shelter

for furtive love, in a song by Vicente's younger Spanish contemporary
Lope de Rueda:

Mimbrera, amigo,	Osiers, friend:
so la mimbrereta.	under the osiers.
Y los dos amigos	And the two friends
idos se son, idos,	have gone away; they are gone
so los verdes pinos,	under the green pines,
so la mimbrereta;	under the osiers;
mimbrera, amigo.	osiers, friend.
Y los dos amados	And the two lovers
idos se son ambos,	have gone away together,
so los verdes prados,	under the green meadows,
so la mimbrereta.	under the osiers.

LTT 400

It is conceivable that *so*, in 'so los verdes prados', is a corrupt reading
(by anticipation of the same word in the next line) of *por* (or that
prados should be *ramos*: 'branches'). But what lifts this poem out of
the realm of the commonplace is precisely the chilling implication
that (like 'les petites marionettes' who 'font, font, font / trois p'tits
tours, / et puis s'en vont'), the way this archetypal pair of anonymous
lovers has gone is that of all flesh.

In a more carefree and less courtly style, a song-book of the next
century alludes darkly to unspecified 'goings on', not under the pines
but among the green olive trees:

> Que no hay tal andar
> por el verde olivico,
> que no hay tal andar
> por el verde olivar.

LTT 277

The olive, as a traditional rural index of wealth and fruitfulness,
frequently appears in association not only with oranges, as in Lorca's
'Baladilla de los tres ríos' (GL 153), but with apples. André Michalski
has made a detailed study of the meaning of the olive and apple
trees (respectively solar or masculine and lunar or feminine) in the
'hermetic garden' which he argues is the scene of an alchemical-
sexual union in the arcane thirteenth-century Castilian poem known

as the 'Razón de amor',[25] citing numerous early and modern references, popular and literary, to olive trees and their fruit as metaphors for the male genitalia. As for the apple—a metonym for Eve and hence a symbol of woman herself—see the Greek and Portuguese songs quoted in Reckert 1980: 217 f. A full study of the olive and apple in traditional verse, called for many years ago by Asensio (269), still remains to be made.

There is more coming and going in the olive groves (and more uninhibitedly identified) in this *cante flamenco*, copied down in Seville at the end of the last century by the great poet Antonio Machado's ethnographer father,[26] and reminiscent of Pedro de Padilla's earlier *niña* who called her handsome friend with her bonnet 'y con mis dedos cinco':

Mira que no soy de aqueyas	Don't think *I'm* one of that kind,
que ban por los olibares	going about the olive groves
con er pañuelo en la mano,	with my handkerchief in my hand,
yamando a los melitares.	beckoning to the soldiers!

Vicente's canebrake song likewise finds a modern echo in an Alentejan folk quatrain, also much less veiled:[27]

Andas morto por saber	You're dying to find out
onde faço a minha cama:	where it is I make my bed:
faço-a à beira dum rio,	I make it on the riverbank
à sombra da verde cana.	in the shade of the green canes.

[25] Michalski's unpublished paper 'La "Razón de amor": alquimia y mozarabía', which he has kindly allowed me to see, helps to interpret the enigmatic 16th-c. poem, quoted in Ch. 1, in which a girl dreams of roses blooming for her and of 'ell vino so ell agua frida'. In the older poem a young man has just lain down for a nap in a grove of olive and apple trees after a vision of two silver vases in the top of one of the latter, the upper vase 'pleno . . . d'un agua fryda' and the other of red wine, put there by the mistress of the orchard, when her arrival makes him revise his plan for a siesta; after the two have lain under the olive tree the *doncella* takes leave of him; a white dove then appears, and after bathing in the cold water flies off, overturning it into the wine in her haste. A comparative analysis of the two poems leaves no doubt about the respective symbolic identity of water and wine and of apple and rose; on the latter two see Wilkins, 108.

[26] Antonio Machado y Álvarez, *Cantes flamencos* (Buenos Aires, n.d.), 83.

[27] *CPBA* i. 699/701. All reticence vanishes in Nuno Bragança's semi-autobiographical novel *A Noite e o Riso* (Lisbon, 1969), 112 ff., when a purposeful 15-year-old proletarian girl marches the upper-class adolescent narrator off to a canebrake on the slum outskirts of Lisbon to initiate him into sex and the realities of life. The author told me he was unaware of the old motif: the topos was not intertextual but real.

Judging from her evident uneasiness at the end of her interrogation of an alternately pale and flushed daughter, the mother in this song of Vicente's must have been as well acquainted with the reputation of the actual riverside bower as she was with what it habitually symbolizes:

—Donde vindes, filha,	'Where have you come from, daughter,
branca e colorida?	all so white and red?'
—De lá venho, madre,	'From down yonder, mother,
de ribas de um rio;	by the riverbank;
achei meus amores	I chanced to meet my love
num rosal florido . . .	in a flowering rose garden . . .'
—*Florido*, 'enha filha	'*Flowering*, my daughter
branca e colorida?! . . .	all so white and red?! . . .'

Cop 240^{r-v}

A cantiga by Joam Zorro provides what might be another answer to the same question, except that this time the question has not even been asked; the reader is thus given cause to wonder whether real repentance is being expressed, or whether the volunteering of such information may not instead be a discreetly veiled defiance of maternal authority (as if to say 'lá vai a laranja ao ar!'):

> Pela ribeyra do rio salido
> trebelhey, madre, con meu amigo;
> amor ey migo que non houvesse:
> fiz por amig' o que non fezesse . . .
>
> CBN 1158
>
> Down on the bank of the river in spate
> I dallied, mother, with my friend;
> I feel a love I would I did not:
> I did for my friend what I would I had not . . .

This mother–daughter dialogue survives in the Alentejo, so thoroughly stripped of all but the purely symbolic by simple replacement that if it were not for the example of Gil Vicente (and the pallor of the rose) it would be hard to recognize the same theme in such an almost completely volatilized state:

—Rosa branca, desmaiada,	'White rose so pallid,
onde deixaste o cheiro?	where have you left your scent?'

—Deixei-o além no jardim,	'I left it out in the garden,
à sombra do limoeiro.[28]	in the shade of the lemon tree.'

A counterpart of this *rosa branca* is the 'cinnamon flower' in a folk-song from Epirus (Theros, 208), whose mother, asking 'Why have you gone so pale, why have you lost your colour?' ("'τί ἐκιτρίνησες καὶ 'τί εἶσαι χλωμιασμένη;"), is told a boy kissed her when she went to the spring for water (spring and fountain being other erotic symbols habitually conflated with the lovers' actual meeting-place).

In Brazilian variants of the same motif it appears in conjunction simultaneously with citrus imagery and the venerable 'blaming the wind' topos:

—Minha laranjeira verde,	'My green orange tree,
porque estás tão desfolhada?	why are you so bare of leaves?'
—Foi do vento desta noite,	'It was the wind that blew last night,
sereno da madrugada.	and the foggy dew at dawn.'

CPB ii. 614

A still more striking parallel is this pair of quadras, once again from the Lower Alentejo, in which a more openly suspicious and too persistently inquisitive mother gets two different answers, the second no less disquieting than the first:

—Donde vens, ó Ana?	'Where have you come from, Ana?'
—Venho da ribeira.	'From the riverbank.'
—Cheira-me o teu fato	'Your dress seems to me
à flor da laranjeira:	to smell of orange blossom:
à flor da laranjeira,	to smell of orange blossom,
à flor do alecrim:	of rosemary in bloom:
donde vens, ó Ana?	where have you come from, Ana?'
—Venho do jardim.	'It's from the garden I've come.'

CPBA ii. 130

---

[28] Heard in Moura (Alentejo), 1973. The gender roles are reversed in the old ballad (R. Menéndez Pidal, *Flor nueva de romances viejos* (Buenos Aires, n.d.), 53) of the page interrogated by the king with whose daughter he has just slept:

—¿Dónde vienes, Gerineldo,	'Whence come you, Gerineldo,
tan mustio y descolorido?	so wan and pale of face?'
—Vengo del jardín, buen rey,	'I come from the garden, sire,
por ver cómo ha florecido:	from seeing how it has bloomed:
la fragancia de una rosa	the fragrance of a rose
la color me ha desvaído.	has ta'en my colour away.'

Vinícius de Moraes found this much worked-over theme still sufficiently worthy of attention to deserve a witty version *a lo divino*:

Virgem! Filha minha	Holy Mary! Daughter mine
De onde vens assim	Where have you come from like that
Tão suja de terra	All covered in earth
Cheirando a jasmim?	And jasmine scent
A saia com mancha	Your skirt stained
De flor carmesim	With crimson blossoms
E os brincos da orelha	And your ear-rings
Fazendo tlimtlim?	Going ting-ling?
Minha mãe querida	Dear mother
Venho do jardim	I've come from the garden
Onde a olhar o céu	Where I went to look up at the sky
Fui, adormeci.	I dropped off to sleep
Quando despertei	And when I awoke
Cheirava a jasmim	I smelled of the jasmine petals
Que um anjo esfolhava	An angel was strewing
Por cima de mim . . . [29]	On me . . .

'Virgem' is of course at the same time the mother's shocked exclamation of dismay and an identification of the girl; the poet may well have been reminded of the Virgin and St Anne by the fact that the daughter in the paired Alentejan quadras (with which, or a Brazilian variant of which, he was surely acquainted) is Ana.

Vinícius's mischievously disemic 'religious' poem is the sublimation of a motif whose more earthily material expression, ever since Pero Móogo, has always made use of such minimally camouflaged images of sexual initiation as torn dresses or a 'camisa de sangre toda manchada' (cf. Reckert 1980: 113 ff.). But it was Gil Vicente who, with a characteristically vivifying synthesis, gathered together all the scattered motifs—garden and riverbank; young girl and rose; the lover, the lemon, and the love-token—and all the rhetorical devices—simple replacement, parallelism, the simultaneity of literal and figurative meanings—and welded the whole into a single poem. With the help of *leixa-pren* and a verbal echo of two lines by his predecessor of three hundred years earlier, Ayras Núnez—'Pela ribeyra do ryo / cantando ýa la virgo', which also circulated in the

---

[29] *Obra poética* (Rio de Janeiro, 1968), 395 ('A Anunciação').

oral tradition of the Peninsula[30]—Vicente calls up again, in his *Play of the Four Seasons*, all the glamour of the old cantigas:

En la huerta nasce la rosa:	In the garden the rose is born:
quiérome yr allá	I will go there
por mirar al ruyseñor	to see the nightingale,
cómo cantavá.	how he was singing.
Por las riberas del río	Along the riverbank
limones coge la virgo:	the maiden is picking lemons:
quiérome yr allá	I will go there
por mirar al ruyseñor	to see the nightingale,
cómo cantavá.	how he was singing.
Limones cogía la virgo	The maiden was picking lemons
para dar al su amigo:	to give them to her friend:
quiérome yr allá	I will go there
para ver al ruyseñor	and see the nightingale,
cómo cantavá.	how he was singing.
Para dar al su amigo	To give them to her friend
en un sombrero de sirgo:	in a hat of silk:
quiérome yr allá	I will go there
para ver al ruyseñor	and see the nightingale,
cómo cantavá.[31]	how he was singing.

Much of this dreamlike atmosphere comes from the sense of suspended time created by mixing verb tenses: habitual present in *nasce la rosa*; implied future in *quiérome yr*; the ballad-type imperfect of make-believe in *cómo cantavá*, but particularly in *limones cogía*, which echoes the preceding *limones coge* as if to make it plain that no real distinction is intended between present and imperfect. The sensation is of entering an enchanted springtime enclosure where the nightingale is seen rather than heard, and the sun stands for ever at noon.

What this magic circle encloses is the familiar *locus amoenus* of

---

[30] Cf. Joam Zorro (*CBN* 1155): 'Pela ribeyra do rio / cantando ia la dona virgo', and the anonymous 1554 *vihuela* song 'Riberas de un río / vi moça virgo' (*LTT* 134). On the diffusion of the first line as a traditional-style formula cf. (as well as the poems by Vicente and Zorro quoted above) Ch. 1, n. 33 and text, and see Reckert 1977: 157 ff., and 1980: 166 f. The same motif appears, with that of the poplar grove (cf. Ch. 1. n. 17) in *LTT* 279: 'Orillicas del río / mis amores he, / y debajo de los álamos / me atendé' (By the riverbank / I have my love; / under the poplars / wait for me').

[31] *Cop* 17^{r-v} To go into the question of this Freudian hat in detail would be superfluous.

medieval rhetoric, with its amenity made miraculously complete by the exclusion of Time.[32] The reason for this sensation is that Vicente is working in a style appropriate to oral tradition: so successfully, indeed, that it has sometimes even been suggested that his poems might not be his at all, but genuinely traditional. The collective mentality he identifies himself with is one that even today is not wholly at ease (as none of us are in our subconscious, or in dreams) with the rigorous distinction between linear historical time and a mythical past constructed from archetypal happenings eternally renewed by ritual.

ORIENT AND IMMORTAL FRUIT

Marvell's vision of oranges on the tree as 'golden lamps in a green night' would be equally applicable not only to the beach fires glowing in the tropical night of Bahia *de Todos os Santos* but to all the magical and symbolic values they both stand for, lighting up, with the sudden clarity of a unifying intuitive perception, the dark places of pre-logical thought. Given the ambivalence of symbolism itself, it would perhaps be too much to expect such beacons to lead always in the same direction.

Citrus trees first arrived in Japan somewhat later than in the Mediterranean, at about the beginning of the second century, when emissaries of the Emperor Suijin returned from the Land Beyond Time bringing saplings, the fruit of which was to be known thereafter as the fruit with the timeless fragrance (*tokijiku no kagu no konomi*). The Land Beyond Time, with its godlike inhabitants, is obviously identifiable with the Taoist Land of the Immortals, which was usually said to be on the Kun Lún mountain range in furthest Central Asia, near the sources of white jade.

This identification leads to others, for it was on Kun Lún that the golden peaches of immortality grew, which were sometimes not golden but jade, and not peaches but pears; and 'the trees which bear golden pears and peaches . . . are only instances of the universal . . . tree of wisdom, the tree of life' (Schafer 1963*b*: 82–5). Kun Lún

---

[32] On the negation of Time in traditional and East Asian world-views see Ch. 3, n. 6. The *locus amoenus* topos itself, whose proliferation in post-Classical literature has been studied by Curtius, is the imaginative projection of a nostalgia for the lost Eden where Time never intruded; its supreme poetic realization is Dante's Earthly Paradise.

itself, then, is in turn related to the Semitic Eden, with its 'ambrosial fruits of vegetable gold', and to that other garden further West where the apples of the Hesperides were known to grow; and the timeless-scented fruits of the citrus—botanically *hesperidia*—are merely these same Protean apples–pears–peaches in yet another guise.

In the West, however, these Orient and immortal fruits, far from being timeless, are as we have seen the inescapable reminders of temporality. Indeed, it was precisely the apple—'gota de siglos que guarda / de Satanás el contacto', as Lorca called it—that brought the curse of Time and mortality upon mankind.

To resolve this paradox it is unnecessary to invoke the Eastern transcendental reconciliation of opposites or even the 'ambivalence principle' inherent in symbolism: it will be quite enough to observe the poetic uses actually made of the fruit with the timeless fragrance in a handful of Japanese texts, ranging from the seventh to the thirteenth century. Its real-life uses were various, according to the poem by Yakamochi, written in the year 749 (*MYS* 482–3), from which I have taken the details of its acclimatization in Japan: the blossoms could be picked to give to young girls, or carried in one's sleeve to scent it, or left to dry for a longer-lasting fragrance; and the small unripe fruits themselves could be strung together to make bracelets of miniature pomanders.

The association of its blossoms with the evanescent youth and beauty of young girls suggests that in practice the symbolic implications of the orange tree are not after all so very different in Japan from those we have found in the West: an impression only strengthened by the following group of three interrelated poems, the first of which is an anonymous ninth-century tanka from the *Kokinshū* song-book (*JCP* 268) spoken by a woman remembering a past lover:

Satsuki matsu	Now that I smell the scent	3
hanatachibana no	of flowering orange	2
ka o kageba	that waits till June [to bloom]	1
mukashi no hito no	I recall the scented sleeves	5
sode no ka zo suru.	of one long ago.	4

Some three hundred years later, in the mid-Classical period of Japanese literature, the poet Shunzei, struck by the poignancy of a present and a past turned to past and pluperfect by the intervening centuries, composed an allusive variation or *hon-kadori* on this poem imagining his own present tense projected into the future perfect:[33]

Tare ka mata	Will anyone again	1
hanatachibana ni	be moved to think of me	3
omoiden	by orange blossom	2
ware mo 'mukashi no	when I too have become	} 4–5
hito' to narinaba.	'one long ago'?	

JCP 267

Shunzei died in 1204, when the poetic career of his gifted granddaughter—known to literary history simply, and oddly (and with the traditional sexism that often condemned Japanese women writers to at least semi-anonymity[34]) as 'Shunzei's daughter'—was at its height. Her own variation on the same ancient poem naturally alludes at the same time to her grandfather's, and if understood not in the obvious sense as a poem about lost love[35] but rather as a reassuring answer to his question—a granddaughterly tribute of affection to his memory—it acquires an unexpected originality:

[33] Brower and Miner (*JCP* 7) point out that 'Japanese verbs... have... seven morphemes expressing... aspect combined with... fourteen... expressing mood. The result... is a particularly fine adjustment of tone (ultimately beyond the reach of translation) and an instrument especially well suited to exploring states of feeling, mind, and being.'

[34] In fairness it must be recalled that the early Classical period in Japan (9th–11th c.) was the only 'Golden Age' of any world literature in which women writers played the leading role. One reason for this, though, was that 'serious' literature—including prose in general—was written not in the vernacular but in Chinese, which enjoyed a prestige like that of Latin in medieval Europe, and which, again as in Europe, it was not thought ladylike to learn. A notable exception was the 8th-c. bluestocking Princess Uchiko, who has been called the greatest Japanese poet of her time, but who—presumably because she did write in Chinese—is not even mentioned in Katō's monumental history of Japanese literature. Dante ascribed the origin of European vernacular poetry to one poet's wish to be understood by a lady to whom 'era malagevole ad intendere i versi latini', and the same prejudice has been called 'perhaps the chief reason why... literature in Japanese in general survived' (Keene, 34; cf. Miner 1989: 7 f.): in both cases a myopic educational policy had ultimately fortunate results. Feminine ascendancy in early Japanese literature, from the oldest example of literary prose fiction extant in the language (*c.*935), is treated from various perspectives in Miner 1990: 18, 28, 184–7, and 208.

[35] *JCP* 289. That this may in fact not be a love poem is also conjectured (if for a different reason) by the authors, for whom 'Shunzei's daughter has made a dream world out of the daylight of the original... We are almost left wondering whether [she]... really had a lover or only dreamed she did when the scent of flowers stirred her memory of the earlier poem.'

Tachibana no	A brief sleep	3
niou atari no	amid the perfume of flowering	2
utatane wa	orange trees:	1
yume mo mukashi no	even in dreams I recall	} 4–5
sode no ka zo suru.	scented sleeves long ago.	

In the East no less than in the West, however, the scent of flowers wafted to one's bed, as another poem by 'Shunzei's daughter' demonstrates, normally has overtones of sensuous languor:

Kaze kayou	The breeze stirs,	1
nezame no sode no	waking me with the scent	} 2–3
hana no ka ni	of flowers on sleeve	
kaoru makura no	and pillow, fragrant	4
haru no yo no yume.	with spring night dreams.	5

JCP 289

Yet another century on, and we find much the same atmosphere in a tanka by another woman poet, Lady Eifuku Mon'in:

Neya made mo	Penetrating even to my bedchamber,
hana no ka fukaki	the scent of flowers
haru no yo no	in the spring night
mado ni kasumeru	comes in through the window
irigata no tsuki.	with the hazy moonlight.

JCP 395

In modern Japanese the unqualified word 'flower' (*hana*) conventionally means the cherry blossom, and is so translated in both these poems by Brower and Miner, who call attention to the poets' synaesthetic hyperbole (cherry blossom being scentless). The erotic suggestion is more overt in a Brazilian variation on the same subtheme (*CPB* ii. 593), from a Western and male point of view and in symbolic equation form, with the familiar heady perfume of orange blossom once again evoked:

Laranjeira ao pé da porta,	Orange tree by the doorway,
na cama me vai o cheiro;	your scent floats in to my bed;
tanta mocinha bonita	so many pretty girls
para mim que sou solteiro.	just for me, because I'm single.

A particularly lovely version of this motif from Trás-os-Montes coincides with others we have seen, from both Greece and Brazil, in substituting carnations for orange blossom:

Tendes cravos na janela,   Carnations in your window:
p'ra dentro, oh! vai o cheiro;   oh, how the scent floats in!
as folhas vos estão caindo   The petals all are falling
nas rendas do travesseiro.   on the lace of your pillow.

                    AMRP

In the following two tankas, on the other hand (which are the oldest we have seen), the mood is already the more typically Japanese one of discreet sentiment. The first was written by the seventh-century poet Mikata shortly after his marriage, when he was ill and away from his wife:

Tachibana no	People rush hither and thither	3
kage fumu michi no	in the lanes, treading on the shadows	2
yachimata ni	of orange trees;	1
mono o zo omou	my thoughts too turn every way	} 3–5
imo ni awazute.	when I remember you in absence.	

                    MYS 200

The second—anonymous, and also from the seventh century—is a wistful reproach:

Ware koso wa	Though you care	} 1–2
nikuku mo arame	no more for me,	
waga niwa no	will you not even come to see	5
hanatachibana o	the orange trees blooming	4
mi ni wa kojito ya	in my garden?	3

                    MYS 917

The apparent contrast between Eastern and Western attitudes is arguably at most a matter of perspective. In all these last few poems the real protagonist is Time: explicit in the sudden remembrance of an old love or a dead grandfather, implicit in the *memento mori* brought to mind by illness and absence or by the fragile and transitory beauty of fallen petals, spring nights, and the springtime of life and love.

The true contrast—of which the East merely prefers to stress one aspect while the West stresses the other—is between individual mortality and the seasonal renewal of Nature. Except for certain sounds (an old song, a street cry, perhaps even the chirring of cicadas in the night), nothing brings back the past so vividly as a familiar scent.[36] The timeless fragrance, returning unchanged from year to year, forms precisely by its immutability an ironic background to human change.

As such it is a link not only between East and West but between traditional and cultivated verse; for this very conflict of irreconcilables—the impersonal continuity so untragically celebrated by traditional symbolism, and the tragic uniqueness of the individual life—is a major poetic theme of Renaissance Europe. In the Iberian Peninsula at least, from the 'Portuguese Wyatt', Sá de Miranda, in the first half of the sixteenth century, to the Baroque poet Rodrigues Lobo in the first half of the seventeenth—but above all with Camões—it could without exaggeration be called *the* major theme.

---

[36] The crypto-Manichaean relegation of smell and taste to inferior rank in a supposed hierarchy of the senses (as Proust well knew) is an uncharacteristically obtuse gambit of philosophy in the civil war with poetry originally declared in the *Republic*.

3

STRUCTURE, STYLE, AND SYMBOL

THE word *structure* has by now lost most of its power either to charm or to alarm, and no longer raises hackles even in the remoter Common Rooms of Cambridge. The sense in which I use it here has less to do with any orthodox structuralist definition than with that of Umberto Eco, for example, to whom it means not the physical consistency of a work—its form—but rather that aspect of it that makes it possible to break the work down into a system of relations and then isolate, among these, the ones that are common to other like systems. Thus, for Eco (1968: 29), 'the structure . . . of a work is what it has in common with other works'.

By *style*, on the other hand, I understand exactly the opposite: in principle, the style of a work is what it does *not* have in common with other works, and constitutes its ultimate and irreducible uniqueness. But on one level these two antithetical concepts coincide. In so far as the whole of a given author's work is a structure differentiating it from that of any other author, we say he has a personal style ('l'homme même'). But a style may also be collective. Just as the individual works of an individual author can be analysed in terms of the relations they share with each other but not with those of another author, so the works of a linguistic or cultural community are reducible to a structure of mutual relations with the whole body of works produced by it and differentiating it from those of other communities. From the perspective of what they have in common, these relations constitute a structure; from that of difference, they individualize a style.

In terms of poetry, I take style to be the differentially characteristic way in which thought is moulded into poetic form, whether by an individual maker or by a particular linguistic and cultural community. And by thought, I mean not just conceptual reasoning but all three of those faculties which, according to Augustine of Hippo, are the manifestations of the Trinity in the soul; and which in addition to Understanding (representing the Son) also include Memory (corresponding to the Father) and Will (equated to the Holy Ghost).

ESPAÑA TODA ES CONCETOS

Augustine's theory is a staple of Iberian literature from the *Arbre de Ciència* of the Majorcan Ramon Llull (1296) and the Castilian Archpriest of Hita's *Libro de Buen Amor* (1330) at least down to the Portuguese Gil Vicente's *Play of the Soul* (1518).[1] In language—the medium through which thought, as defined above, is turned into poetry—these three 'powers of the soul' correspond to the communication of conceptual propositions, images, and affective states.

The Golden Age of the traditional lyric in the Iberian Peninsula coincides with that of the song-books of the late fifteenth- and early sixteenth-century *vihuelistas* or lutenists, with which it shares the medieval heritage of what Francisco Rico (683) calls the 'honda homología estructural de las literaturas de la minoría sabia y de la mayoría iletrada', in the form of a starkly non-metaphorical style most conspicuous in the initial theme stanzas—*cabezas* or *motes*—of the villancico, which, strictly speaking, *are* the villancico. As we have seen, these are in any given poem the part most likely to have been taken from oral tradition, or the one to which any literate poet deliberately seeking to write in the traditional idiom would be most anxious to give the appearance of traditionality.

Where metaphor is found—and it increasingly is, as the vogue for traditional-type verse passes from the composers of songs for *vihuela* accompaniment to the playwrights of Spanish Golden Age drama—is in the glosses: the added stanzas commenting and expanding on the first and genuinely or purportedly traditional one. The ever greater proportion of metaphor in these added stanzas composed by highly conscious artists keeps pace (though always more soberly) with the parallel evolution of courtly verse, from the spareness and austerity of the great Catalan Auziàs March and the early Garcilaso to the metaphorical exuberance of Lope de Vega and Góngora, both of whom were themselves important contributors (Lope one of the most prolific and felicitous of all) to the corpus of traditional lyric. The

---

[1] For an analysis of the dramatic structure of this morality play correlated to the three powers, the Trinity, and the threefold path of mysticism, see Reckert 1977: ch. 3: 'El Drama Doble de las Tres Potencias del Alma'.

theme stanzas, on the other hand, continue up to the late seventeenth century quite immune to the successive waves of Petrarchan, Mannerist, and Baroque imagery, and as obstinately bare of figurative ornament as in the days of Juan de Mena's or the Marquess of Santillana's *arte menor*.

The reason, I think, is that they possess secret inner resources that are not dependent on fashion and changing intellectual climates: because those resources are essentially non-intellectual ones. It is just this that constitutes the main difference between traditional and courtly verse: a difference disguised by their frequent mutual contamination; by the fact that they coexist not only physically—in the miscellaneous song-books that are our principal source of fifteenth-century poetry—but also, at their common apogee, chronologically; and finally by the fact that both are non-metaphorical. The last of these affinities is purely fortuitous, and the first two are largely so.

The only substantial surviving body of Peninsular lyric poetry earlier than the Court song-books is that of the Galician and Portuguese *trovadores*: equally non-metaphorical, and divided in much the same way into the elaborately 'literary' Provençal-influenced *cantigas d'amor* and the *cantigas d'amigo*: heirs to the kharjas, and modelled more or less (usually, one suspects, less) directly on the poetry of oral tradition. From the late twelfth to the early sixteenth century, and from West to East of the Peninsula—in the alembicated casuistries of the *cantigas d'amor* as in the earnestly rhetorical *canciones* and *decires* of Juan II's Court poets; in March and Mena; in Santillana and the Manriques, uncle and nephew—the conceit (or concept) reigns supreme: 'España toda es concetos';[2] and such imaginative elements as can be found in 'serious' verse before Garcilaso brought Petrarchan metaphor home from Italy in his luggage are provided chiefly by allegory.[3]

Roman Jakobson's theory of the metonymic and metaphoric poles of figurative language has been challenged or substantially amended by the analyses of, among others, Kenneth Burke, Jacques Lacan,

---

[2] The other half of the saying was 'Italia toda es hablar': admiration for the elegance of Italian style was tempered by a suspicion that it was a cover for frivolity (the authentic voice of the future Counter-Reformation can already be heard here dourly judging that of the High Renaissance).

[3] Relevant dates: Juan II (1405–54); Auziàs March (1395?–1462); Santillana (1398–1458); Mena (1411–56); Gómez (1412?–90?) and Jorge (1440–79) Manrique; Garcilaso (1503–36).

and David Lodge, who has demonstrated that in literary discourse (including the theatre and the cinema), metonymy is in the long run practically indistinguishable from disguised metaphor,[4] to which it can thus hardly be considered 'polar'. For our purposes it might be preferable to speak of metonymic and *analogical* poles, since as well as metaphor properly speaking, and allegory—both analytical, intellectual methods of comparison—analogy includes also the intuitive and synthetic method that is the symbol.

For allegory itself is of course pre-eminently conceptual: the product more of subtle intellects than of supple imaginations; while the traditional lyric, measured by Dámaso Alonso's sixfold typological scale of styles according to their relative conceptual, affective, and imaginative content (Alonso 1989: 410–19), displays an almost total subordination of the concept to image and emotion. What is singularly characteristic of traditional style is that, since the images are symbols and not metaphors, the emotion, thanks to the archetypal nature of symbolism, is impersonal and collective. Whereas allegory represents the concrete by way of abstractions, symbolism does the opposite; but in the West, at least, the two—as joint heirs of medieval poetics[5]— are in effect the obverse and reverse of the same coin, since the Middle Ages viewed everything concrete as a manifestation of some archetype.

In Symbolism with a capital S, the poet can create his own private symbols, whose decipherment depends on the context or on the keenness of the reader's intuition. But in a traditional and impersonal kind of poetics such as we are concerned with, the symbolic motifs are constant and belong to the common domain, and simple replacement can therefore be used more freely in full confidence that they will be recognized. Given the vastness of the realm of traditional symbolism in both space and time, it seems legitimate to interpret such symbolic constants as vestiges of a primitive mode of thought in

---

[4] David Lodge, *The Modes of Modern Writing* (London, 1977), 79–124. In this sense, metonymy is only a relative concept. In the pre-permissive days of the cinema, for example, the visual metaphors of rockets exploding in the sky or waves breaking on a beach were commonly used to represent sexual intercourse; but if the lovers are on a beach on the night of a fireworks display, the metaphors become at the same time what might be called contextual metonyms.

[5] Peter Dronke has conclusively dispelled the odd notion (held, surprisingly, by such different scholars as C. S. Lewis and Eco) that symbolism is incompatible with medieval poetics; see Dronke 1970: 193 f., and the important review article by Francisco Rico.

which Aristotelian logic had not yet opened a breach between objects and our apprehension of them, and the relations between different phenomena were felt not abstractly but as solid realities. In the (by Aristotelian standards) alogical thought that underlies this kind of symbolism it is not really a matter of comparing autonomous entities, because the symbol is not consciously distinguished from what it represents.

The works of Seznec and Curtius, of Malraux and Focillon (see below, Ch. 5, n. 39) have demonstrated the astonishing survival and metamorphosis of ancient forms through the constant renewal of their contents: the old bottles are for ever being filled with new wine. To suggest that the style of the traditional lyric is the product of a *solera*, and that it retains traces of archaic pre-logical thought processes of which the substance has long since been lost, is not to return to Herder and the discredited Romantic apparatus of the *Volk*. From Lévy-Bruhl to Lévi-Strauss—from *La Mentalité primitive* to *La Pensée sauvage*—many perspectives changed. We now know that totemism is far from universal; that the psychology of the child and that of the primitive are not all that much alike, nor those of the primitive and the civilized all that much different (or at any rate, that the difference is more of degree than of kind); and that the non-Aristotelian logic of primitives, to judge by the evidence of linguistics and structural anthropology, does not exclude a high degree of abstraction—without which, indeed, language itself could not exist.

Thought, by its very nature, was fated from the outset to be the first victim of a sort of primeval dissociation of sensibility; for thought (the purely mathematical kind—including music—excepted) cannot be formulated without language; and language contains built-in tensions tearing it apart simultaneously in the directions of the concrete and the abstract: of synthesis and analysis. While 'la esencia del lenguaje', in the words of Octavio Paz (1956: 93 f.) 'es simbólica, porque consiste en representar un elemento de la realidad por otro', its function is not limited to the symbolic—to the naming of entities—but includes the asserting of something *about* them; and as discursive reason is inherent in syntax, 'the form language imposes on experience is necessarily discursive' (Langer, 237). Once the implications of this imposed form have been absorbed, the seed of logic begins irresistibly to germinate.

All this being said, it must be added (unless one is a McLuhanist) that for the seed to bear fruit there must be not only language but written language; and it is with the rise of literate cultures that the real parting of the ways is reached. 'Ever since Parmenides,' Paz adds, 'our world has been one of clear-cut distinctions between what is and what is not. . . . This first uprooting—for it was a wrenching of being out of primordial chaos—constitutes the basis of our thought. . . . The identity of contraries postulated by the Eastern tradition is also a central affirmation of many Western mystics and poets. But among us this is a subterranean vein that contradicts the principles our culture is founded on.'

It was possible for Breton, in the second Surrealist Manifesto, to propose as an aim of art the transcendental reconciliation of dualities; but a Mexican like Paz, or a Brazilian, is more aware than any Western European or Anglo-American can be of the gulf between the world with which Paz so insistently identifies himself—'*nuestro* mundo', '*nuestro* pensar', 'entre *nosotros*', '*nuestra* cultura'—and the one inhabited by the many among even his own compatriots who share neither the Judaeo-Classical past nor the technological present of his *cultura*, and whose *pensar* is radically different from the analytical reasoning he has inherited with that culture.

Yet even in Europe a literate majority has in many places only come into being within living memory. Within another lifetime (and here McLuhanism is possibly a little less implausible) it may be a thing of the past. For the moment, at least, there still exists, in villages and countryside, a substantial population whose thought processes are mythic: that is to say that in their vision of people and objects they incline to synthesis, global identification, and symbolism; and in their vision of time to an unconcern with temporality which is exemplified at one extreme by the ritual re-creation of archetypal past events (real or imagined) in preference to linear history, and at the other, as we have seen, by such a purely stylistic matter as the morphology of verbs.

'Purely stylistic' is of course only a manner of speaking. If style is the way thought takes poetic shape, then the primary aim of stylistics must be the surely not insignificant one of tracing the conformation of thought in a poem; and for revealing the qualitative rather than quantitative concerns of the mythopoeic mind, the non-temporal treatment of verbs is as effective as the whole myth of the Eternal Return. Both are equally symptomatic of a concentration of interest in how an event occurs and what comes of it, rather than in the mere sequence or seriation of events; for to anyone in whom the principle of cause and effect has not been instilled by the dominant culture, it is the whats and hows that count: the whens and whys, in so far as they are grasped at all, can be little more than a matter of idle curiosity.

In a similar way the non-*personal* treatment of verbs in Chinese and Japanese—languages as unrelated syntactically and morphologically as they are akin lexically and culturally—reveals the basic non-individualism of Far Eastern civilization (though 'basic', as the Japanese poems we saw at the end of the last chapter show, certainly does not mean total). If the mythic mind is not greatly interested in the whys and whens, to the Eastern mentality it is the *who*s and whens that are of little concern. The labyrinthine complexities of Japanese verb inflection, for example, meticulously distinguish caused from spontaneous actions (as well as probable from certain, and complete from incomplete ones), while remaining vague with regard both to the time of occurrence and to Lenin's question 'who whom?'

While the insistence of traditional narrative verse on treating verbal tenses as aspects, in the Greek or Slavonic manner—thus giving the mistaken impression of a confusion of tenses—has been the subject of considerable study,[6] the same phenomenon in the traditional lyric has attracted virtually no scholarly attention. And this is unfortunate, because it is precisely there, through its relation to symbolism, that its true significance and its place in the organic continuum of traditional style become clear.

The literate mind, bedevilled by its knowledge of the separateness or separability of phenomena, is forced to work by successive analysis and re-synthesis. Things fall apart, and metaphor is a subconscious (as myth is an unconscious) attempt to recover the fragmented unity and restore the centre by reversing the analytical process: to reconcile, by discovering—or inventing—unsuspected similarities, the differences that cannot be simply ignored. Its aim is reassurance that there is hierarchy and order in the universe: form and meaning, and not just the aimless hurrying of atoms to which analysis has reduced it.

---

[6] Notably by J. Szertics, *Tiempo y verbo en el romancero viejo* (Madrid, 1967), and Stephen Gilman, *Tiempo y formas verbales en el 'Poema del Cid'* (Madrid, 1961), for whom 'the reader who goes from the present tense to the preterite and back again by way of illogical imperfects feels himself in another world'. Wang (1974: 9), in his study of the *Shi Jing*, the oldest monument of Chinese verse, notes 'inconsistency of time . . . as one of the characteristic signs of oral-formulaic poetry'. On its occurrence in the medieval cantigas see Reckert 1980: 26 ff.

Art being by nature concrete rather than abstract, and synthetic rather than analytical, the literate poet, aware that A irremediably exists as distinct from B, has to reconstruct his own pseudo-synthesis by asserting that A, though we know it is not B, is *like B*. The true opposite of metaphor is irony, a still more sophisticated device (and therefore rare in traditional style) intended precisely to jolt complacency by demonstrating the difference between reality and appearance. Whereas the metaphors of a Góngora, for example, pretend to discover patently outrageous similarities, irony pretends to accept 'accepted' ones while hinting at their falsity and suggesting that A, however much it may be made to *seem* like B, is still not B. The opposites coincide in John Berryman's *Dream Songs* (1964), which 'are not meant to be understood, you understand. / They are only meant to comfort [*metaphor*] and terrify [*irony*]'.

It is Góngora's peculiar achievement to have invented metaphors that allowed him to give impossible comparisons a specious validity by formulating and then apologetically withdrawing them, on the journalistic principle of the bold statement later retracted in fine print: something, at least, is bound to stick. A similar desire can be detected behind the defiance of a time-obsessed Quevedo, in the face of his appalled awareness that he himself is 'un Fue, y un Será, y un Es, cansado', pitting will against understanding in the bold affirmation that after death his flesh and bones, though turned to ash, will not cease to feel: 'serán ceniza, mas tendrán sentido'.

But in art, cunning can be a match for boldness; and the achievement of a Vicente, or the Lope of the *letras para cantar*, or Lorca, is not the less because they chose instead (or were chosen by) the way of the symbol. Their hard-won identification with the mythic pre-literate consciousness that has never quite lost its original vision—its primal and wholly amoral innocence—is itself a triumph of the intellect, for virtue comes hardest to the fallen. Only the most sedulous worshipper of the *Volksgeist*, however, would deny that theirs was a fortunate Fall, and that their work—and we ourselves—are the richer for its fruitful tension between the mythic and the discursive.

BEYOND PITY AND TERROR

Of myth it has been said that because 'it places our true being not in the forms that shatter but in the imperishable out of which they again bubble forth', it is eminently untragical: 'both pitiless . . . and terrorless..., with the joy of a transcendent anonymity regarding itself in all the...egos that are born and die in Time' (Campbell 1956: 45 f.). Symbolism too, like myth, wears the archaic smile. Like myth, it comes from before the Fall, and has of its nature no share in Original Sin: in the knowledge of good and evil, of time past and time future, of change and decay and death. That is to say, of the differentiation of phenomena.

At first glance nothing could seem more mythic, by these criteria, than the symbolic 'La Lola' in Lorca's *Poema del cante jondo*:

Bajo el naranjo lava	Under the orange tree
pañales de algodón.	she is washing cotton nappies.
Tiene verdes los ojos	Green are her eyes
y violeta la voz.	and violet her voice.
¡Ay, amor,	Ah, love,
bajo el naranjo en flor!	under the orange tree in bloom!
El agua de la acequia	The water in the stream
iba llena de sol,	was flowing full of sun,
en el olivarito	in the little olive grove
cantaba un gorrión.	there was a sparrow singing.
¡Ay, amor,	Ah, love,
bajo el naranjo en flor!	under the orange tree in bloom!
Luego, cuando la Lola	Later on, when Lola
gaste todo el jabón,	has used up all the soap,
vendrán los torerillos.	the little bullfighters will come along,
¡Ay, amor,	Ah, love,
bajo el naranjo en flor!	under the orange tree in bloom!

GL 199

Mythic or not, however, Lola is no transcendentally anonymous *niña*, much less a *dona virgo*. Unlike Gil Vicente's temporal fusion, the time scheme in Lorca's poem is one of sharp, if unstated, contrast. It is not only that, despite the reassuring timelessness of the undifferentiated descriptive present and imperfect in the first two stanzas, Lola's washing of her baby's *pañales* bears witness to an irreversible past event (perhaps not unrelated to her behaviour with other *toreritos* in an earlier poem which we shall see shortly): the last stanza, too, with its successive temporal adverbs 'then' and 'when', and the finality of *gaste todo*, gives the sense of an ending. The drowsy tedium of motherly duties is about to give way to a future of excitement and (for all the pretence of domesticating the passing *cuadrilla* of bullfighters with an offhand diminutive) deliciously unpredictable danger.

Lorca's poem may have been suggested by some lines of Lope de Vega's about a certain María who was ready to run away with the raggle-taggle cart-drivers who called her Mariquita ('Ladybird'):

> Mariquita me llaman
> los arrieros;
> Mariquita me llaman . . .
> voyme con ellos.

Frenk, 176

The generic situation and *dramatis personae*, however, have the look of a topos: in the Welsh poem quoted in Chapter 1, for example, a girl washing her lover's shirt approached by a horseman 'on a steed / broad in shoulder, proud in speed' (*ysgwydd lydan, buan, balch*), who instead of inviting her to ride off with him, rather oddly asks her to sell him the shirt (conceivably to take over its owner's powers).

More disturbing than the uncomplicated Lolas and Mariquitas, always prepared to be off with the first *torerillos* or carters who pass their way, is the fair-faced *niña* who shuts her ears to successive invitations to go away with bullfighters, horsemen, and even a romantic young man bringing flowers, and goes on coolly picking olives with the grey arm of her lover the wind clasped round her waist:

La niña del bello rostro	The girl with the lovely face
está cogiendo aceituna.	is picking olives.
El viento, galán de torres,	The wind, gallant of towers,
la prende por la cintura.	seizes her by the waist.
Pasaron cuatro jinetes	Four horsemen passed by
. . . . .	. . . . .
'Vente a Córdoba, muchacha.'	'Come away to Cordova, girl.'
La niña no los escucha.	The girl doesn't listen to them.
Pasaron tres torerillos	Three bullfighters passed by
. . . . .	. . . . .
'Vente a Sevilla, muchacha.'	'Come away to Seville, girl.'
La niña no los escucha.	The girl doesn't listen to them.
. . . . .	. . . . .
pasó un joven que llevaba	a young man passed by, carrying
rosas y mirtos de luna.	roses and moon myrtle.
'Vente a Granada, muchacha.'	'Come away to Granada, girl.'

Y la niña no lo escucha.   And the girl doesn't listen to him.
La niña del bello rostro   The girl with the lovely face
sigue cogiendo aceituna,   carries on picking olives
con el brazo gris del viento   with the grey arm of the wind
ceñido por la cintura.   clasped tight about her waist.

   Árbolé arbolé   Trees, trees,
seco y verdé.   dry and green.

                    GL 315

  The concluding couplet shows once again the preoccupation with
fertility and barrenness that underlies Lorca's constant symbolic
references to vegetation. Once symbols are converted into 'forms that
shatter' and 'are born and die in Time', then symbolism ceases to be
pitiless and terrorless, and *can* become the vehicle of tragedy:

   La manzana es lo carnal,   The apple is carnality,
   fruta esfinge del pecado   the sphinx-fruit of sin

   .   .   .   .

   La naranja es la tristeza   The orange is the sadness
   del azahar profanado,   of orange blossom profaned,
   pues se torna fuego y oro   for that becomes fire and gold
   lo que antes fue puro y blanco.   which before was pure and white.

                    GL 106

The ripening of what was pure and white into a thing of fire and gold
is seen as tragic because it is regarded not as a fulfilment but as
merely a passing phase in the irreversible process of dissolution.
  Wherever celibacy is exalted as an end—an escape, in G. M.
Hopkins's words, to 'fields where blows no sharp and sided hail'—
rather than as a means (whether to sanctity or to service), we may
reasonably suspect that the real motive for it is a subconscious hope
of halting this process: that what is really being sought is a way back
into the lost Eden where the sun stands still. It is this that lends
a special poignancy to an anonymous villancico from Alonso de
Mudarra's *vihuela* book of 1546:

       Gentil caballero,   Courteous gentleman,
       dédesme hora un beso,   now give me a kiss,
       siquiera por el daño   if only for the harm
       que me habéis hecho.   that you have done me.

       Venía el caballero,   The gentleman was journeying,
       venía de Sevilla;   on his way from Seville;

en huerta de monjas	in the nuns' orchard
limones cogía,	he was picking lemons,
y la prioresa	and the Prioress
prendas le pedía:	asked him for compensation—
'siquiera por el daño	'if only for the harm
que me habéis hecho.'	that you have done me.'

LTT 87

The theme stanza here may well be traditional. It is equally likely that the whole poem was written as a unit. What is certain is that the gloss, up to the last two lines, has been deliberately engineered to look as if it were unrelated to the theme stanza. Glosses on genuinely traditional themes often do have only a notional and rather forced relevance to them, and here the poet's stratagem—an unwitting revival of kharja technique—adds to the shock value of his ambiguous ending. More than that, however, the entire gloss is a tissue of ambiguities. 'Huerta de monjas', for one thing, means both the convent orchard and one of *jeunes nonnes en fleurs*. At the same time it is Hopkins's 'Heaven-Haven': the timeless Eden rediscovered, the enchanted garden of innocence—*hortus conclusus*—where the *caballero* has trespassed.

As for the *limones*, they are literal on one plane of meaning, while on another they are the simplest of simple replacements, assuming our familiarity with traditional symbolism. And the concluding lines 'siquiera por el daño / que me habéis hecho' remind us with a jolt, by referring us back to the first stanza, precisely what kind of compensation it is that the perhaps still youngish Prioress is demanding from the 'courteous gentleman': ostensibly for trespass, but actually for his discourtesy in smuggling Time back into the magic circle and forcing her to become aware of the difference the years have already made between herself and the fresh young novices who are now as she once was.

One further ambiguity still remains. In addition to its literal meaning of compensation for damages, the word *prendas* in this poem has another meaning, which, though equally literal, assumes, like the simple replacement *limones*, previous acquaintance with a particular convention: in this case the convention that just as the picking of fruit or flowers is invariably symbolic in poems of this kind, so the compensation or *prenda* exacted is always at the same time a love-token or *prenda de amor*. In Gil Vicente's *The Old Man and his Garden*,

for example, after a *niña* has been caught picking roses, the young
gardener demands appropriate compensation—but only, he chival-
rously adds, if she is not already committed elsewhere:

> Cogía la niña
> la rosa florida;
> el ortelanico
> prendas le pedía—
> si no tiene amores;[7]

and another *niña* in an anonymous poem of the same period explains
none too convincingly to her mother that she has come home without
her hair-ribbon and the belt from her dress because a less considerate
vineyard-keeper, in similar circumstances, had insisted on his due:

> Viñadero malo
> prenda me pedía;
> dile yo un cordone,
> dile yo mi cinta ...
>
> *LTT* 22

(The refrain repeatedly makes the point that *niñas y viñas*—girls and
vineyards—are equally difficult to guard.)

We have come full circle, back to the Seville *galán* with his gentle
reproof 'You came, my lady, into another's orchard ... : you should
have left the token of true love', and to the Chinese suitor who, also
as a love-token (and reversing the gender roles), gave his lady jewels
for her belt. And in the process we have been reminded that a *prenda*
is first of all an article of clothing: a *prenda de vestir*.

Behind symbolism lies the shadow of sympathetic magic: the
lingering subconscious belief, born of semantic confusion, that if
phenomena are not really separable, and a symbol *is* the thing
symbolized, then control over one is also control over the other. An
action or a time can only be symbolized by another action at another
time: the creation of heaven and earth, say, by a ritual dance, equating present to past; or the hoped-for coming of the rains by the
pouring of libations onto the fields, equating present to future. But to

---

[7] *O Velho da Horta* (*Cop* 203ab). The words *rosa, flor, horta* (and its synonyms *horto*
and *jardim*), *pomar* ('orchard'), and *cheiro* ('perfume'), occurring 30 times in this brief
playlet, end by transforming the *niña* into an implicit synecdoche of the garden itself,
just as happens with Melibea's *huerto* in the *Celestina*, and later, in *Don Duardos*, with
Flérida's garden: see Ch. 4, below.

symbolize a tangible object, such as an animal or a human being, almost anything will do. Sometimes the mere knowledge of its true name is enough to confer magic power over it; or again, as with the painted bison of Lascaux or Altamira, the symbol may be a pictorial or plastic representation. Most typically, however, it is a part or possession: a lock of hair, the *cinta* or *cordón* given as a token[8] (or got by false pretences, like Melibea's in the *Celestina*) . . . or even a lover's shirt; which may account for this near panic insistence on the return of an embroidered *camisón* which has evidently been taken without the owner's permission:

> Dame el camisón, Juanilla,
> mas dame hora, Juana, la camisa.
>
> Dame el camisón labrado,
> mas la camisa que me has tomado;
> dame hora, Juana, la camisa.
>
> Dame el camisón, Juanilla,
> mas dame hora, Juana, la camisa.
>
> Frenk, 1665

To trace the clothes-washing motif from Nausicaa to King Dinis's thirteenth-century *louçana* who went to wash shirts at dawn on the windy hillside, and thence to Lola, bright and fierce and fickle, washing nappies in the sunlit stream under a flowering orange tree, would take us far afield:[9] among the examples that come to mind is Mallarmé's 'petite laveuse blonde' (obviously a country cousin of Baudelaire's 'petite mendiante rousse'):

> Quand, sous l'eau claire où tu t'inclines
> Pour laver (et non pour te voir)
>
> .   .   .   .
> Tu ris au soleil du rivage . . .
>
> 16

The antithesis of this modest *petite laveuse* is Lola herself on her earlier appearance:

---

[8] Torner (146–9) cites 18 references to *cintas* (meaning variously hair-ribbons, neckbands, or sashes) as love-tokens in poems from different parts of the Iberian Peninsula, Spanish America, and the Canary Islands, and from the 13th c. to Lorca's *Yerma*.

[9] On the ritual background to the poetic symbolism of the washing of clothes, hair, and the body, see Reckert 1980: index, s.v. *Lavagem*.

La Lola	Lola
canta saetas.	is singing *saetas*.
Los toreritos la rodean,	The bullfighters gather round her,
. . . .	. . . . .
La Lola aquella, que se miraba	That Lola, always looking at herself
tanto en la alberca.	in the washing-tank.

GL 185

Diverging and converging strands of this theme involve Susannah and Bathsheba; Venus and Diana; mermaids, naiads, dryads—and by extension any young woman who goes to fetch water from a fountain or spring. One strange and beautiful example will therefore have to suffice: another of the many traditional wedding songs in which the Spanish-speaking Jews of Morocco have taken symbols—the link between all art and its lost ritual origins—and re-ritualized them:

Debajo del limón	Under the lemon tree
dormía la niña,	the girl was sleeping,
y sus pies en el agua fría;	her feet in the cold water;
su amor por ahí vendría:	her love came along that way:
—¿Qué hases, mi novia garrida?	'What are you doing, my fair bride?'
—Asperando a vos, mi vida,	'Waiting for you, my life,
lavando vuestra camisa	washing your shirt
con xabón y lexía.	with soap and bleach.'
Debajo del limón, la niña,	All under the lemon tree, the girl,
sus pies en el agua fría:	with her feet in the cold water:
su amor por ahí vendría.	her love came along that way.

LTT 499

Water, as one of the most fundamental of all symbols, partakes in superlative degree of the symbolic capacity for reconciling opposites: life and death, exuberant fecundity and virginal purity. For Lola, washing *pañales* under the orange tree in bloom, the water in the stream 'iba llena de sol', while for the unawakened *niña* under her lemon tree it is icy cold: a parallelistic version of the same song (*CRHJ* 31) even insists on the point by alternating *agua fría* with *agua helada*.

It is not these by now excessively familiar symbols, however, that give this song its special air of mystery, but the fact that even more than Gil Vicente's equally mysterious 'En la huerta nasce la rosa' (and unlike 'La Lola'), it represents the total convergence of three different time planes. Its use as a wedding song is a clue to this fact;

the mixing of verb tenses confirms it. As much as the surrealist bison of Altamira (or Picasso's horse in *Guernica*), painted in simultaneous front and rear view, this is a total unified vision of the object depicted; rather than the relation of a temporal succession it is, like the battle scenes in the *Poema de Mío Cid* analysed by Eugen Lerch, the description of a group of related events viewed not serially but as a whole.[10]

On one time plane—that of the past—the *niña* waits without knowing it for a fated lover (whom she nevertheless recognizes the moment he arrives on the scene). On another, corresponding to the present, they have already met and pledged their love (*novia* here meaning 'fiancée'), and her power over him is symbolized by her possession of his shirt. On yet a third plane—that of the future which is about to be made present by the wedding ceremony—they are at last married, and the *novia* (now meaning 'bride') is proudly and lovingly carrying out the homely domestic task of washing her husband's shirt.

The symbol is pre-literate man's oldest and most effective instrument for interpreting the universe and manipulating his environment. By the same token it is also the raw material of all the arts, with their utilitarian beginnings in cave painting, in the making of cult objects, and in propitiatory song and dance. This being so, the inextricable intermingling of vegetation and sexuality in primal symbolism is hardly to be wondered at; for all these activities are goal-seeking, and their goal is the preservation and continuance of life.

This is the meaning of the painted bison and the carved amulet, of the rain-making chant in the cornfields and the ritual couplings in the rice paddies. And it is this—the continuity of life itself—that is most insistently celebrated by the symbols of traditional verse. Birth and death are temporal accidents in the impersonal and undifferentiated collective flow: lullaby and lament for 'the egos that are born and die in Time' yield precedence to the eternal epithalamium for *la niña*.

[10] Cf. Gilman, op. cit. (above, n. 6), 30, 117n.

II. STRANGE ISLANDS, GARDENS
OF DESIRE

... las ínsulas extrañas,
los ríos sonorosos,
el silbo de los aires amorosos

    .   .   .   .

en el ameno huerto deseado...

        San Juan de la Cruz

4
ÍNSULAS EXTRAÑAS

'LAS ínsulas extrañas', St John of the Cross explains in the commentary to his *Cántico Espiritual*, are so called because 'they are seagirt, and beyond the seas, and very far away'. Half a century earlier in Gil Vicente's *Lusitania*, Venus—herself daughter and mistress of divine *ínsulas*—had commanded the marriage of Portugal and the daughter of the Sun to be solemnized to the tune of a villancico which, she said, 'we use in Greece' (and with which we too are already acquainted). Once 'turned into plain Castilian', it epitomizes all the strangeness and remoteness of those far and lonely 'islas de la mar':

> Vanse mis amores, madre,
> luengas tierra van morar:
>
> .   .   .
>
> Yo soñara, madre, un sueño,
> que me dio en el coraçón:
> que se yvan los mis amores
> a las islas de la mar:
>
> .   .   .
>
> ¿quién me los hará tornar? . . .
>
> *Cop* 245cd

An *island* is defined, tautologically, by its isolation: the fossil metaphor forces us to recognize that an outcrop of land in the midst of the waters, an oasis in the desert sands, a clearing in the forest, a city enclosed by its walls, and even the smallest walled garden (or *hortus conclusus*), are at the deeper level of the symbol identical.

'Oasis' would in fact be the best definition for the most ancient of all iconographically documented gardens, such as the one depicted in an Egyptian mural of the fourteenth century BCE: a rectangular pool full of fish, birds, and lotuses, and surrounded by fig trees and palms (Fig. 1). It is exactly this plan, adopted and adapted during the next eight hundred years by the Assyrian invaders of Egypt and their

Persian successors, that will subsequently spread both westward and eastward to culminate in the sixteenth and seventeenth centuries in the gardens of the Alhambra and the Taj Mahal.

The leading part in this eight-century evolution fell to the Achaemenid Persians, who added to the lotus its symbolic equivalent, the rose—by antonomasia the *flos florum* of the West—and divided the pool into quarters by means of perpendicular canals, whose evidently cosmological significance is reminiscent of the four rivers of Eden: one scholar, recalling the tradition that equated these rivers to the four branches of the Cross—the new Tree of Life—quotes the seventeenth-century Rosicrucian De Bry's characterization of a rectangular garden, quartered by paths emanating from a central tree or fountain, as by its nature a foretaste of Heaven.[1]

Still further east, the earliest mention of a garden in China is in poem 24 of the *Shi Jing* (twelfth–fifth centuries BCE), and refers to a simple kitchen garden whose wall a girl begs her suitor not to climb over and trample the tender young tree her parents have planted (the metaphorical significance of this *hortus conclusus* needs no commentary).

In Japan, finally, the oldest 'garden' recorded in historical documents is in reality nothing more than a forest clearing made among the pines of the Ise peninsula about the year 20 BCE to enclose the shrine of the Sun Goddess, to this day the most sacred place of Shintoism. In surrounding it with a fence, the builders of this shrine were following the established practice of symbolically delimiting any numinous space or object (such as those typical representatives of the *axis mundi*, an isolated tree or a rocky crag) that might serve as the dwelling of a divinity.[2]

---

[1] Comito, 44. On the evolution of the oasis garden see Kuck, 23 ff.; 40. The *flos florum* topos is discussed by Dronke (1965: i. 181–92; see also Leo Spitzer, ' "Fleur et rose" synonymes par position hiérarchique', in *Estudios dedicados a Menéndez Pidal*, i (Madrid, 1950)). Arthur Cooper, recalling the Rose of Sharon and those of Persian and Arabic poetry, and noting that what is apparently the first mention of roses in Chinese poetry is by the Central Asian Lǐ Bó, conjectured that rose symbolism might all emanate from the Middle East (personal communication).

[2] Holborn, 15 ff. Cf. Kuck, 66. Quoting Varro's definition of *templum* as 'a place whose limits are defined', Comito (31; 50) cites the medieval cartographic convention of showing the presence of a garden by a fountain or tree enclosed by a fence: a practice perhaps attributable to the sense of a boundary separating sacred space from the amorphous profane world outside. In early Shinto, such spaces often contained a single tree, rock, or pillar, intended for temporary occupation by the numen (*kami*): see Pilgrim, 262, and Ch. 6, below. The tree as archetypal axis of the world is the subject

Seven hundred years later, however, when the Japanese—emerging from their own literal and cultural isolation—decided to imitate the sumptuous imperial gardens of China, the name they gave the result was 'islands'; and while the name lasted for only a couple of centuries, the model was religiously maintained until the move of the Shogunate, another millennium later, from Kyoto to Edo—the future Tokyo—where the topography did not favour the by then classical pattern of a great central lake with one or more islands.[3]

ISLES OF THE BLEST

I say 'religiously' because in the context of general mythology those islands correspond to the Earthly Paradise, which traditions as ancient as they were universal agreed in situating on a height—stylized iconographically in the form of a conical mountain—rising from the middle of a remote island lost in the seas at the world's end. We can see it in any illustrated edition of the *Divine Comedy*: often in a reproduction of Domenico di Michelino's fresco in the Duomo of Florence, with Dante in the foreground holding the manuscript of his *Comedy*, and behind him the Mountain Isle, with Adam and Eve still naked and innocent at the foot of the Tree which—like the slowly dancing tree of Ō-oka Makoto, or the mountain itself—is one more of the innumerable manifestations of the axis or navel of the Earth.

In the local context of Sino-Japanese culture, the lake and its islands represented the magic floating archipelago of the Isles of the Immortals, from whose highest peak, on the isle of Péng Lái, souls deserving of salvation ascended directly to Heaven. The mountain landscape motif typical of later Chinese iconography first appears—even before its incorporation in the imperial gardens—in bronze thuribles of the third century BCE,[4] representing Péng Lái, and in a funeral portrait on silk, of the same century, in which the soul of the deceased appears trudging up its slopes (this painting, the earliest known Chinese portrait, will be discussed in the next chapter).

Like the other islands of the group, Péng Lái ('Tangleweed'

---

of E. A. S. Butterworth's monograph *The Tree at the Navel of the Earth* (Berlin, 1970); other manifestations of the axis are discussed below and in Ch. 5.

[3] For *shima* ('island') = 'garden' see Holborn, 25, and Kuck, 69; on gardens in Edo, Kuck, ch. 22; on other aspects of the matters discussed in the next four paragraphs, Ch. 5, below.

[4] Cf. Rawson and Legeza, pl. 5.

or 'Tumbleweed') was conical, its appearance suggesting a vase emerging from the sea; and it was believed, no doubt because of this resemblance to a receptacle, to be the place where the elixir of life was stored. A Western parallel can be found in a reference by the Greek alchemist Zosimus (third century CE) to an altar in the shape of a vase, full of the 'Water of Wisdom', by whose beneficent action those who 'desire to obtain virtue . . . are transformed, on leaving their bodies, into spirits' (Centeno 1981: 20).

In addition to the five (or, according to variant traditions, three or four) islands that made up the archipelago, one of the canonical books of Taoism speaks of another fabulous peak, 'Mount Vase' or 'Mount Gourd' (Hú Lǐng):[5] in this case not insular, but even so, as the name indicates, with similar characteristics. From a round orifice or chalice on its summit—the 'Hollow of Fecundity'—issued the 'Divine Spring', whose waters (divided into four streams like the rivers of Eden or the symbolic canals of the Persian garden) preserved the vital forces of the inhabitants, who went naked and lived to the age of a hundred without ever growing old (Liè Zǐ, 5.6). Traditional Chinese art therefore not infrequently identifies a Taoist sage by two symbolic 'attributes' hanging from his belt: a gourd and an amulet of the sacred mountains (Keswick, 37).[6]

The initially puzzling wasp-waisted double gourd makes sense as a *yin-yáng* symbol, if less (from a Western point of view) in its other role as a functional equivalent of the microcosmic grottoes thought to lie under the mountains: crystal-lined geodes that expanded to the size of the universe to accommodate the sage when he retired inside them to meditate. The Taoist belief in total spatial and temporal

[5] An alternative name for Péng Lái is Péng Hú: of three characters pronounced / hú /, two properly mean 'gourd' and the other 'vase', one of the former sometimes being used for the last. On the etymology of these and other names of the archipelago see Schafer 1985: 51–60.

[6] These are not the mythical archipelago but the five actual mountains that dominate and symbolize the four quarters of the Empire, plus the centre: an immemorial division obviously related to the image of four rivers or canals issuing from a central fountain. According to the *Canon of Records* (7th c. BCE), a legendary emperor six centuries earlier had made sacrifice on the summit of all five mountains. The rite was subsequently centred on that of the East, Tài Xan; but in eleven hundred years only four sovereigns felt worthy of celebrating it, one (who did so five times, and even attempted to repeat the original complete itinerary) being the great Wǔ Dì, referred to below. On these matters, and the metonymic relation between the five 'Notable Mountains' (*Míng Xan*) and Péng Lái, see Kroll, 167–70, 194, 201, and 209 f.; for a comprehensive historical-iconographical treatment of the entire subject, Kiyohiko Munakata: *Sacred Mountains in Chinese Art* (Urbana-Champaign, Ill. 1991).

relativity exemplified by this idea will be studied in greater depth in Chapter 6.

Vessels in all their various forms, such as the vase or chalice, have been called the central symbol of the feminine, and woman 'the vessel par excellence . . . , the life-vessel as such' (Neumann 1974: 39; 42). The translator of the sixteenth-century Chinese erotic romance *Jin Píng Méi* ('The Flower in the Golden Vase') explains that '*píng*, vase à col étroit, évoque le réceptacle de la fécondité . . . , mais . . . aussi . . . l'organe sexuel féminin': the identical meaning attributed by Taoist metaphorical language to the terms 'receptive vase' and 'golden lotus'[7] (the latter, as it happens, the singularly appropriate name of a principal female character in the *Jin Píng Méi*).

The lake, whose presence in the gardens of East Asia was *de rigueur*, stood for the primal One or *Tài Yi*: the Grand Monad from which the *yin* and the *yáng* were born; and it was so indispensable that where the terrain or the aesthetic or philosophico-religious principles of the garden's owner made the habitual sheet of water inappropriate, it was necessary to resort to a 'lake' of sand, carefully combed into the shape of waves which were retouched daily (and still are even today in the famous Zen temple gardens of Kyoto), and among which were placed a few rocks disposed in such a way as to recall the far-off archipelago of Péng Lái. Even today as well, one can buy small pictures of the magic island in Tokyo gift shops; and Japanese trippers returning from a day excursion to the country often bring home a few stones specially chosen for making a miniature reproduction of it on a tray filled with sand or water.

Since the archipelago of the Vases may well represent the most deeply implanted vision of Paradise in the history of mankind, it will not be irrelevant at this point to dwell briefly on its own history.[8]

[7] *Jin Píng Méi* (*Fleur en Fiole d'Or*), i, p. xlii; Rawson and Legeza, 25. Taoist art attributes female symbolism to vases in general. In an ancient Canaanite rain-making ritual, vases with plants ('gardens of Tammuz') were thrown into the water by groups of women (Frye 1982: 152); where this rite survives in the West it is customarily celebrated on Midsummer Night (Wilkins, 134), but the plants still include the basil allusive to Adonis (= Tammuz). Citing the invocation of the Virgin as *Vas spirituale*, *Vas honorabile*, *Vas insigne devotionis*, etc., Wilkins (58; 93) adds that the central bead in the rosary often is vase-shaped, and that *vas* was the name given to the centre of the mandala (in the East often a lotus; in the West a rose) by Christian alchemists; see also Durand 1969: index, s.v. *vase*. Aguirre and Hauf (94) quote a Spanish ballad in which Christians, Moors, and Jews join in throwing various plants into the water 'the better to honour the feast' of St John (on Midsummer customs see below, Ch. 6).

[8] For a full discussion of the origins and esoteric significance of the islands that make up the legendary 'principalities of the sea', including Péng Lái, see Schafer

As early as 104 BCE the great Emperor Wǔ Dì, of the Hàn dynasty—the 'Divine Warrior' in whose fifty-three-year reign the Chinese dominions achieved not only a greater expansion than in the previous twenty-seven centuries, but the consolidation of a social structure that was to hold together essentially intact for another twenty—ordered a park to be laid out in the vicinity of his palace grounds at Cháng An (the future starting-point of the Silk Route that was to link China with the Mediterranean), containing an extensive lake whose tree-covered rocky islands—among them an artificial mountain more than two hundred feet high—were intended to reproduce the conditions (and, by inference, the magical virtues) of the archipelago that successive expeditions over the preceding hundred years had failed to locate. For a dynasty such as the Hàn, capable of sending an entire army across almost two thousand miles of desert to the shores of the Caspian, not even an unsuccessful enterprise could fail to be commemorated with due magnificence.

Exactly half a millennium later, it happened that another emperor —who made up for a lack of his remote predecessor's military and administrative gifts by unbounded megalomania—was engaged in repeating the latter's experiment (though with unprecedented grandiosity, and purposes more exhibitionistic than magico-religious) at the very moment when the first emissaries from the 'emergent nation' that was Japan arrived at his Court. Yáng Dì was an emperor not without qualities: his public works included perhaps the second greatest of all the achievements of Chinese engineering, the Grand Canal (and he was even, as we shall see later, a by no means contemptible poet); but within ten years his overreaching was to lead to the premature fall of the Suí dynasty.[9] By then, however, the

1985: 49–121. The following necessarily oversimplified résumé is based chiefly on Holborn, 27; Keswick, 38, 40, 80; Kuck, chs. 4–7, 13–14, 20, 23, and 25; and Loewe, 37–40; cf. also Reckert 1977: 122–7; 147 ff. Gernet, bk. 2, ch. 2, deals with 'A Grande Expansão dos Han na Ásia'. The name of this powerful dynasty (206 BCE–220 CE) is even today a synonym in the East for 'Chinese': in China itself the Hàn people (ethnic Chinese) are distinguished from the non-Hàn 'nationalities'; and in Japan the graphemes of the written language, imported from China from the 6th c. on, are 'Hàn characters' (kan-ji).

[9] The cautionary tale of his labyrinth or 'Palace of Going Astray' (Mílóu), with its thousand doors and ten thousand windows, built at such 'great expense of jade and gold . . . that the royal treasury was left utterly empty', is related in the preface to Owen 1989. In Yáng Dì's own time his Grand Canal was a more impressive engineering feat than even the Great Wall, the major part of which is now known to date from the early 15th c. rather than the 3rd BCE (see Arthur Waldron, The Great Wall of China: From History to Myth, Cambridge, 1991).

dazzled Japanese had long since gone home with the plans in their briefcases, and the firm resolve that their own empress too must have an 'island'.

It was common knowledge that the floating mountains that made up the archipelago of the Immortals rested on giant sea tortoises, and that the elect were transported to Péng Lái (in Japanese, Hō Rai) on the wings of cranes. As the original esoteric meaning was gradually lost sight of, the lake gardens of Japan began to include, from the sixteenth century on, the more and more purely decorative motif of rocks in the form of cranes and tortoises (Fig. 2); and in modern Japanese the very expression 'cranes and tortoises' (*tsuru-kame*) has come to be a conventional formula of congratulations or good wishes.

The islands themselves, in the course of time, have undergone an analogous process of aesthetic secularizing, to such an extent that the most distinguished Japanese garden designer of this century has called some of his most boldly abstract projects (including some for Zen temples) 'Hō Rai': no doubt with the aim of stressing their residual link with the ancient tradition whose vestiges would otherwise be hard to detect. At the opposite extreme, some current over-literal attempts to represent realistically (rather than merely to hint at) actual cranes and tortoises suggest that this motif may now 'lack the precision it needs to convey the original aesthetic function' (Slawson, 129); but its continuing prestige is clear from the sale in 1990 of an eighteenth-century Korean 'crane-and-tortoise' vase to a Korean buyer for the record price of almost a million pounds.[10] And it may be supposed that the numinousness inherent in all gardens (affirmed by Pliny when the Japanese were still at the stage of the sacred forest clearing) is ultimately immune to the vicissitudes of time.

Here it is necessary to clarify an aspect of East Asian culture that has led to fundamental misunderstanding. One of the constants of that culture in China and Japan alike, not only in its literary and philosophical expression (poetry of the haiku or the jué jù, aphorisms of Confucius or the Tao) but also in the visual and plastic arts (tray landscapes, lakes of sand or moss a few square yards in size, thuribles in the shape of mountains, gourds adorning the staff of a Taoist sage), is miniaturization.

---

[10] See Geraldine Norman, 'Nouveau Far Eastern Rich', *The Independent*, 14 Dec. 1991, 39. The same decorative motif occurs in Hokusai's print *Cranes on a snowy pine* (see the catalogue of the 1992 Royal Academy Hokusai exhibition, no. 65).

The hasty judgement of the West sometimes takes these procedures for signs of a basically frivolous aestheticism, and their products for little more than exotic trinkets. In reality, their wholly serious objective—often explicitly justified in theory together with the related goal of emptiness, sought through deletions or omissions[11] —is the most rigorous condensation and intensification of the secret qualities and virtues understood to be inherent in the objects evoked. 'Representations of potent sites in miniature', Maggie Keswick observes (38), 'were ... not aesthetic in origin, but were pieces of practical magic'; and the traces of this original attitude have not yet altogether disappeared.

A case in point is that of the engaging and ill-starred eighteenth-century dreamer Fù Shěn,[12] whose *Chapters from a Floating Life* record (with deliciously Freudian details *avant la lettre*) his childhood compulsion to invent a miniature fantasy world, seeing mosquitoes as cranes and flower-beds as forests; and his touching pleasure, when a grown man, in making a tray landscape through which he imagined himself wandering in spirit with his adored wife (who died young) as if they had been transported to the Isles of the Immortals. Even for this pure aesthete, determined to make his life a work of art in the face of constant misfortunes, and obliged by obscure childhood traumas to do so by taking refuge in a diminutive universe of his own making, it is the time-honoured traditional motifs—the cranes, the lush vegetation, the mountain isles of Péng Lái—that spontaneously come to his mind as the most natural language in which to express his most intimate concerns.

Fù's obsession is interpreted by the Sinologist Stephen Owen (1986*a*: 102–7) as a desire to escape from the real world and, by shrinking, to encompass infinite space at the same time as he enjoys a private space of his own: an attitude confirming the view of Gaston Bachelard (who does not share the prevailing Western distrust of the minuscule in the arts) that 'la miniature sincèrement vécue ... détache du monde ambiant' (150), and that by activating 'des valeurs profondes', it paradoxically constitutes 'un des gîtes de la grandeur' (142; 146).

[11] Cf. Ch. 1, n. 35, above, and see O-Young Lee, *Smaller is Better: Japan's Mastery of the Miniature*, tr. R. N. Huey (Tokyo, 1987). In the Japanese view, merely to say 'small is beautiful' is not enough.

[12] On this personage, one of the most appealing figures in all of Chinese literature in his century, see Keswick, 85 ff., 181, 186 f., and 196 f., and esp. Owen 1986*a*: 100–13.

Miroslav Holub, a practising scientist as well as a fine poet, places the phenomenon in a broader human context, arguing that 'the scientist who models the incomprehensible complexity . . . of organic and inorganic processes in a . . . little experiment, and . . . then presents a paper . . . which is nothing more than a miniature excerpt of [it] . . . is . . . like the builder of miniature railroads in miniature landscapes. Indeed, so is the artist, who gives a little version of the state of things in . . . colours . . . , notes, or . . . verses.'[13] The artist Fù Shěn himself seems to be hinting at a whole philosophy of life when he sums up his ideal of garden design (60) as 'to give the feeling of the small in the large and the large in the small, the real in the illusion and the illusion in the reality'.

A curious parallel with Fù's childhood vision of the miniature 'forest' (an extreme case of the garden 'où les enfants regardent grand', as the poet Pierre de Boissy calls it in a line quoted by Bachelard) is the experience of a contemporary Western author (Holborn, 69 ff.), who, after observing the pine forest surrounding a temple garden in Kyoto, looks down and sees the same scene repeated in the tufts of moss at his feet: the two facing photographs he reproduces (Figs. 3–4) graphically justify his moment of vertigo.[14] Even more remarkable is the coincidence of this real-life experience with passages from two nineteenth-century novels mentioned by Bachelard (151) among other 'textes . . . où . . . une touffe d'herbe est un bosquet': one by Thomas Hardy, unidentified, in which 'une poignée de mousse est un bois de sapin', and the other, *Niels Lyhne*, by the Dane J. P. Jacobsen (a *livre de chevet* of Rilke's), describing the Forest of Happiness, where 'la mousse vigoureuse' similarly 'ressemblait à des sapins'.

Pictorial representation of the Islands is likewise not limited to tourist kitsch. The oldest true landscape painting in China, dating

---

[13] 'The World in Miniature', in *The Dimension of the Present Moment*, ed. and tr. David Young (London, 1990), 78 f. Pointing out that some structures can be established with coarse measurements and then repeated in successively finer scale with ever greater definition, Holub goes on to relate pleasure in miniaturization to an intuitive recognition of the 'self-symmetry' of structures with this quality (Mandelbrot's 'fractals': cf. Ch. 5 n. 23, below).

[14] The moss in Holborn's photograph appears to be the so-called 'cedar moss', whose plants indeed resemble diminutive Japanese cedars (*Cryptomeria japonica*). The garden designer David Slawson (189) reports a similar experience when planting moss in a Japanese garden: 'from . . . a couple of feet above the freshly planted moss, the tiny seedlings that grew up . . . from the dappled green carpet seemed to tower high above a rolling landscape of hills and fields'.

from the eighth century (if we discount the much earlier funeral portrait mentioned before), habitually includes the familiar conical mountains as a background; and beginning in the fifteenth (the 'Japanese *Quattrocento*' in both the chronological and the qualitative sense) Japanese landscape painting too is increasingly permeated by the esoteric symbolism of Zen,[15] transposed forthwith into the three-dimensional art of the garden as well, in the form of lakes and rivers of sand or moss, stone 'waterfalls' and boats, and the inevitable islands.

It is without doubt in the justly celebrated garden of the Ryōan temple in Kyoto—probably built in the year of Columbus's American landfall—that this evolution reaches its apogee: in this case only qualitative and not chronological, since most of the other famous Zen gardens of the old capital are later than that of Ryōan and derive from it. In the Ryōan-ji the concrete representation of the ancient myth is simply transcended, becoming etherealized in the form of a metaphysical design of pure abstractness (Figs. 5–6) which, like a musical composition or a mathematical formula, represents nothing but itself; but which, as has been well said, teaches the supreme lesson of the harmony of the universe.[16]

THE MAGIC MOUNTAIN

'Ínsula divina' is Camões's term for the Isle of Venus (the subject of the next chapter). As a synthesis of the numerous forms taken by the primordial Island Mountain, the epithet will serve; but even the most minimally detailed summary of these would have to include not only Mount Sinai, effectively islanded by the desert, and Dante's Mount of Purgatory, crowned by the Earthly Paradise, but also, at a humbler level, the simple conical stone which from Cuzco to Delphi and from

[15] Strictly speaking, the word 'symbolism' is not applicable to Zen, a radically anti-symbolist philosophy in which everything is what it is, no more and no less, and 'the world, emptied of symbols, does not need to be interpreted any more' (Faure, 350). A case in point is the Ryōan temple, discussed below in the text. The attitude of Buddhism in general to symbols is studied by William R. La Fleur, *The Karma of Words* (Berkeley, Calif., 1983).

[16] Kuck, 167. If Western art compels our admiration rather than our participation, 'the fifteen stones of the Ryōan-ji . . . , irregular in shape and position, allow us to participate in the creation of the garden' (Keene, 13): the language of the Japanese garden, like that of Japanese poetry, is a 'cool medium' (see 'Bashō's Pond', in Ch. 7, below; and on irregularity and asymmetry as ideals, Ch. 1, n. 20).

Jerusalem to Peking (Neumann 1974: 260) likewise represents, on a microcosmic scale, the axis or navel of the world.

And not only to Peking but to Japan, as witness the example unearthed in 1903 on the probable site of the estate of an uncle of that empress whose ambassador had brought back to her, about the year 610, the report of the ill-fated Yáng Dì's grandiose park at Lò Yáng. This Japanese specimen is a stone fountain in the form of a cone slightly over two metres high, with spouts for the distribution of water in the predictable four directions, and carved designs suggesting a central peak surrounded by other lower mountains (Fig. 7). Its owner was known as 'the Lord of the Island' (Kuck, 68 f.): a sobriquet no doubt due to his ownership of this uncommon artefact.

There is unlikely to have been any great difference between the uncle's fountain and the replica of the Buddhist *axis mundi*, Mount Meru or Sumeru, which his niece is recorded as having ordered in 612, quite possibly from the same sculptor, for her own 'island' then in the planning stage. The distinction between Péng Lái and Sumeru, already confused in Chinese iconography before they entered that of Japan as Hō Rai and Shumisen, became in practice a purely nominal one, with the latter coming to be used for the most part in specifically Buddhist contexts.[17]

As well as a miniature image of the primeval Mountain, the conical-iconical stone is also, for that very reason, a symbol of the Magna Mater, being at once her material manifestation and her earthly dwelling. If the evidently more phallic than omphalic shape of the supposed Ὄμφαλος τῆς Γῆς may at first glance make its identification with a mother figure puzzling, other factors help to explain it. Apart from the metonymic link between the goddess and her dwelling, this ambiguous form can be interpreted not only as a phallic symbol but as the representation of a breast,[18] and hence as a

---

[17] Cf. Kuck, 44 and 393 n. 17; Holborn, 27; Keswick, 80. It is significant that in Indian Buddhist tradition the cosmic mountain of Meru is surrounded by four others that 'establish an orientation to . . . the compass points and the divinities that preside over them' (Mabbett, 66); cf. n. 6, above. For the sacred mountain, replicated in decreasing scale by the sacred city, temple, and altar, see Eliade 1954: 12–15; cf. *The City as a Sacred Center: Essays on Six Asian Contexts*, ed. Bardwell Smith and Holly Baker Reynolds (Leiden, 1987).

[18] On the superficially surprising identity of penis and breast as *axis mundi* see Neumann 1973: 32. Columbus, thinking he had reached the axis, concluded that the Earth was not a sphere, but pear-shaped like a woman's breast, the nipple being the part nearest to Heaven: cf. Ch. 5, n. 40.

synecdoche of the Mother Goddess herself. 'Navel', moreover, is a known euphemism (at least in the Song of Songs) for the vulva.[19]

Among the numerous manifestations of the Great Mother, the most universally venerated was perhaps Ishtar, otherwise Astarte, Astaroth, Aphtorete, Aphrodite—or as Camões calls her, 'Venus, who brings loves along with her', and who, he says, fashioned amid the waters her *insula divina* expressly for the bodily refreshment of Gama's weary mariners. For John of the Cross, in contrast, the *insulas* of his own poem are understandably a simple metaphor for that God in Whom he finds 'all the strangeness of islands never before glimpsed', and Whom the soul, in view of the 'strange news' it has had of Him, calls 'ínsulas extrañas'.

Sainthood apart, Juan de Yepes, as he was called *in saeculo*, is one of the supreme lyric poets of all time.[20] As an interpreter of his own poetry, however—and notwithstanding the limpid prose of his commentaries and the evident fervour of his conviction—he is not always entirely successful in transmitting that conviction to the reader; and it must be granted that though based on a long tradition, both Judaic and Christian, of allegorical and typological interpretations of his main source, the Song of Songs, his valiant attempt at Christianizing the immemorial identification of the Island with its *numen loci* does not quite work.

The poetic intuition of a Camões, on the other hand, untrammelled by doctrinal commitments, is at liberty to lay equal stress on the inherent erotic as well as maternal and initiatory aspects of the myths of the Great Mother and the Island or Magic Mountain that both represents and belongs to her. This process literally culminates on the summit of a 'monte alto, & divino' in Canto X of *The Lusiads*. But the climax is prepared for by a series of topographical images which, though in principle objective descriptions of the Isle of Venus, at the same time covertly but unmistakably allude (as a Camonian scholar, J. H. Sims, observed some years ago) both to a woman's body and to the act of love.

---

[19] Cf. Carr, 157 and n. 1. The Hebrew word used in the Canticle, *xarr*, is extremely rare and hence ambiguous. Among other meanings proposed by translators and exegetes (acc. Carlo Suarès, *The Song of Songs* (Berkeley, Calif., 1972), 140 ff., cit. Shuttle and Redgrove, 20), is 'door'.

[20] Competent English translations of his complete poems—which can be read in not much more than an hour—have been made by Roy Campbell and, more recently, Lynda Nicholson.

The vision begins to take shape even before the arrival at the Island, with the phallic prow of Vasco da Gama's ship parting the sea before it as it plunges across the curving bay into the future (see below, Ch. 5, n. 6 and text) towards the white beach 'painted with blond shells by the Cytherean'. If the 'enseada curva' suggests, both etymologically and by its adjective, a breast (Portuguese *seio*, from Latin *sinus*: 'bay' or 'bosom'), it was from a shell that the Cytherean goddess was born: specifically, a scallop shell: '*venerea concha*, nom d'un coquillage dont la forme'—as the Latin etymological dictionary explains—'évoque le sexe de la femme'. The scallop was also called *pecten* by the Romans, and in Greek κτείς: both words whose primary meaning was 'comb', and both themselves metaphors for the pubis; in the colloquial Latin of Plautus, moreover, *concha* has the same sense. In this context one is reminded of the mysterious *coquillage* ('un, entre autres') that Verlaine found troubling; but the same metaphors are used in a less veiled way by Manuel Bandeira in two poems: in one the Brazilian poet recalls the colour of the king's daughter's hair as he saw her riding by, and wonders whether that of her 'marvellous comb' is the same colour; in another, 'Água-forte' ('Etching') he evokes both comb and shell:

O prêto no branco,	Black on white,
O pente na pele.	Comb on skin.
. . . .	. . . .
Em meio do pente,	In the middle of the comb,
A cóncha bivalve . . .	The bivalve shell . . .[21]

Once we penetrate into the interior of the Island itself, the whole of it a vast garden, we discover 'shapely hillocks' (with 'pleasant valleys' between them); 'scented pomes'; 'fair lemons' and 'pyramidal pears'; 'tangled thickets'; and finally, for the second time in the poem, a 'purple lily' (the euphemistic metaphor used in Canto I for the sex of Venus). The sexual symbolism of fruit, as we have seen, is universal; and lemons, from Camões to Lorca and from the folk poetry of Greece to that of the Sephardic Jews of the Maghreb,

---

[21] Bandeira, i. 241; 292. Among the many names given to it by the esoteric language of Taoism, 'the female [sexual organ] is . . . "the pink shell"' (Rawson and Legeza, 25). Cf. Bachelard, ch. 5, 'La Coquille'; Delcourt, 51; Durand 1969: index, s.v. *coquille*; Eliade 1979: ch. 4: 'Notas sobre o simbolismo das conchas'; and Grigson, 38 f. On symbolic implications of the spiral in shells see Glucklich, 261, 267, 271; those of spirals in general are discussed in the following chapter.

are a standard metaphor for breasts (though Columbus found the 'pyramidal pear' more appropriate).

As for the 'tangled thickets', or *espessa mata*, these anticipate the 'monte espesso . . . e mato'—the hillside thick with undergrowth—that Gama must traverse before he can attain the summit of the Isle of Love and receive the reward reserved for him by Supreme Wisdom. The name of the Chinese Isle of the Immortals, Péng Lái, we recall, means precisely 'tangled undergrowth'; and it is curious to find here yet another convergence of Camões's poem, the Chinese myth, and the biblical epithalamium: in translations of the verse of the Song of Songs corresponding to the consummation of union ('I have eaten my honeycomb with my honey'), the Hebrew word *ya῾ar* is invariably rendered by the equivalent of 'honeycomb'; but on fifty-seven of its other fifty-eight appearances in the Bible it is translated by some such word as 'thicket' or 'undergrowth'. The Hebraist Lloyd Carr (129) notes that in the erotic poetry of the ancient Middle East in general, 'honey' and 'thicket' are both 'euphemisms for the female genitalia'.

The metaphorical anthropomorphosis—specifically, gynaecomorphosis—of geographical and geological forms seen as goddesses or simply women is both ancient and world-wide. In Taoist tradition the five sacred mountains (above, n. 6) were identified with the body of the legendary founder of the Tao, Lǎo Zǐ (otherwise Lao Tzu) in his macrocosmic epiphany (cf. Faure, 340). The Taoists held the view that 'a human body [is the] image of a country' (*yi rén zhi shen, yi guó zhi xiang*): 'a landscape with mountains, lakes, woods, and shelters'.[22] But whereas *rén* means simply 'human being', the 'body' originally represented by *shen* is in fact that of a pregnant woman: The Body by antonomasia, by means of which the principle of the continuity of life is realized.[23] The Taoist teaching was that 'those who nurture the

[22] Schipper, 355–8 (with a 'map' of one such landscape).
[23] The character *shen* ('body'):

1–2: 9th–10th-c. BCE inscriptions showing a human figure with distended abdomen trying to keep its balance, feet apart and one arm in the air; 3: seal style, 2nd–3rd c. CE; 4: modern form (now also meaning 'self', or, as an adjective, 'personal'). Of the five sacred mountains (cf. n. 6 above), the most numinous was Tài Xan, a name apparently meaning simply 'Great Mountain'; by the 2nd c., however, etymologists equated *tài* ('large') to *tai* ('womb'), and *xan* ('mountain') to *chǎn* ('generative'): cf. Kroll, 175.

Immortal Embryo, the Real Self, are mothers and should adopt a female personality. . . . The Taoist's body in this world is the body of a woman, a mother with child' (Schipper, 364 f.).

Two drawings will suffice to illustrate the survival of these metaphors in the visual arts: André Masson's well-known *Cascade*, in which a telluric and aquatic female figure blends into a background of nature; and *Landscape Figure*, by Peter Reddick, which can be read alternately as a landscape of rolling hills and brush (Camões's *fermosos outeiros* and *espessa mata*) and as a languorously recumbent nude (Fig. 8). Such visions are the pictorial equivalents of those evoked in two poems by Jorge Guillén: 'Más esplendor' (1984: 402 f.)—

> ¡Cuántos valles detrás y cuántos aires
> En torno de tu cuerpo,
> Campo también, país y suma cándida! . . .

> How many valleys behind, how many breezes
> blowing all round your body:
> countryside too; a country: candid summation! . . .

—and 'El manantial' (1984: 37), in which this theme converges with the feminine symbolism of water:

Mirad bien. ¡Ahora!	Watch closely. Now!
Blancuras en curva	Curving whitenesses,
Triunfalmente una	triumphantly one,
. . .	. . .
Guían su equilibrio	deftly balancing
Por entre el tumulto	amidst all the tumult
. . .	. . .
De un caos ya vivo.	of a chaos now alive.
El agua desnuda	The naked water
Se desnuda más.	strips more naked still:
. . .	. . .
Manantial, doncella:	a maiden spring;
. . .	. . .
Y emerge compacta	and she emerges, compact,
Del río que pudo	from the slim, curving river
Ser, esbelto y curvo	she could be:
Toda la muchacha.	the girl, entire.[24]

---

[24] Here Guillén has superimposed metaphor on symbol: this *muchacha* is a poem emerging intact from the turbulent chaos of poetic composition.

João Cabral—who, as it happens, dedicated one of his first poems to Masson—characteristically notes difference as well as similarity[25] between the terms of this comparison in 'Imitação da Água' (267):

De flanco sobre o lençol,	On your side on the sheet—
paisagem já tão marinha,	landscape already seascape—
a uma onda deitada	a wave stretched out
na praia, te parecias.	on the beach was what you seemed.
. . . . .	. . . . . .
Uma onda que parara	A wave that had stopped short
. . . . .	. . . . . .
no alto de sua crista	at the very top of its crest
e se fizesse montanha	and turned into a mountain,
. . . . .	. . . . . .
mas que ao se fazer montanha	but while turning into a mountain
continuasse água ainda . . .	went on being water still . . .

That the same motif continues to be used in the East as well as the West is evident from the perhaps more exotic and certainly more explicit verses of the Japanese modernist poet, critic, and translator, Horiguchi Daigaku (1892–1981):

Ah, the curves of a woman's body,
swelling, undulating; the tangled bush
a neat triangle, a sunny island
floating in a smooth, milky sea.

. . . . . .

In the middle of the island (the pivot, ah! of all aesthetics),
in the shadow of the trees growing lush in the valley,
the tapering roof of the island guard's house
appears and disappears;
the tapering peach-coloured roof, ah!
appears and disappears[26]

If the definitive formulation and the most circumstantial working-out of the equation 'Island = Woman' is still that of Camões, in the *Cántico espiritual* of his younger contemporary John of the Cross, mountains and islands are only two among the abundant images that

[25] On Cabral's two-way comparisons see below, Ch. 6.

[26] Horiguchi Daigaku *Zenshishū* (Tokyo, 1971), 40: 'Landscape' (full Japanese text in the Textual Appendix). Horiguchi, the best-known Japanese translator of French literature and a friend of Cocteau, would certainly have known Baudelaire's 'La Géante', and (having spent time in Brazil as a young man in 1913–25) possibly Bandeira's 'Água-forte' as well.

the enamoured Soul draws on to apostrophize the object of its headlong flight towards union with an unequivocally masculine God:

Mi amado, las montañas,	My Beloved, the mountains,
los valles solitarios nemorosos,	the solitary valleys forest-clad,
las ínsulas extrañas,	the islands far and strange,
los ríos sonorosos,	the rivers sonorous,
el silbo de los aires amorosos ...	the murmuring of breezes amorous ...

Alonso 1946: 282

What is most truly 'strange' about these verses, however, is the alternation of mountains, islands, and valleys—all well-known feminine symbols—with those no less recognized masculine ones, rivers and the wind. And later in the Canticle, the consummation of this novel variant on the classical hierogamy will be announced in an equally novel way by the entry not of the Bridegroom, but of the Bride, into the pleasant garden of her desire: 'en el ameno huerto deseado'.

At this point St John is following closely the text of the *Canticum Canticorum* (and indeed, of the *Shîr ha-Shîrîm* itself, for in the passage the Saint is paraphrasing here the Vulgate, which he is using, does not diverge substantially from the Hebrew original, with which he will also have been familiar). But the fidelity of a genuine poet to his sources is as freely interpreted as it is freely assumed; and the fact is that this surprising transformation of one of the most universal feminine symbols into a metaphor for God owes nothing to the biblical model. On the contrary, it is a direct inversion of the sense of the corresponding verses of the *Canticum*. Where the Castilian poem reads 'Entrado se ha la esposa / en el ameno huerto deseado', in the Bible it is the Bride who invites the Bridegroom into the garden which is only His, and for Him: 'Veniat dilectus meus in hortum suum'. Once again it is the etymological dictionary that elucidates the mystery: *hortus*, like its Greek equivalent κῆπος, 'quelquefois ... désigne le *pudendum muliebre*'.[27]

---

[27] An elaborate medieval example of this trope is found in the *Cosmographia* of Bernardus Silvestris, whose Edenic garden of Gramision, 'espace clos et privilégié, fertile ..., à la fois un jardin et ... un sexe féminin', is characterized as an 'endroit secret et retiré' and a 'repli caché': 'une toison le couvre ..., une forêt l'entoure'; and of the thirteen plants growing in it, ten are either aphrodisiacs or used in gynaecology (Jean Jolivet, 'Les Principes féminins dans la *Cosmographia* de Bernard Silvestre', in *Actes du 7e congrès international de la philosophie médiévale* (Louvain-la-Neuve, 1986), 296–305).

St John's *insulas* have no parallel in the Song of Songs, the poles of which are a concrete City—Jerusalem, where the Bride lives—and a metaphorical Garden: the *hortus conclusus* that is herself, but also the new Eden into which the whole of the countryside around them is transformed, and which is ultimately the same thing, since *paradisus* derives from the Old Persian *pairideaza*, meaning simply an enclosed precinct or walled garden.

HORTUS CONCLUSUS

The gynaecomorphic vision of Nature is extensive to the urban landscape as well: the prototype of the City is also a simple enclosure: sacred or defensive, or both at once; but in any case uterine. It is not by chance that the Egyptian hieroglyph for 'town' was used metaphorically to mean 'mother' (Lewis Mumford, *The City in History* (London, 1966), 13). At a deeper level, the apparent polar opposition of City and Garden can be seen as a transcendent identity, as is shown in William McClung's study of the literary and artistic *fortuna* of Jerusalem and Eden, which documents the long-standing identification of these supposed poles in the collective imagination of the West.[28]

In the iconography of the Buddhist East, on the other hand, Paradise is customarily represented in the schematic form of a mandala, which as an abstract diagram is especially well suited to the figurative representation of a garden indeed enclosed, but whose enclosing wall implies neither reclusion nor exclusion of a forcible kind. As Eugenio Battisti says in his preface to the Italian translation of McClung's important book (7), any form of enclosed space can assume the charisma of the Earthly Eden, though 'con il rimpianto di un paradiso originario le cui...mura coincidevano con i confini dell'universo'.

It was for the consoling of just such a *rimpianto* that China developed over the centuries, in the art of painting as in that of the garden, a subtly knowing illusionist technique which consists in calling attention to the real existence of a wall at the same time as it

---

[28] On the early lack of distinction between the ideas of city and garden see McClung, ch. 3. A. Bartlett Giamatti, *The Earthly Paradise and the Renaissance Epic* (Princeton, NJ, 1966), 114–18, notes the convergence of the City of God with Paradise in the 'rosa sempiterna' of the final canto of the *Divine Comedy*.

hints at its essential unreality, by transforming it into what is in effect a horizon.

In painting, the principal method employed for this purpose is the typical play of alternating full and empty spaces that makes a Chinese painting instantly recognizable as such.[29] As for the garden, at least three different strategies may be used to obtain what is known as the 'borrowed landscape' effect: three ways, that is—not mutually exclusive—of subverting the solidity of the barrier whose existence is nevertheless, paradoxically, indispensable for the creation of that effect. The smooth and impassive surface of the wall may be perforated by sudden unexpected openings, not infrequently in the form of lotuses, shells, gourds, or vases (Fig. 9), opening on the unknown. Or it may be partly hidden behind scattered bushes and plants that seem to blend imperceptibly, with no break in continuity, into the surrounding vegetation outside the wall. Or it may simply dissolve, as in one of the most famous gardens in the garden city of Suzhou, laid out in 1140, in which the pearl-grey wall becomes almost invisible in the half light of early morning or evening, fading to a vague mist hardly distinguishable from the sky, so that 'the wall which encloses and divides space also serves to extend it symbolically beyond all bounds'; a similar effect, also ultimately indebted to Chinese painting, is found in the 16th-century Daisen'in garden in Kyoto, whose white wall, behind the foreground of a crane island and a miniature pine, appears as a misty sky, giving the impression of 'an immense landscape that does not stop at the wall but continues on through the mist'.[30]

It seems obvious that these means, though in principle aesthetic, in fact transcend the sphere of aesthetics and are directed (like the placing of the islands in the sea of sand at the Ryōan-ji) towards an ulterior end. The *trompe-l'œil* of the Chinese (and, *ipso facto*, the Japanese) garden, far from being futile tricks, imply a special ontology: a dialectics of the open-and-shut, no doubt esoteric, but by no means exclusive to the East, at least since the Renaissance: in Palladio's *Villa Rotonda* of 1559, for example, 'the garden's boundaries no longer fence it from a radically different world outside,

---

[29] On this technique, reflecting an idea common to Taoism and Zen, see Cheng 1979; for paintings employing it, Cheng 1980. On its more general philosophical, philological, and psychological aspects see above, Ch. 1, nn. 18 and 35.

[30] Cf. Keswick, 18; 135; Slawson, 119 f.

but ... localize a potency ... now perceived to be universal'.[31] The essential difference between the European and Sino-Japanese traditions is that in the latter the practices described are underwritten by a conscious and explicit philosophical teaching.

It is in fact in the oasis gardens of the *Middle* East (and in the Arab-inspired Mediterranean gardens deriving from them) that the function of the wall has always been to exclude hostile Nature in order to affirm Man's possession of that part of it that he has succeeded in enclosing and domesticating. In China, on the contrary, what the garden designer wishes to keep *extra muros* is rather the agitation of everyday human life, precisely in order to return the interior to the legitimate possession of Nature, of which Man forms a part and with which he seeks to feel in harmony and equilibrium.[32]

As for Japan, the aesthetic expression of this metaphysical concept of equilibrium—between Man and Nature, the closed and the open, what is hidden and what revealed—is exemplified by the case of the celebrated sixteenth-century Master of the tea ceremony, Sen no Rikyū, in whose garden there was a hedge that concealed a famous view of the sea. It was only when guests bent over a stone fountain to perform the ritual hand-washing that preceded the ceremony that the distant panorama was revealed through a gap in the hedge. When pressed for an explanation, their host contented himself with reciting a familiar haiku:

Umi sukoshi	A little of the sea
niwa ni izumi no	in the garden: just the size
ko no ma ka na.	of the lake in the fountain.

A Western exegesis may prove less impenetrable to Western readers than Master Sen's 'explanation'. What happens is that the guest, suddenly catching sight of the immensity of the sea after beholding himself reflected and, as it were, summed up in the water of the fountain, realizes as a good Buddhist that the relation of this water to that of the sea is an emblem of his own pettiness, but at the same time of his oneness with the universe.[33]

---

[31] Comito, 162. The same is already true a century earlier of the villa of Lorenzo il Magnifico at Vicenza (ibid. 6).

[32] Cf. Kuck, 55; Keswick, 31.

[33] Cf. Kuck, 197. Having refused his daughter to the Shogun Hideyoshi as a concubine, Sen held a final tea ceremony for his disciples and presented each with one of the utensils, keeping only the bowl, which he broke before taking leave of them and carrying out the shogun's sentence of suicide. His portrait ('Hat on his head and fan in

The post-modernist architect Charles Jencks turns to a structural anthropologist, Edmund Leach, for the elucidation of a paradox which is at base neither architectural nor anthropological but semiotic: the inevitable dilemma faced by anyone who seeks to create a space which, as in the Chinese garden, is intended to symbolize by means of a repertoire of formal devices the multiform oneness of the universe, and has therefore to oscillate constantly between opposite poles—the solid and the empty, present and absent, inside and outside, *yáng* and *yin*—thereby generating a kind of 'symbolics of negation' in which to call attention to one of these poles is at the same time to evoke the other. For Leach it is the artificial boundaries Man feels obliged to invent in order to divide and, if possible, control the flow of Time, that create in him the disquieting contrary obligation to transcend them by means of rites of passage or initiation. Applying the same notion to Space, Jencks necessarily arrives at the conclusion that the Chinese garden performs a spatial function parallel, and rigorously analogous, to the temporal function of those rites of transcendence.[34]

'All of Holy Scripture [*ha K^ethubîm*] is holy, but the *Shîr ha-Shîrîm* is most holy', the mystical rabbi Aqiba proclaimed in the second century.[35] The rabbinical tradition, unlike the majority of Christian exegetes, seems indeed never to have felt it necessary to deny the undeniable eroticism of the Song of Songs before being able to affirm its holiness, originating perhaps in a fertility rite prior to the consolidation of Judaism itself, and common to various peoples of the ancient Middle East.[36]

Even more than the soberly unadorned history of Eden related in twenty-five brief chapters of Genesis, it is the *Canticum* that is the obligatory starting-point for any reflection on the symbolism of the garden in Western culture. If the condensed narrative of Genesis is a seed (whose growth potential, including an implicit element of eroticism, Milton in particular was adept at realizing), the Canticle is

his hand', the epigraph reads, 'The solemn image . . . captures what he always was') can be seen in *Japan: The Shaping of Daimyō Culture*, ed. Yoshiaki Shimizu (New York, 1988), plate 38.

[34] Jencks, in Keswick, 196 ff.; cf. Leach, ch. 7.

[35] *Mishnah, Yadayim* 3: 5 (cit. Carr, 70 n. 2). The great mystic was taking a stand against the *exclusively* natural interpretation that threatened to prevent admission of the Canticle to the biblical canon.

[36] According to a controversial but widely held theory (cf. Carr, 49), the germ of the *Shîr ha-Shîrîm* itself was a Babylonian ritual in which a hierogamy was celebrated between Ishtar, personified by her priestess, and the king.

the mature fruit: complete and self-contained like the *botri vineae* it speaks of.

Many poets both before and after John of the Cross have harvested that vineyard,[37] just as others before and after Milton have drawn inspiration from Eden. To establish a manageable corpus, I shall limit myself to the former, and to the same coordinates as hitherto: the sixteenth century and the Iberian linguistic domain; which leads us more or less automatically, by a process of elimination, to Gil Vicente.

Vicente refers explicitly to the Song of Solomon on five occasions, each time to invoke the Virgin as a 'garden enclosed' (*huerta cerrada* or *orto cerrado*), in accordance with the long-established typological interpretation that identified her with the Bride in the *Canticum*. The most elaborate citation comes almost at the beginning of his career in a modest and apparently ingenuous little song included in the *Castilian Shepherds' Play*—the first authentic theatrical work to be written in Portugal—and consists of a paraphrase of selected verses from the second and fourth chapters of the biblical text, addressed to 'the comely shepherdess / whom Solomon called his Spouse / when he used to sing ('cuando canticava') of her':

Llevántate, amiga mía,	Arise, my beloved,
columba mea fermosa,	*columba mea* most comely,
amiga mía olorosa;	my beloved so sweet-scented;
tu boz suene en mis oídos,	let thy voice sound in my ears:
qu'es muy dulce a mis sentidos,	it is most sweet to my senses,
y tu cara muy graciosa.	and full of grace thy face.
Como el lilio plantada,	Like the lily planted,
florecido entre espinos;	flowering among thorns;
como los olores finos,	like the finest perfumes
muy süave eres hallada.	thou art found most smooth.
Tú eres huerta cerrada	Thou art a garden enclosed
en quien Dios venir dessea:	wherein God desires to enter:
tota pulchra amica mea,	*tota pulchra amica mea,*
flor de virgindad sagrada.	flower of sacred maidenhood.

Cop 4d–5a

---

[37] Stanley Stewart (*The Enclosed Garden* (Madison, Wis., 1966), pp. xiii–xiv; 191), with no pretensions to an exhaustive inventory, lists Robert Grosseteste, Guillaume de Lorris, Chaucer, Dunbar, William Neville, James I, George Herbert, Marvell, Richard Rowlands, William Prynne, St Teresa of Ávila, Joseph Beaumont (the sources of whose long poem 'Psyche' would merit study in view of its striking resemblance to Vicente's *Auto da Alma*, mentioned above in Ch. 3), and Monteverdi's *Vespro della Beata Vergine*.

The first half of this song is an abridgement of three verses of the second chapter: 'Surge ..., amica mea, columba mea, formosa mea ...; sonet vox tua in auribus meis: vox enim tua dulcis, et facies tua decora ... Sicut lilium inter spinas ...'. Then, substituting new elements that accentuate the concrete and sensorial (*mis sentidos*; *plantada*; *florecido*) for some of the verbal and semantic repetitions of the Latin, Vicente passes directly from *lilium*, in the second chapter, to *hortus conclusus*, in the fourth.

Gil Vicente's characteristic attachment to the life of the senses, through which the concrete is apprehended, leads him to distil the suave perfumes of the biblical garden and diffuse them throughout his own poem, scenting even the lines not taken from the Canticle. But even in these verses of his own making he is still, no less than John of the Cross—and with remarkable formal intuition—following closely the internal organization of his model. Two groups of Latin verses are exactly matched by his two blocks of verse in Castilian; but the fragrance that pervades these can already be found floating, no less diffuse, throughout the eight chapters of the Canticle, in which the scattered allusions to fresh or heady perfumes and to the flowers, fruits, scented woods, aromatic plants, and gardens that exhale them, total nearly a hundred, with a notable concentration in the second and fourth chapters: the very ones the poet has chosen to paraphrase in the respective halves of his song.

As his dramatic technique matures, simple paraphrases of this kind, not infrequent in his earliest works, are quickly outgrown, and biblical material is skilfully integrated into the structure of the plays and interpreted with ever greater freedom, not to say licence. Even the farce of *The Old Man and His Garden*, a still relatively early play of his middle period, begins with a highly irreverent secular gloss on the paternoster, heralding the playwright's increasing detachment from his origins in liturgical drama.

The special relevance of this miniature farce to our subject, as the title suggests, lies in its relation to the Garden theme, starting with the analogous secularization, or rather *re*-secularization, of the Garden ≈ Woman metaphor, which almost a millennium and a half of sacred allegory had applied successively to Israel, the Church, and the Virgin. The process already experimentally applied to a single song is now extended to an entire short play, in which, as we have seen (above, Ch. 3, n. 7), the words 'flower', 'rose', 'scent', 'orchard', and 'garden', with various synonyms and cognates such as *horta*, *horto*, or *jardim*, appear no less than thirty times. Even *Paraíso* figures (along with seven of the occurrences of *rosa* and *flor*) among the hyperbolic *piropos* the besotted Old Man showers on the more or less innocently provocative object of his senile infatuation, and which, with the other words mentioned, make her a synecdoche of his garden, to which her mother has sent her for sweet herbs.

In *The Shepherds' Play*, the 'flor de santa virgindade' is still, naturally enough, the lily, which predominates almost exclusively in the Song of Songs. Yet the biblical 'lily of the valley' translates a Hebrew word probably related to the Egyptian name of the lotus, nenuphar, or water-lily (Carr, 88). In German, on the other hand (to complicate matters further), the lotus is a 'lake rose' (*Seerose*); whereas in Luther's translation of the Canticle it is in turn St Jerome's *lilia* that become German *Rosen*.

Functionally, lily, lotus, and rose are identical symbols, if only because the *coincidentia oppositorum* characteristic of symbolism is common to all three. If the rose is the Virgin's flower, it is also that of Aphrodite (and of prostitutes); if the lily is a synonym for virginity, it is no less true 'qu'on attribue le lis à Vénus et aux Satyres': what makes the lily symbolically interchangeable with the lotus is simply 'le bouton fermé . . . dont l'ouverture . . . est la réalisation des possibilités antithétiques de l'être'.[38] We cannot fail to recognize here, repeated on the scale of an individual flower, the same dialectic of shut and open, of the hidden revealed, that we saw before on the scale of the garden—which is not surprising, since flower and garden are both, in their way, mandalas.[39]

But *The Old Man and His Garden* brings another innovation no less significant than its 'realization of the antithetic possibilities' of the secular recycling of an ancient sacred metaphor: it is the first in the long series of European dramatic works inspired by the *Tragicomedia de Calisto y Melibea*, otherwise *La Celestina*: often considered the most important prose work in the Spanish language with the exception of *Don Quixote*. Gil Vicente himself not only evokes the figure of

---

[38] Chevalier and Gheerbrant, s.vv. *lis* and *lotus*. For the equivalence Western lily = Eastern lotus = Western rose, see *IETS* (s.vv. *lily* and *lotus*).

[39] Cf. n. 7, above. On the lotus as mandala see Jung's commentary on the ancient Chinese *Secret of the Golden Flower* (77–151). Indian iconography emphasizes the sexual aspect of the lotus mandala: the Hindu goddess Lakshmi and her Buddhist counterpart are typically shown holding a lotus in the gesture known as the 'link' (*kataka*), and symbolizing marriage (Campbell 1982: ch. 3: 'The Lotus and the Rose'). The Chinese word for 'lotus', *lién*, is a homophone of 'link', as in 'linked verses' (*lién jù*: cf. Ch. 1, n. 28, above), and hence a standard pun for sexual union.

1. Egyptian mural (Thebes, 1420–1375 BCE) (Kuck, 41).

2. Péng Lái 'islands', Tenryū temple lake (Kyoto, 9th century): possibly Chinese, and the only extant specimen of Sòng dynasty rock art (Kuck, 302).

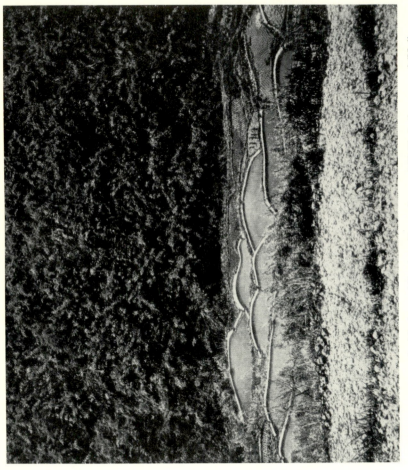

3. Japanese pinewood with rice paddies in valley and stony hillside in foreground (Holborn, 69).

4. Zen temple garden (Ryōgen' in, Kyoto, *c.*1502) with cedar moss and stones (Holborn, 68).

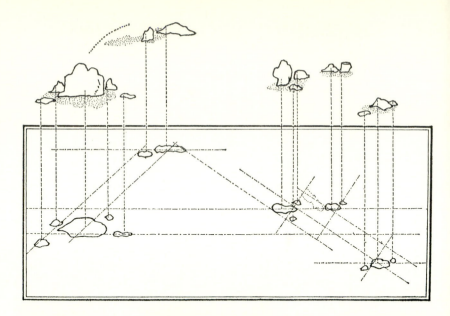

5 and 6. Ryōan temple (Kyoto, *c.* 1492): diagram and projection of the five groups of 'islands' (Kuck, 165); detail of the right-hand three groups (Holborn, 61).

7. Conical stone fountain (National Museum, Tokyo, *c.*615) representing the Buddhist *axis mundi*; probably the only extant work of its kind in the Táng period Chinese style (Kuck, 284).

8. Peter Reddick, 'Landscape Figure' (Adam, 128).

9. Lěng Méi (18th century), Lotus gate (National Palace Museum, Taiwan), metonymically assimilated to the roses on the trellis and the graceful chess players.

10. Funeral portrait of the Countess of Dài (Mǎ Wáng Tui, c. 168 BCE): courtesy of Michael Loewe.

11. 'Bond of Union' (© 1956 M. C. Escher / Cordon Art, Baarn, Holland. Collection Haags Gemeentemuseum): reduplication of spirals representing the fusion of sexual duality in a superior unity; cf. ch. 5 n. 26.

'Madre' Celestina again in the bawds who appear in four other plays after the Branca Gil of *The Old Man*, but also refers, in *The Gypsies' Play*, to Melibea. It is clearly Melibea's *huerto* that has suggested to him the idea of the Old Man's *horta*, which a few years later is to flower anew in Vicente's masterpiece, *Don Duardos*, transformed into the infanta Flérida's 'huerta muy guardada'.

The metaphoric and metonymic identification of Flérida's garden with her person has been pointed out by Thomas Hart;[40] for *La Celestina* the equivalent identification is confirmed in Jorge Guillén's poem 'Huerto de Melibea' with Calisto's passionate cry, '¡Oh Melibea, toda huerto mío!' It is curious to find in this work by one of the finest poets of this century—himself author of a great *Cántico* as well as an admirer of John of the Cross and editor of the *In Cantica Canticorum Salomonis explanatio* of Luis de León—the implicit affirmation of a hidden link (seemingly unnoticed by historians of Spanish literature[41]) between the *Celestina* and the two previous 'Canticles', those of the Bible and of John of the Cross. Compare:

1. 'que voy, voy de vuelo' (Guillén) < 'Apártalos, amado, que voy de vuelo' (St John) < 'Averte oculos tuos a me / Quia ipsi me avolare fecerunt' (*Canticum*);
2. 'Escucha...Ya va a llegar, ya le veo / Venir por la senda' (Guillén) < 'Vox dilecti mei; ecce iste venit / Saliens in montibus' (*Canticum*);
3. '¡Brisa! Muy delgada, / Mueve apenas las hojas. / ¡Este calor tan grato por la noche!' (Guillén) < 'los aires amorosos, / la noche sosegada'; 'el aspirar del aire...en la noche serena'; 'aspira por mi huerto, / y corran sus olores' (St John);
4. '¡Terrible tu presencia / Misma, tu aurora misma!' (Guillén) < 'progreditur quasi aurora..., / Terribilis ut castrorum acies' (*Canticum*).

It is time to draw these various strands together. The myth of the Earthly Paradise attains to its highest poetic realization as a universal

---

[40] *Gil Vicente: Casandra and Don Duardos* (London, 1981), 40 ff.

[41] Of nine titles listed under 'Garden' in Joseph Snow's *Annotated Bibliography* of the *Celestina* (Madison, Wis., 1985), only one considers a possible influence of the Canticle, but only to dismiss it: see W. E. Truesdell, 'The *Hortus Conclusus* Tradition, and the Implications of its Absence in *La Celestina*', *Kentucky Romance Quarterly*, 29 (1973).

archetype in the *Divine Comedy*. But a myth is at base little more than a theme: a melodic line, requiring not only the plenitude of an orchestrated realization but the free unfolding of a gamut of potential variations. The linearity of myth then yields to the plurivalence of the symbol: the Earthly Paradise engenders on one hand the garden enclosed of the *Canticum*, and on the other the topos of the *locus amoenus*; and both then subdivide again. The latter, the delectable natural enclosure ideally propitious to love (*dignus amore locus*, in the words of Petronius[42]), is transformed in the course of time into the landscape-metaphor of a woman's body, as in the Isle of Love in *The Lusiads*; while the *hortus conclusus*, as we have seen, is already disemic in the Bible, where, just as in the *Celestina* or in *Don Duardos*, it stands both for the beloved woman's garden and at the same time for her body.

What is it that makes a city, a garden, and an island ultimately identical? 'Ce qui sacralise avant tout un lieu', Gilbert Durand remarks (1969: 281), 'c'est sa fermeture.' That is to say, its *isolation*. Which brings us back to our starting-point: now, however, enhanced by a new symbolic vision: that of the sacred or numinous, incarnate in a *numen loci* which if not eternal is at least feminine, and has a history going back some thirty centuries. A vision, moreover, that includes the implicit hope, or even the tranquil confidence ('fe de vida', Guillén would say) that sooner or later the garden of desire, and the flower that sums it up—whether lily, lotus, or rose—will open:

> Yo vi la rosa: clausura   I have seen the rose: first
> Primera de la armonía,   closure of harmony,
> Tranquilamente futura . . .   tranquilly future . . .[43]

---

[42] *Carm.* 131 (cit. Curtius, 195 f. On the false etymology *amoenus* < *amor* cf., ibid., 192; 197 n. 22).

[43] *Cántico*: *fe de vida*, 243. Compare the closed, inward-turned schema of the consonants in ll. 1–2 (r—s ← → s—r / m—r ← → r—m) with the open-ended linearity of l. 3 (*tra* → *t-ra*), maintained throughout the remaining seven lines. Robert Havard has identified the mandala as the central structuring principle of the great Castilian poet's work.

5

THE ISLE OF VENUS
(ICONOGRAPHY OF AN ARCHETYPE)

И море, и Гомер — всё движется любовью.
And the sea, and Homer—all is moved by love.

Mandel'shtam

The road that leads from self
to self goes round the world.

Keyserling

YES—oh, dear, yes (to paraphrase Forster's wry comment on the other main narrative genre), the epic, too, tells a story. To be sure, the epic of the Lusiads, and even those of Odysseus and Aeneas, in so far as they are the stories of voyages regarded—or at least represented—as belonging to History, differ in principle from Dante's professedly allegorical pilgrimage or that of the Soul in Gil Vicente's eponymous play,[1] in both of which the poet uses the story to say something else (or something more). In the purportedly historical epic, that is, the narrative of the journey does not set out to do more than give an account of that journey as such, which is thus in the strictest sense the meaning—in semiotic terms, the signified—of the narration (though not, as we shall see, of the poem).

In the *Commedia* or the *Auto da Alma*, on the other hand, the journey is at once a signified and, *ex professo*, a signifier: the words signify the journey, which in turn purports to signify a universal and transcendental truth, encoded not in the words but in the actions and situations they describe.

'Littera' (according to Nicholas of Lyra) 'gesta docet; quod credas, allegoria'; and Dante himself, in his Epistle to Can Grande,[2] makes it

---

[1] See above, Ch. 3, n. 1.
[2] The persuasive arguments advanced by Dronke (1986: 103–11) against the traditional attribution of the *Epistola* to Dante do not, of course, invalidate the statement quoted.

clear that in his poem, 'primus sensus est qui habetur per litteram, alius qui habetur per *significata* per litteram'. Both senses, of course—the literal and concrete no less than the allegorical—are equally valid. The American Dante scholar Demaray has in fact shown that the poet's imagined pilgrimage through the other world reflects not only (like Vicente's play) the 'pilgrim's progress' of mankind through earthly life, but also, stage by stage, the great circular pilgrimage of the Middle Ages in which the pilgrims of all Europe, following in the footsteps of the ancient Hebrews *in exitu Israel de Aegypto*, plodded through the deserts of Sinai and Palestine to Jerusalem before re-embarking for the holy places of Rome.

But just as the allegorical elements in the narrative of a journey-as-signifier (even one represented as telling the whole truth and nothing but the truth: 'tudo sem mentir, puras verdades') do not invalidate the letter, so the letter, in that of a journey-as-signified, does not rule out a possible extraliteral dimension—at least not when the 'story' is also a poem. As Camões's contemporary Sidney pointed out, Aristotle's thesis admits of a corollary: if Poetry is indeed more philosophical than History, because it universalizes its signifieds, it can also be considered more historical than Philosophy, because it concretizes its own universals.

Despite the ingrained Portuguese habit of prizing it as much for its historical as for its poetic virtues, no one is likely to be so ingenuous as to take *Os Lusíadas* literally for History (or even Philosophy). As Frei Bartolomeu Ferreira was at pains to make clear when he signed the *nihil obstat*, it is nothing but poetry and feigning ('Poesia & fingimento'); and the reason why every poet (as Fernando Pessoa said) is a feigner, is that the very nature of poetic communication will not allow him to express a univocal, literal signified without at the same time using it as a second-degree signifier to create, by metalepsis, new imaginative, affective, and even conceptual signifieds. This is no doubt why the word *fictio* was considered, from the early Renaissance on, the most appropriate translation of the Aristotelian *mimesis*.[3] As far as Camões is concerned, at least, one cannot but agree with his great exegete Faria e Sousa that he never said anything with only one meaning ('no dixo . . . cosa alguna con un sentido solo').

---

[3] Cf. *Princeton Encyclopaedia of Poetry and Poetics* (Princeton, NJ, 1975), s.v. *feigning*. For the earlier and later vicissitudes of the difficult distinction between fiction (or feigning) and lying in Western literature see Curtius, 203–7, 217 f., 398, and 593; for Eastern views cf. Miner 1990: index, s.v. *fictionality*.

FROM *MYTHOS* TO *PRAXIS*

To say 'the words signify the journey' is no more than to paraphrase Nicholas of Lyra's more lapidary and elegant 'littera gesta docet', except for the overtones of 'docet'; but these are not without relevance. What is meant by the *gesta* is, in Aristotelian terms, the *mythos* of the poem: the series of concrete happenings that structure the narrative, and which in *The Lusiads* (or the *Odyssey*, or the *Aeneid*) are those of the voyage. And no matter how historically justified their presence in that literal and linear narrative, or how functionally indispensable their role in it, they are none the less, in the long run, *significant* happenings. What they signify, metaphorically or metonymically, is an inward action (in Aristotelian terms once more, a *praxis*) definable as learning.

Nicholas of Lyra speaks of the teaching function of the letter. In our own day it is an eminent Hellenist who stresses the pedagogical importance, in the *Odyssey*, not only of the literal narrative but of the *gesta* themselves, with 'the myriad overtones of the journey, the return, and what they jointly tell of human possibility' (Finley, 25); and of their importance not only for the reader or hearer but for the hero himself who lives the *gesta*. It is unnecessary to be either a deconstructionist or a cabbalist to recognize that every genuine reader of a genuine literary work (one that Barthes would have considered *scriptible*) becomes perforce a collaborator in the writing of the work. If the protagonist journeys, the reader—and even the author—also journey, as Dante suggests in his exhortation:

> O voi che siete in piccioletta barca
> desiderosi d'ascoltar, seguite
> dietro al mio legno . . . [4]

In consonance with this teaching function (which is not to be confused with a didactic intention), history, in Homer, is filled with 'illustrative figures'; but precisely because they are illustrative, 'history as such is not their home, rather history become paradigm'.[5]

---

[4] *Paradiso*, II. 1–3. For the poet's own journey in *The Lusiads* see *Os Lusíadas*, VII. 78–9, and M. Clara Almeida Lucas, 'A Viagem de Vasco da Gama: Estrutura da Narrativa Mítica', in Reckert and Centeno, 57–62.

[5] Finley, 41. 'The decline of paradigmatic history, and our growing consciousness of historiography's irreducible element of fiction, are . . . contributions to what Wilde called "the decay of lying"' (Kermode 1973: 43).

History become paradigm, of course, is nothing but a special case of the signified become signifier. This is the meaning of Dante's enigmatic pronouncement: 'Expositio littere nichil aliud est quam forme operis manifestatio'. The literal voyage signifies, 'mimetically', the complex spiritual evolution that is the internal *praxis* of the whole *Divine Comedy*; but the various figures Dante encounters on his way, while no less 'illustrative' than those of the *Odyssey*, are at the same time almost all real historical persons. That is, they are *figurae* even in the technical rhetorical sense of the word, studied in Erich Auerbach's well-known essay—and which as it happens coincides not only with the 'allegoria de li teologi' of Dante's *Convivio* but even with the concept of allegory *tout court*, as understood in our own time by the school of Walter Benjamin (cf. Merquior, 104–13).

As we have already seen, however, it is not necessary for the gesta (or the agents or figures of the gesta) to be 'feigned': that is, mere pretexts for a second-level discourse. Any journey that teaches is perforce a signifier, even if in principle it makes no claim to be considered anything more than a signified: it is simply that in the latter case its mode of signifying will no longer be metaphorical—by similarity of the journey to what it 'really' signifies—but rather metonymical: by superimposition, on what the journey *is*, of what it *also* signifies.

Eliot equated lyric poetry to the first person of the verb (the poet speaks of himself), dramatic to the second (the poet places his characters in a dialogic, 'I-you', situation), and epic to the third. Another possible correlation would be with the three main tenses of the Indo-European verb: epic = past, lyric = present, and dramatic = future. If it is true, as Thornton Wilder said, that 'on the stage it is always *now*', the 'now' is a constant becoming, which, like life, projects itself forward in time. Moreover, it can be argued that the dialectical rhythm of learning (which is that of human life itself, habitually allegorized in terms of a quest, pilgrimage, or initiatory journey) coincides with the deep structure of drama (cf. Reckert 1977: 60–8).

The heroic poem whose *mythos* is constituted by a voyage thus has obvious points of contact with dramatic poetry. Indeed, it has been reckoned that more than 60 per cent of the *Odyssey* is direct discourse, setting up a second-person relation and a virtual present tense in the process of becoming future. The comparable proportion in *The Lusiads* (which I calculate at some 57 per cent) has an almost identical effect. It is obvious, as well, that the very concept of movement towards a goal, and the shape of a ship's prow itself—both implicit in the narrative of a voyage—allude metonymically (even in the absence of any metaphorical intention) to futurity.[6]

Now here, in the case of the *Odyssey*, we are confronted with a paradox: if the goal the hero's ships are making for is indeed, in temporal terms, the future, in spatial terms it is the homeland left behind ten years earlier when the expedition departed for the war. The *Odyssey*, as it happens, is the only survivor (and, it is perhaps safe to conjecture, the supreme example) of a lost epic genre related not just to voyages but specifically to the return voyage: the *nostoi*, or 'home-comings'. The word *nostos* apparently comes from the same root as νόος (Classical νοῦς): 'understanding' or 'intelligence' (Finley, 65); and it is only thanks to the trials and ordeals he has suffered in the course of his *nostos* that Odysseus achieves the ultimate νόος that is self-knowledge.

On the other hand, understanding is itself a prerequisite for the return: thus it is only after Tethys has demonstrated the nature and workings of the 'grande machina do mundo' to Gama that she allows him to descend from the 'monte alto, & divino' and undertake his homeward journey. Now that he has learned, he is fit to embark for his own Ithaca: 'Agora, pois que tendes *aprendido*..., Podeis vos embarcar...pera a patria amada'. It is as clearly a post-initiatory leave-taking as the concluding inscription of the alchemical emblem book *Mutus Liber*: 'oculatus abis'.

What is involved, in short, is a circular process—or rather, as in Hegelian dialectics, an ascending spiral—leading to the rediscovery of the point of departure, which may equally well be either the hero's earthly 'patria amada, & proprios lares' or the holy City whence his soul descended—'santa Cidade / Donde esta alma descendeu'—and whither it may yet return if it can only discover the 'maneira / Pera subir aa patria verdadeira': the way back up to its own 'true homeland'. For there is naturally more than one *patria* one can go 'back' to: the original one, like the Ithaca of Odysseus or Gama's Lisbon; or the Heavenly home, like that of the *Alma* in Gil Vicente's play, or Ō-

---

[6] For George Steiner (1972: 62), the metaphysically and logically 'scandalous' capacity of language 'to articulate a future...and...exist in advance of that which it designates' is intimately linked with sexual activity 'through its verbalized imaginings...[and] the...pre-physical and para-physical erotic exchange in which it takes place'.

oka's Pluto; or even, like the Rome of Aeneas, a new *patria* conceived of as the victorious restoration of the former one lost or destroyed.

For the 'fortes Lusitanos', however, the real goal of their 'Tam incertas viagens, & remotas' is neither the triumphant return to the longed-for land of their birth, 'o terreno / Em que nacêrão, sempre desejado', nor Heaven, nor yet (though it is not a little reminiscent of Virgil's 'recidiva Pergama') the 'Novo Reino' which in fact they later 'entre gente remota edificárão'. Despite the innumerable echoes of the *Aeneid* in Camões, his own poem is at base perhaps more Homeric—and certainly more Dantesque (as well as hardly less Ovidian[7])—than Virgilian: in part, no doubt, because its foundations go deeper into a archetypal subsoil.

THE WAY TO THE CENTRE

The archetypal journey is the quest for the Earthly Paradise, approached by a spiral path leading to the summit of the cosmic mountain-island: 'the primeval ocean . . . gives birth to the primeval hill, which cosmologically signifies the earth and psychologically is consciousness rising up out of the unconscious . . . ; [it] is an "island" in the sea, as consciousness is in the unconscious'; in ancient Egypt it was believed to have been the first land to emerge from the primordial waters, and was symbolized by an obelisk whose name derived from the verb 'to rise up'.[8] Itself the product of an epiphany, this mountain-island is in its turn, as Northrop Frye observes (1971: 203), a place of epiphanies, where the 'apocalyptic' world and the cyclical world of nature converge. We can now examine its various components one by one.

1. The EARTHLY PARADISE stands for many things: as Paradise lost, for the childhood of mankind and prelapsarian innocence; as Paradise to be regained, for Knowledge (νόος) and the full realization of mankind's adult potential; as both at once, for primal Wholeness, lost and to be regained: the garden where the Tree grows whose fruit, initially the symbol of *gnosis*, ended, thanks to a pre-logical intuition as accurate as it was naïve, by becoming a symbol of

---

[7] On the significance of metamorphosis and its role as a constitutive element in *The Lusiads*, see Reckert 1973.

[8] Neumann 1974: 241, who cites as 'the most perfect architectural example of this symbolism' the stupa of Borobudur, in Java, where an 'ascending spiral leads from . . . the world to the invisible Buddha'.

eros. As the archetype of the *locus amoenus*, therefore, it is also the seat of that Love which is, in the purest sense of the word, irresponsible. The Ancients, linking *amoenus* with *amor*, made the Earthly Paradise the topographic counterpart of the Golden Age in which Love had indeed been all amenity, and not yet the subject of contracts and commitments, or the guilty cause of jealousy, cruelty, suffering, betrayals—in short, of what Camões, in a definitive summing-up, calls 'mudanças e enganos': that is, change (Spenser's 'mutabilitie') and deceit (or, more simply, mistakes).

2. The SPIRAL PATH likewise sums up a whole complex of forms and motions both spatial and temporal, material and spiritual, ascending and descending. It is the exactly adequate figure and the natural model for both evolution and involution (as well, obviously, as convolution). It governs the development (a word that is itself a fossil metaphor) of the snail shell and the ascent of the spiral staircase; the entrance into the labyrinth and the exit from it; the winding and unwinding of ritual dance—in fact, everything either centrifugal or centripetal. In the millennia before the discovery of spiral nebulae or the double helix of DNA, the symbolic implications of the spiral were intuitively recognized alike by the most archaic and the most advanced societies: by Siberian shamans no less than by philosophers and artists such as Schelling and Hegel, Goethe and Coleridge. Even today its power of attraction can be seen to affect a whole range of attitudes, extending from the most serious scientific or artistic experiments (biophysical researches of D'Arcy Wentworth Thompson or Crick and Watson; mathematical and pictorial vortexes of Gödel and Escher; Klee's mandalas; the labyrinths of Borges) to the wildest and most charlatanesque speculations of astrology, occultism, and UFO-mania.

The generic term 'spiral' comprises three distinct species: the Archimedean, like a coiled snake; the equiangular, corresponding to the shell of a snail or whelk; and the helix, which suggests a serpent twisting round a central axis—the cosmic tree, the lingam, the caduceus of Hermes—and which is not, strictly speaking, a true spiral at all, since its teleological orientation, instead of converging on or diverging from that centre, is purely vertical. The very ancient and universal symbolism of the spiral is based almost entirely on the last two types: the helix, as the only inherently three-dimensional spiraloid, and the equiangular 'spira mirabilis', which, as Wentworth Thompson pointed out (175), is a spatial form linked to a temporal process. If the great biologist found it necessary to rap some other eminent scholars over the knuckles for their 'mystical' extrapolations from this fact,[9] one wonders what he would have made of recent suggestions (noted in passing—with picturesque *obiter dicta*—by Shuttle and Redgrove, 191) that certain Stone Age spiral designs represent flying saucers.

As we saw in the previous chapter, shells in general are a ubiquitous female symbol. Venus is born from a shell-womb; poets such as Verlaine, Ungaretti, and Bandeira see the shell as a vulva; and Philip Rawson (54) recalls that the equiangular spiral shell in particular is associated with birth and growth. As for the labyrinth, its spiral form hints at the initiatory element of ordeal or trial involved in the difficult and perilous access to the centre (cf. Eliade 1954: 18, and Wosien, 26 f.), comparable to the arduous ascent of the cosmic/conic mountain.

The relevance of these symbolic aspects of the spiral to Camões will become apparent in due course; of more obvious pertinence is the view of human life (collective and individual) as a journey starting from the primordial Paradise and Unity and ultimately spiralling back to a Paradise and a Unity enhanced (Goethe uses the alchemical term *Steigerung*) by the ordeals suffered and the lessons learnt on the way: thus—to borrow Hegel's characterization of his own method of argument—the return to the beginning is also an advance.

For M. H. Abrams (184), Hegel's concept is a specifically Romantic one in which the Plotinian doctrine of a circular return to Unity and the Good after a passage through multiplicity (understood as a separation from the Good) merges with the modern idea of linear progress, and spirals upward to a superior form of unity: superior in that it incorporates all the intermediate differentiations. The same idea already occurs in Chinese philosophy, however, by the end of the second millennium BCE in the *Yî Jing*, for which, though 'the beginning of the circle is from one perspective the same as the end . . . , from another, the two are . . . distinguished by the journey in between' (Colegrave, 55).

Applied to a specific case, this abstract principle can lead to the

---

[9] Among them, quite unjustly, Sir Theodore Cook, whose *The Curves of Life* (1st pub. 1914) remains the *locus classicus* for the study of spiral forms in Nature and art, and who was himself annoyed (16) by 'zealous inquirers so overwhelmed with the significance and ubiquity of this formation that their contributions to knowledge have been . . . weakened by their mystical or spiritual extravagances'.

surprising conclusion that while the intrinsic value of the phenomena of birth and death is metaphysically equal, in relative terms 'death at the end of a given cycle is higher than birth into the same cycle', by reason of 'the pitch of the evolutive screw'.[10] Jung's theory of the 'individuation process', which conceives of dreams as a helix simultaneously climbing upward and revolving round a hidden axis of meaning which in the course of a lifetime gradually reveals itself as the dreamer's essential Self, is an analogous idea.[11]

The possibility of a literally cata-strophic or 'down-turning' inversion of this process—the rolling backward of the wheel, dispersion instead of individuation—reminds us forcibly of two fundamental symbolic aspects of the spiral: its directional ambivalence—up or down, forward or backward, inward or outward—which seems almost automatically to impose a translation into subjective and evaluative terms (Heaven or Hell); and its dynamic energy, exemplified in the expansion of stellar nebulae and the contraction of whirlpools (Wosien, 99) and ritually invoked by the winding and unwinding of the wheel in the labyrinthine steps of sacred dance. Lord Clark (202 ff.) has studied Michelangelo's discovery of this same dynamism in the 'heroic spiral', a motive which 'was to dominate sculptural representations of energy during the baroque period', and which in painting, inspired by the example of the Sistine Last Judgement, extends from Tintoretto to Blake.[12]

3. The CONICAL MOUNTAIN, as *axis mundi*, is a variant of the World Tree (the tree not only of knowledge but of immortality), with which it often appears in a complementary relation (Eliade 1964: 492; cf. 266–74) apparently intended to reinforce by reduplication its symbolic message. It is curious to compare a photograph of Mount

---

[10] Matgioi (i.e. Albert de Pouvoirville), *La Voie Métaphysique* (edn. not specified), 137, cit. Guénon, 98. Seen from above or below, the screw ceases to have a pitch, its coils being reabsorbed into the circle that originally generated them. Guénon (110 n. 1) compares this perspective of the helix to the archetypal serpent uroboros, with its tail in its mouth, as opposed to the snake coiled round a tree (below, nn. 25–6).

[11] Cf. Cook, 26; von Frantz, *passim*. The Brazilian avant-gardist Lins based a novel explicitly on the helix, whose directional ambivalence leads to an erotic 'epiphany' of conjunction and dissolution—a 'Paradise', but with elements of Hell, and only provisional: a point on the continuously turning helix (cf. Gregory Rabassa, 'Osman Lins and *Avalovara*', *World Literature Today*, 53: 1 (Winter 1979), 32).

[12] Compare the extraordinary paintings by a contemporary of Camões reproduced in Sylvie Deswarte, *As Imagens de 'As Idades do Mundo' de Francisco de Holanda* (Lisbon, 1987). On Holanda see J. B. Bury, 'Francisco de Holanda and His Illustrations of the Creation', *Portuguese Studies*, 2 (1986).

Sinai (Demaray, fig. 13)—the model for Dante's mountain, and prototype of the axis in the Western tradition—with one of a typical Japanese sacred mountain (Blacker, fig. 2), each girt by the serpentining spiral terraces of its respectively Christian or shamanistic pilgrims' way.

By a happy coincidence, the direct link connecting the motive of the Mountain, as the point of tangency between Heaven and Earth, with the dynamism of the 'heroic spiral', can be neatly exemplified by reference to three Venetian churches. The monumental Baroque retable of San Moisè, by Heinrich Meyring (otherwise Arrigo Merengo), represents Mount Sinai, with Moses on its peak receiving, *de excelsis*, the Tables of the Law. On the other side of the Grand Canal, crowning the high altar of Santa Maria Gloriosa dei Frari, is the earliest (1518) of Titian's masterpieces: his grandiose Virgin of the Assumption, her arms raised in the act of taking flight. The dramatic impact of this picture has been attributed to its composition 'based on the dynamic line curving upward from the ... leg of an Apostle ... through his upstretched arm, and then through the body of the Virgin to the face of God the Father' (Hugh Honour, *The Companion Guide to Venice* (2nd edn., London, 1967)).

But it is in the tiny secularized church of Sant'Andrea in Zirada—almost lost to sight among the tourist buses of the Piazzale Roma coach station—that we find the striking conflation of these two works in one by the Flemish sculptor Josse Le Court (otherise Giusto Le Corte, 1627–79). Inspired simultaneously by Titian's Virgin and Meyring's massive crag, Le Court substitutes the Virgin for the Prophet on the summit of the mountain, thus restoring to it at one stroke both its function as point of departure for Heaven, and the figure of the Great Mother, now in her Christianized form.

Just as the cosmic Tree has its microcosmic replica in the sapling that the shaman transforms into a spiral stairway to Heaven by carving notches round its trunk (Eliade 1964: 76; 191; 194), so the cosmic Mountain has its own in the conical stone that, like earthly mountains and the caverns in them, symbolizes both the dwelling and the material manifestation of the Magna Mater. The disturbingly rounded and fleshy form of Le Court's 'mountain' does in fact vividly suggest a human torso with opulent hips; and in the centre of its base—defended, as it were, by a crucifix blocking the entrance, and no doubt meant to serve as a reliquary—there appears, precisely, a cavern or grotto.

If, as we saw earlier, the conventional interpretation of the conical stone as navel of the earth is implicitly phallic—Gilbert Durand, for example (1969: 142), refers to 'le cône, la pierre "levée" masculine'—we have also seen that the navel itself can be, as in the Song of Songs, a symbolic euphemism for the vagina. Once again we are reminded that a primary function of the symbol (suggested by the etymology of the word itself) is the reconciliation of polarities which though apparently antithetical are in fact complementary.

4. The ISLAND. In the same way as the mountain crowned by Paradise-to-be-regained rises from the middle of an island, the island in turn rises from the middle of the sea: according to Christian tradition, at the exact antipodes of the centre of the terrestrial hemisphere, which is Jerusalem. To seek the Island is therefore to seek a centre. But another centre and another Jerusalem also exist, even more sublime and more 'enhanced' than those that have been lost: they are the heavenly ones still to be gained. 'Exist' is not in fact the right word, for what is in question is not existence but essence. From the summit of the mountain, the elect are transported to the 'cidade Hierosolima celeste': the eternal and essential Paradise of which the terrestrial one is only a *figura*,[13] and which will be the ultimate objective no less of Camões (as is shown by his most famous lyric poem, the gloss on the 137th Psalm) than of Dante.

But the goal of a nation, as a collective social organism belonging by its nature to the world and to History, cannot be so ambitious; and in so far as the true hero of *The Lusiads* (as its title 'The Sons of Lusus' implies) is the Portuguese people, for whom Gama and his companions are no more than a synecdoche, the true goal of their 'home-coming' can therefore be no more or less than the Island and its Mountain. It has been noted that the climate and vegetation of the Isle of Love are identical to those of Portugal (an idealized Portugal described in terms of a *locus amoenus*), while those of India—which the poet knew from hardly less intimate experience—have come straight out of the pharmacological and botanical treatise of his contemporary Garcia de Orta.

That India is not the mariners' real goal, at least, goes without

---

[13] In the *figura* there is no question of a choice between literal and figurative senses: both are present; the earthly Jerusalem was no less a historical reality for being a *figura aeternae Jerusalem* (Auerbach, 68; 74). See also Fergusson, 126 ff.; Demaray, 62 f.; 94 ff.; and cf. Guénon, pp. xi–xii. As the transcendental signified and its *figura* are equally real, this trope appears to be a special form of metonymy.

saying. On their departure from Calicut, with the ostensible mission of their voyage completed and no inkling as yet of the last and most marvellous adventure of all, still awaiting them, a pervasive listlessness seems to hang in the air: a feeling of let-down, as if they were asking themselves 'Was that all we came for, then?' The choice of vocabulary, the very movement of the verse, seem to be hinting at something incomplete: a partly failed enterprise, even a kind of anticlimax. In a scene parallel to but sharply contrasting with the euphoric moment when the expedition weighed anchor in the Tagus at the beginning of the voyage, Gama releases a few black hostages, takes on board a few captives from Malabar and a quantity of pepper, and sails away down the coast, having concluded that his attempts to do business with the 'heathen king' are leading nowhere: 'Partese costa abaxo, porque entende / Que em vão co Rei gentio trabalhava'. At this stage the main purpose of the return itself, for the 'fortes lusitanos', seems to be to get back home to their families and tell them all about their 'rare pilgrimage': 'chegar . . . / A seus penates caros & parentes, / Pera *contar* a peregrina, & rara / Navegaçam'.

There is an obvious parallel in these lines with Dante's vision of himself as a pilgrim who, on reaching the 'temple of his vow', is already beginning to look forward to the moment when he can tell what it was like: 'quasi peregrin che . . . nel tempio del suo voto . . . spera già *ridir* com' ello stea' (*Para.* XXXI. 43 ff.). Nor is this the only parallel. It has often been observed that at the more dramatic moments in his narration, Dante the pilgrim and protagonist of his own poem becomes one with Dante the poet and citizen, whose earthly *patria* has been reduced to a 'serva Italia, di dolore ostello' (*Purg.* VI. 76). In much the same way the pilgrim and protagonist Vasco da Gama, after being granted by Tethys the wisdom that is the reward for his pilgrimage, gives place to the poet and citizen Camões, who launches out on a fierce diatribe against his native country, sunk in abject, vile, and lacklustre joylessness: 'metida . . . na rudeza / Dhūa austèra, apagada, & vil tristeza' (X. 145. 6 ff.).

EROS AND GNOSIS

The 'varios çeos' the Portuguese are privileged to see are not the same heavens Dante traverses in his flight upward through the nine celestial spheres of Ptolemaic cosmology. Gama, as the representative of an earth-bound historical people, must content himself with the vision of these in the form of a model: the crystal globe which Tethys—in her turn only the representative of Venus—reveals to him on the highest peak of the mountain. Just as with Dante, however, the revelation he and his companions are granted is at once double and single. It is that of Knowledge, imparted by the lesson of the crystal globe; and it is also that of Love, imparted by the other lesson that consists in the union of the heroes with the nymphs: two lessons that are at the same time initiations.

But Love and Knowledge—*eros* and *gnosis*—are ultimately one and the same thing; and never more than in the context of the Earthly Paradise, where, as the Vulgate says (echoing ἔγνω in the Septuagint,[14]) 'Adam vero *cognovit* uxorem suam Hevam'. One contemporary Hebraist in fact holds that among the meanings of the word *daath*—'insight'—which occupies the central position in the cosmic tree of the cabbala, between *binah* ('understanding') and *hokhmah* ('wisdom'), is precisely this form of 'knowing'.[15]

If the Greeks—with the passion for analysis that was both their glory and in the long run their undoing—conscientiously split love into *eros* and *agape*,[16] the post-Classical West, instead of following their example, has opted for synthesis. And to synthesis, indeed, the Greeks themselves have in the end capitulated, rather oddly choosing not ἔρως but ἀγάπη as the name of that love which is at the same time, like the revelation granted to Vasco da Gama, both double and single: that love which, in the words of a Brazilian poet, 'moves the stars / and shuts the lovers up in a bedroom' ('êsse amor que move as estrêlas / e fecha os amantes num quarto'[17]).

Homer, at least, was already well aware that *eros* was *gnosis*, and *gnosis*, *eros*: as John Finley has said (47; 109) after half a century dedicated to the study of Homeric epic, 'the theme of the *Odyssey* is

---

[14] The New Jerusalem Bible replaces the familiar 'knew' of the Authorized Version (presumably for the benefit of readers unfamiliar with the expression 'carnal knowledge') by the aseptic 'had intercourse with'.

[15] D. Bakan, *Sigmund Freud and the Jewish Mystical Tradition* (New York, 1955), 278 f. (cit. Shuttle and Redgrove, 227).

[16] As well as στοργή and φιλία. The *Septuagint* may have adopted the 'rather colourless' ἀγάπη (uncommon in earlier Greek) because the other words did not lend themselves to the variety of meanings of the single Hebrew one; comparison of the Hebrew OT and the Septuagint shows the ἔρως/ἀγάπη distinction 'was not part of the Hebrew mind up to . . . the early centuries of the Christian era' (Carr, 62 f.).

[17] Lêdo Ivo, 'O Sol dos Amantes', in *Um Brasileiro em Paris* (Rio de Janeiro, 1968), 44.

instruction', and 'the knowledge of the world with which Odysseus will return includes love'. Dante, whose *Purgatorio* has been aptly defined (in three nouns that deserve equal emphasis) as 'the epic of the transformations of love' (Fergusson, 45), was no less certain of the identity of the two concepts, fusing them in that of 'intelletto d'amore', and affirming that 'amor e cor gentil son una cosa'— *gentilezza*, in the terminology of the *dolce stil nuovo*, meaning the most exquisitely cultivated intelligence of the heart.

The same conviction is evident also in the scheme of hierarchical parallels which Camões pointedly introduces into the design of his last two cantos. Just as in Dante the souls of the elect enjoy the *beatifica visione* of God in different degree according to their capacity, Camões informs his readers that their understanding of his verses will depend on their capacity for love: 'segundo o amor tiverdes, / Tereis o entendimento dos meus versos'; and in the twofold revelation granted to the Sons of Lusus a similar criterion of differing degrees of merit and reward applies. In Canto IX, the sailors and nymphs consummate their love 'in the shade, among the flowers', while Tethys and Gama pass their own day engaged in the same 'sweet games, and in continuous pleasure'—but in her gold and crystal mountain-top palace.

In just the same way, in the rigorously parallel scene in the following canto, after the banquet in which the entire company have shared the collective revelation of the future history of Portugal contained in the prophecies sung by an 'angelic Siren', Tethys leads Gama by the hand to the still higher peak where Supreme Wisdom grants him his vision of the crystal globe of the universe, with its nine spheres.

It was the scholar poet Jorge de Sena who first observed that the publication of *The Lusiads* coincided (accidentally, no doubt, but significantly) with the centenary of the first printed edition of the *Divine Comedy*. It was also Sena's combined poetic insight and intellectual stature that gave respectability to a semi-clandestine current of esoteric exegesis of Camões's poem that had long coexisted with the triumphalist official fanfares extolling it as the Bible of the Nationality. A similar line of interpretation is represented by the more recent researches of Yvette Centeno (1981: 29), for whom 'the aim of the voyage is transformation. When the nuptials have been consummated, the banquet takes place, [and] the knowledge that has been gained is shared.... As in all voyages of this kind, what matters is the outward journey, which alone makes transformation possible:

once the Centre has been reached, there is no return—or only an apparent one.'

The reason why there can be no real going back is that not only is the traveller who returns no longer the one who originally set out, because he brings back with him all he has seen and learnt and suffered, but that the place he returns to is itself no longer the one he left, because it too has been transformed (*gesteigert*, Goethe would say). And not only by the intervening time but even more by the new angle of vision (the new *knowledge*) with which it is perceived. It is just this that Eliot means by

> We will not cease from exploration
> And the end of all our exploring
> Will be to arrive where we started
> And to know the place for the first time.

THE ICONOGRAPHIC PERSPECTIVE—I

The theme of the Isle of Love alone, studied from this perspective, would make another book. I shall limit myself to suggesting some parallels (which may seem not only esoteric but, from a Western viewpoint, exotic) between it and other yet more distant islands—in Camões's words, 'as Ilhas mais remotas do Oriente'. For the Centre where the metamorphosis referred to by Yvette Centeno takes place—Paradise regained, the island mountain where Heaven and Earth meet in an 'epiphany [which] may be presented in . . . terms . . . of sexual fulfilment' (Frye, 1971: 205)—is by general consensus situated in the 'desejada parte Oriental'.

If *epifania* is the very word used by Sena[18] to characterize the Isle of Venus episode—a 'magnificent epiphany . . . , a victorious exaltation of sex'—the same idea underlies the ancient Egyptian hieroglyph that signified the primeval 'hillock of appearance' and 'to appear in glory', and represented a hill crowned by the rising sun.[19]

Ex Oriente lux is an idea so deeply rooted in the unconscious of mankind that both for Homer and, a millennium later, for Clement of

---

[18] *Grande Dicionário da Literatura Portuguesa*, i (Lisbon, 1977), s.v. *Amor*. 'Epifania' is also the word used for the terrible erotic denouement of Lins's *Avalovara* (above, n. 11).

[19] John A. Wilson, 'Egypt', in Henri Frankfort *et al.*, *Before Philosophy* (Harmondsworth, 1949), 60.

Alexandria, πρόσω—'in front'—was synonymous with 'East': that is, with light and the birth of day, with life and the birth of life (and thus, paradoxically, with the past[20]); and by the same token the words for 'left' and 'North' in many languages share a common etymology. In the typical medieval *mappamundi*, too, the East was at the top, crowned by the image of Christ as *sol oriens* or *sol iustitiae*; and churches were 'oriented' so as to allow the faithful to face eastward: 'Orantes convertunt se ad orientem . . . ut sol iustitiae oriatur super eos' (cf. Singleton, iv. 160 f; 694). Until at least the end of the second century BCE (as we saw in Chapter 4) even the Chinese—and the Japanese until much later—placed Paradise to the East of the known world, in the archipelago of the Vases.

The iconographic history of Péng Lái, it will be remembered, begins early in that century (and on a considerably more modest scale than that of the lake islands in Emperor Wǔ Dì's park at Cháng An) in what is believed to be the oldest extant Chinese portrait, a T-shaped silk triptych with maximum dimensions of roughly one metre by two, unearthed in the course of the extensive archeological excavations made in central China in recent years (Fig. 10).[21]

This painting depicts a recently deceased lady of the Hàn dynasty Court, ascending the 'Vase' of Péng by a spiral causeway on her pilgrimage to Paradise. She has been identified as the widow of the first Count of Dài, Chancellor of the Kingdom of Chángsha from 193 to 186 BCE: hence thirty-five years before Wǔ Dì's accession to the throne. What we might call the deep structure of this portrait, discovered in a tomb dating from c.168 BCE, does not differ in essence from that of Domenico di Michelino's fresco in Santa Maria del Fiore. Five elements in the painting are directly relevant to *The Lusiads*: a pre-initiation banquet, an ascending spiral path, the nine celestial spheres, a heavenly mermaid, and—more unexpectedly, perhaps—a pair of dragons.

1. At the base of the T, a BANQUET SCENE represents the ritual meal that precedes the ascent to the summit of the mountain. Such pre-initiatory meals, functionally analogous to the banquet served to

---

[20] For Homer see Norman Austin, *Archery at the Dark of the Moon: Poetic Problems in Homer's 'Odyssey'* (Berkeley, Calif., 1975), 90; for Clement, Guénon, 21. To the Chinese the East was sometimes in front and sometimes to the left, but always associated with the sky and the solar principle, *yáng*: cf. Marcel Granet, *La Pensée chinoise* (3rd edn., Paris, 1968), 302 f.

[21] The following description is taken from Loewe, 45–52.

Gama before his own final climb to the 'erguido cume' where he is initiated into the secrets of the great globe 'composto / de varios orbes', are even today an essential prelude to the 'heavenly journey' of the shaman. Eliade (1964: 76 f.), mentions the Siberian belief that the shaman has a 'celestial wife' who, before the last and most arduous stage of his pilgrimage to the highest Heaven, serves him 'an exquisite banquet . . . and sleeps with him', as proof 'that he shares . . . in the condition of semidivine beings, that he is a hero who . . . therefore enjoys a second life, in the heavens'.

No one who is familiar with *The Lusiads* can read these words without remembering Camões's 'Semideoses immortais' and 'Heroes esclarecidos' whose prowess made them godlike—since (according to a standard euhemeristic theory) 'the search for knowledge—either profane or religious—is a road to immortality and is connected with the cult of the Muses', who 'awaken in the human heart . . . a nostalgia for heaven . . . ; impart . . . wisdom, a pledge of immortality . . . ; summon to themselves in the starry spheres the soul which has sanctified itself in their service; and cause it to share in the . . . life of the Immortals'.[22]

It is significant that even the residual shamanism of Japan, in full retreat before the onslaught of microchip technocracy, still holds to its ancient objectives: 'the ascent to Heaven, and thence upwards through nine more paradisal levels, the meeting with godlike beings, the eating of paradisal food, the conferment of secret knowledge' (Blacker, 197).

2. An inclined SPIRAL PATH up which the pilgrim toils: a spiral design on the pavement serves as a shorthand indication of the tortuousness of the way itself. The road to the centre, Eliade observes (1954: 18), is difficult because, like the 'danger-ridden voyages of . . . heroic expeditions . . . , it is . . . a rite of the passage . . . to reality and eternity. . . . Attaining the centre is equivalent to . . . an initiation.'

The comparison with 'heroic expeditions' is apt. Among several forms of mirror construction in *The Lusiads*, such as the reduplication of characters and episodes, the most striking is the *mise en abyme*: the incorporation in a given structure—a picture or literary work, for example—of a smaller one that is a replica of it in miniature.[23] In the

---

[22] Cf. Curtius, 234 f., based on Franz Cumont, *Recherches sur le symbolisme funéraire des romains* (Paris, 1942).
[23] See Moura 1980: 67–86. In linguistic terms the simultaneous relation of whole to whole and part to corresponding part is analogous to that of signified and signifier in

light of this, it becomes evident that the hierarchical ranking of the 'sweet games' and of the revelation of the crystal globe (a microcosmic *mise en abyme* of the 'grande machina do mundo') is not due solely to such superior merit as Gama may possess: it is that he reflects and epitomizes all his companions, in the same way as they (and he) are 'miniature replicas' of the whole Portuguese people. Likewise, all the ordeals of the voyage up to the arrival at the Island are reflected and summed up in the 'monte espesso . . . & . . . mato / Arduo, difficil, duro a humano trato': the tangled undergrowth and the mountain, inhumanly harsh and steep, the conquest of which will at last make the hero, immortalized by his 'esforço & arte'—his effort and skill—worthy to contemplate secrets impenetrable to the 'vain science / of miserable deluded mortals'.

3. TWO DRAGONS with tails interwined, further linked together by the coils of a scarlet serpent, occupy either side of the shaft of the T. Dragon and serpent being minimally differentiated iconographic variants of the same symbol, their simultaneous presence in a single image (and in perhaps their most frequent role, as guardians of access to the *axis mundi* and to immortality: cf. Guénon, 112) is an overdetermination of meaning which suggests that the union of the dragons—underlined, so to speak, by visual rhetoric—in turn stands for the conjunction of feminine and masculine: *yin* and *yáng*.

In the same way as the dance is a kinetic realization of the idea of spirality (as in a poem by Nerval in which a line of girls 'forme un serpent qui se meut d'abord en spirale et puis en cercle'[24]), the dragon-serpent ('sujet animal du verbe *enlacer*' and 'complément vivant du labyrinthe', in the words of Gaston Bachelard) is its zoomorphic realization.

More important: it is the realization of all the potentialities implicit in its directional ambivalence. In the form of the uroboros, for example, grasping its tail in its mouth, it isolates a single phase of the helix, turning it, like the dance, into a circle; but a circle that, again like the dance, also has a temporal dimension. As an image of cyclical

C. S. Peirce's 'icons'; in terms of optics it consists in a 'processus de *redoublement* indéfini des images'; in philosophical terms it is one of (potentially) 'infinies manipulations d'emboîtement des similitudes' (Durand 1969: 234; 243); in physics and mathematics it corresponds to the infinite regress of non-linear dynamics ('chaos theory') associated with Mandelbrotian geometry. Chinese boxes, Russian dolls, and the Quaker Oats carton of our childhood are familiar examples of the open-ended variety.

[24] J.-P. Richard, in Nerval, *Œuvres*, Pléiade edition (Paris, 1975), i. 212.

time,[25] 'le serpent qui se mord la queue..., c'est la dialectique matérielle de... la mort qui sort de la vie et la vie qui sort de la mort';[26] and its circularity is itself a spatial metaphor for the cyclical 'rebirth' of the serpent that sheds its skin. In most cultures it is therefore 'l'animal polymorphe *par excellence* and 'le doublet animal de la lune' (Durand 1969: 364; 369).

Subjective interpretations of this polymorphism affect even so objective a phenomenon as spatial direction, as when the intrinsically neutral concepts of up and down, or higher and lower, are endowed with positive or beneficent and negative or maleficent values such as those normally attributed to the 'metaphysically identical' phenomena of birth and death. Guénon (110) remarks that symbols are at times reduplicated in order to reflect these two antagonic aspects, as in the caduceus.

At other times, as seems to be the case in our painting, doubling reflects rather an intention of fusing sexual duality in a higher unity. It is precisely the caduceus that exemplifies, for Gilbert Durand (1969: 329; 366 f.), 'l'androgynat lunaire'. For one thing, the serpent reconciles in itself the sexual opposites, being both female (because lunar) and, in form, suggestive of a penis. But even the staff it twines round, apart from its obvious phallic implications, is also the cosmic tree or axis—and hence a symbolic alternative to the Magna Dea or Magna Mater whom we know in one of her many other forms (for she is no less polymorphous than the serpent) as Venus.[27]

Here, then—just as with the serpent and the dragons appearing

---

[25] More exactly, archetypal time, which might be imagined, in contrast to both linear and cyclical time, as cylindrical, composed of the sum of all the circles of the latter stacked one on another and extending simultaneously towards past and future for ever. Since any point on any of these circles is not merely equivalent but identical to the corresponding point on all the others, however (all moments, as Fernando Pessoa said, being 'always, always... the same moment returning'), the apparent cylinder collapses into itself, and archetypal time amounts in effect to the abolition, pure and simple, of Time itself, Cf. n. 10, above.

[26] Gaston Bachelard, *La Terre et les rêveries du repos*, cit. Durand (1969: 364), who adds that in traditional Chinese thought, dragon, serpent, and fish were interchangeable symbols 'du flux et du reflux de la vie': an equivalence that reappears in a print by Escher (Hofstadter 1979: fig. 6) showing a 'uroboric' dragon, with its tail in its mouth (for 17th-c. German examples see Centeno 1976: 55 ff.); another well-known Escher print, *Bond of Union*, with the faces of a man and a woman composed of intertwined spirals (Fig. 11), illustrates the sexual fusion referred to below.

[27] For the identity of axis and Magna Dea see Colegrave (45); for that of Magna Dea and Magna Mater, Harding (ch. 4); for that of Magna Mater and Venus, Harrison (268–85).

together in our painting, or the cosmic tree growing out of the top of the cosmic mountain, both being mere variants of the world axis—is another case of overdetermination or emphatic reinforcement. As Neumann shows (1974: 18), the Great Mother is herself an avatar of the uroboros—'the most perfect example of the still undifferentiated primordial archetype'—in an evolutionary progression 'from the uroboros through the Archetypal Feminine to the Great Mother and further differentiations'.

4. The SUN and MOON, represented by a large red disc or orb and a crescent, in the upper corners of the crosspiece of the T, entangled in the branches of the world tree and accompanied by eight smaller red discs. Early Chinese literature contains numerous references to nine or sometimes ten 'suns', the word used being the familiar *yáng*: the masculine principle. The moon, appearing on the left and balancing the sun on the right, suggests (like the intertwined dragons) a hierogamy or cosmic wedding of *yáng* and *yin*.

The analogy with the ten celestial spheres of Ptolemaic cosmology is the more striking in the light of a similar painting discovered in an adjoining grave, and in which a number of stars have been introduced between the spheres of the sun and moon, recalling the firmament or 'heaven of fixed stars' that appears in both Dante and Camões. Most Western historians of science, Joseph Needham remarks (*Science and Civilization in China*, iii (Cambridge, 1959), 198 n. k), would no doubt ascribe the coincidence of Chinese and Ptolemaic cosmologies, with ingenuously chauvinistic Eurocentrism, to Greek sources; but even apart from the practical obstacles to such influence before the journey to Western Asia of the 'Chinese Marco Polo', Zhang Qian, who only returned some forty years after the date of our painting, this conjecture is not compatible with chronology. Eudoxus, working in the half-century immediately before Zhang, only managed to produce a rough hypothesis of a system of concentric spheres; in the mean time the theory of the 'grande machina do mundo' celebrated by Camões had already been anticipated in a Chinese ode of *c.*300 BCE entitled 'Questions about the Heavens'. Another poem—this one perhaps contemporaneous with the two paintings—tells of a shamanistic pilgrimage in which the traveller refers not only to the nine suns but by implication to the cliffs that extend, like the 'monte espesso' of Venus's island, from the Valley of the Dawn (compare 'quella valle', in the *Inferno*, I. 14) to Heaven.

5. A BEAUTIFUL WOMAN, apparently young, surrounded by birds,

occupies the top centre of the picture, her body ending in a serpentine tail that emerges from the mouth of a dragon on the right (balanced by another on the left, with wings). Loewe conjectures that she is a second version of the candidate for immortality herself, shown now at the moment of literally shuffling off her mortal coil with the same ease as a serpent shedding its skin, and revealed in her true and imperishable youth and beauty; two other eminent Sinologists,[28] however, have independently identified her with the goddess Nǔ Gua. In the light of all the foregoing it is not surprising to learn that Nǔ Gua is a Chinese manifestation of the Magna Mater. More significantly, she is a Great Mother who still retains a 'uroboric' sexual ambiguity, anterior to the primordial differentiation of *yáng* and *yin* (cf. Colegrave, 51).

THE MYTHIC-HISTORICAL PERSPECTIVE

Some seventy years after the Countess of Dài's portrait was painted, China began seriously to direct its attention, with that 'volonté de la conscience et volonté de la découverte' we like to think of as typically Western, to the West. By the end of the century, the expeditions and emissaries sent out by Wǔ Dì had already established a Hàn presence on the frontiers of the Hellenized world of Bactria, Scythia, and Parthia. Less than two centuries later, only the Caspian and the mountains of Armenia were to separate the world empires of the Hàn and the Caesars (C. P. Fitzgerald, *A Short History of China* (4th edn., London, 1966), 167).

Meanwhile, along the Silk Route that linked Cháng An to the coast of Syria, trade had begun to develop, and with it the interchange of ideas and even creeds. The world axis itself migrated westward, along with the Earthly Paradise, to the Kun Lún mountains, in Central Asia;[29] and there arose a popular cult (afterwards adopted and made official, as is customary, by the ruling class) of Xi Wáng Mǔ: that is, the Queen Mother of the West. For information about this goddess I continue to resort to Loewe (ch. 4).

Xi Wáng Mǔ dwelt on the summit of the mountain of shaman serpents, seated (as some held) on a dragon, in a cavern; or else (as

[28] The Japanese Doi Yoshiko and the internationally known Chinese scholar Guo Moro (Kuo Mo-jo), cit. Loewe, 143.
[29] Eliade (1984: 40 f.) gives a garbled account, confusing Kun Lún (which he misspells 'Kun Lün' and places in 'the Western Ocean') with Péng Lái.

others said) at the top of the cosmic tree or pillar, surrounded by birds, where she rewarded the elect souls who succeeded in climbing up to her eyrie with the gift of immortality. Hàn Wǔ Dì himself, six years before building his giant model of the magical archipelago of the Eastern Sea, and perhaps already with some idea of playing both ends against the middle (or else, Lord of the Middle Kingdom that he was, of maintaining a dignified impartiality), was understood to have been granted the inestimable boon of a birthday visit by this Great Mother.

The goddess arrived promptly at the seventh hour of the seventh day of the seventh month, accompanied by her escort of birds and enveloped in a purple cloud, and was regaled with jujubes and grape wine: exotic Western delicacies no doubt tactfully allusive to the divine guest's home territory.[30] In the course of a prolonged audience in the Hall of Flowery Delights, the emperor respectfully but persistently entreated the goddess to supply him with the elixir of immortality; but after several evasive references to other highly regarded old-time elixirs—the Scarlet Honey of the Cloudy Mountains, the Purple Honey of the Blossoms of the Centre, etc.— she limited herself to repaying his jujubes and wine by sharing with him seven small but delicious peaches. When the emperor announced his intention of planting the stones, however, the Queen Mother smiled with maternal irony and advised him that the resulting peach trees would only bear fruit every three thousand years. She then remained a while longer conversing with him about everyday affairs and the administrative problems of the Empire, but declined any further discussion of more transcendental matters.

Thus far the testimony of two third-century chronicles, three hundred years or more after the events related, the implications of which I take to be as follows. What the emperor fails to realize is that the peaches he has just eaten represent the tacit granting of his request. They are nothing less than the famous golden peaches of Samarkand or Kun Lún: the 'Orient and immortal fruit', with which we are already familiar, that grows on the tree of Life and Knowledge. (see Ch. 2, above, and Schafer 1963a.) The emperor's very incapacity to realize this—proof that he is not in a state of grace sufficient to profit from the 'elixir'—automatically invalidates its efficacy; and the

---

[30] The vine is said to have been brought to China in 126 BCE by the explorer Zhang Qian on his return from the West.

goddess, recognizing in the failure of the ritual meal what in Catholic terms would be called an 'imperfect Communion', abandons with a sibylline smile any thought she might have harboured of a possible hierogamy like that of Tethys with the 'semideus imortal' Vasco da Gama. Wǔ Dì, for all his military and diplomatic triumphs—an 'esforço & arte' no less great than those that enabled Gama to 'liberate himself' from the law of Death'—has yet not acquired the *quantum satis* of divinity needed to reach the heights of Kun Lún: his cosmic wedding with the Great Mother will not now take place. No wonder, then, that (as the chronicle reports) 'after she had gone away, the emperor was sad for a long time'.[31]

The gods' sense of distributive justice is notoriously weak, and that of the goddesses perhaps even more so. At any rate, in contrast with the emperor's discomfiture, it is recorded that a simple courtier (who, as it happened, had advised the monarch on the correct protocol to be observed for the reception of the goddess) managed to steal one of the golden peaches and achieve the immortality of which his sovereign had not been found worthy. A feminine whim of the goddess, or the inscrutable mystery of Grace without merit? This curious postscript to the great emperor's bitter-sweet birthday party inspired, eight hundred years later, a poetic journey that justifies a digression.

The poet-monk Guàn Xiu (832–912) represents the Taoist-Buddhist syncretism characteristic of the late Táng. For some four hundred years he enjoyed a prestige comparable to that of his now more celebrated predecessor Lǐ Bó, whose name he found singularly apt because of its suggestion of whiteness (see above, Ch. 1, n. 11); but it is as a painter that he is now best known. His 'Dream of a Journey to the Immortals' belongs to a genre then already nearly a millennium old, cultivated since Hàn times, but whose origin goes back to even more ancient songs commemorating shamanistic journeys to Paradise.[32] He tells of a dream pilgrimage to Péng Lái, where he

---

[31] The Divine Warrior was also a man of culture: author of a poem on the Autumn wind that is still a standard anthology piece, and founder of the world's first university; a clue to the character flaw that disqualified him in the eyes of the goddess may, however, be found in his shabby treatment, a decade later, of the great historian Sīmǎ Qian, who had had the honour of accompanying him on his pilgrimages to the sacred mountains, but whose disinterested arguments in defence of an unjustly disgraced general earned him the enraged emperor's sentence of castration. The Chinese Livy (a sobriquet justifiable on various counts) could have opted for suicide, but was determined to finish his *magnum opus*.

[32] Information about Guàn and his poem is summarized from the analysis in Schafer 1963*b*, with minimal extra comment.

tries to emulate Wǔ Dì's counsellor by stealing the peaches and pears of immortality, now seemingly transplanted from Kun Lún, and guarded by a white dragon, the temporary metamorphosis of a sylph or 'rainbow maiden'.

The pilgrim knows he has reached the Earthly Paradise when he meets a renowned Taoist sage of Antiquity and a band of sylphs who are amusing themselves by knocking down the pears. He then comes to a palace in the middle of a lake formed by iridescent streams (which Chinese pictorial conventions allow us to imagine as sinuous, and hence as further, 'overdetermined' metamorphoses of the dragon-sylph of the rainbow). In the palace orchard are the peach trees of Life, with serpentine limbs; and here the pilgrim takes advantage of the drowsiness of other guardian sylphs (also transformable into dragons if need be) to attempt his raid on the forbidden fruit. No doubt as punishment for his daring, however, and because, like Wǔ Dì, he lacks the required spiritual qualities, he staggers and almost collapses on the ground.

Schafer ingeniously translates Guàn's quatrains (three pentasyllabic and the last heptasyllabic) in five different styles—word for word, plain, self-explanatory, mock heroic, and beatnik—'to hint at the possibilities of the exploration of imagery in depth': an experiment that implicitly authorizes me to propose my own version:

> [In] dreams [I] come [to an] isle [in the] midst [of the] sea,
> enter [a] certain white silver house,
> happen on [a] gentleman [of the] Way,
> [who] says [he is] Eighth Sire Lǐ.
>
> Three [or] four girl fairies,
> bodies clad [in] lapis-lazuli garments,
> hands holding gleaming moon beads,
> knock down golden-coloured pears.
>
> [The] nacreous land has no dust.
> Going [on], [I] come [to the] shore [of a] jade pool;
> under thick-set cedrela trees,
> [a] white dragon comes [to] sniff [at the] human.
>
> Lofty palace halls [are] wrapped [in] purple mist;
> [in] golden canals, rainbow water [flows over] jade sands.
> [the] gate-keepers, fairy slave girls, sleep entwined;
> [I] furtively snatch [at] coiled peach-trees, almost fall [to] earth.

The poet being a monk, one might wonder just what the forbidden fruit really was, and whether the failure of his enterprise may not have been due to his confusing the sweetly entwined limbs of the girls with the sinuous branches of the trees (as could well have happened to Gama's sailors, who were no monks, with the scented pomes, fair lemons, and pyramidal pears of the Isle of Love).

THE ICONOGRAPHIC PERSPECTIVE—II

Apart from their common unpredictability, Venus and Xi Wáng Mǔ do not seem to be directly linked (iconographically, at least), unless by way of Inanna or Ishtar, the most ancient and strictly maternal avatars of Venus, in the times when she—so maritime to us—was still a mainland Asiatic divinity, *anadyomene* not from the sea but from an earthen mound (χῶμα τῆς γῆς[33]). However many impeccably Hellenic islands might claim her (and Cyprus hardly qualifies as such), the Greeks never lost sight of what Rome in due course recognized explicitly: that she had once been the *Dea Syria*.

On the other hand, if Kun Lún is further from the sea than almost any other spot on the face of the inhabited planet, even there it was felt necessary to isolate (or insulate) the cosmic mountain in the middle of a large lake: a procedure perhaps reflecting a deep-rooted intuition that in transcendental contexts water and earth only acquire full symbolic force at those places where they come into conjunction.[34] This would explain why these contexts often involve floating islands such as Péng Lái, the island of the winds in the *Aeneid*, or Venus's isle in *The Lusiads*.

More immediately apparent than Xi Wáng Mǔ's relation to Venus is her kinship with the mysterious lady in the portrait, also accompanied by 'lunar' birds,[35] as well as associated with serpents and dragons (and endowed with a serpent's tail), and who has in turn been identified with Nǚ Gua. But Nǚ Gua herself, despite her still

[33] See Harrison, 309–14, and cf. Harding, 98 f.

[34] Centeno 1981: 24 ff. Like its counterpart Kun Lún, the Zoroastrian cosmic mountain, Ushidhāo—identified as Kūh-e-Khwāja ('The Mountain of the Lord'), from which the Magi kept watch for the Messiah's star—is an island, rising from a lake on the Iranian–Afghan frontier (Phyllis Ackerman, 'Some Problems of Early Iconography', in *A Survey of Persian Art from Prehistoric Times to the Present*, ed. Arthur Upham Pope and Phyllis Ackerman, ii. Tehran, n.d., 875).

[35] On the 'lunar' nature of birds (linking them with the various avatars of the moon goddess) and their role as attributes and messengers of the divinities with whom they tend to coalesce, see Harding, 51 f. Doves—the most ubiquitous—are the representatives of Ishtar and Aphrodite as well as of the Holy Ghost and the Gnostics' *Sophia*.

uroborically undifferentiated gender, is sufficiently evolved to bear a notable resemblance to the Nabatean Venus known as Atargatis or Derketo, the cosmic mother-goddess with a dolphin's tail; while a comparable sexual ambiguity to Nü Gua's is found both on Venus's own island of Cyprus, where there was a cult of a bearded Aphrodite or *Aphroditos*, and in Asia Minor, where the Great Mother had androgynous characteristics (Delcourt, 43–51).

It is in the subtle distinctions between understanding (νόος) and wisdom (the *hokhmah* of the cabbala), or between knowledge painfully earned (initiation; γνῶσις) and that gratuitously 'infused' (intuition or *daath*)—it is, finally, in the positive or negative value assigned to knowledge itself—that we find an even more fundamental ambiguity. To resolve it we can make use of the by now familiar symbolic complex of the dolphins and dragons. To the extent that knowledge is prized and sought after or feared and rejected, so its source will be an object of veneration and love or of dread and hatred. Once all the dragons, serpents, fish, dolphins, mermaids, and sirens are recognized as so many metonyms of the archetypal feminine, whose manifestations include Magna Mater in her various forms, the paradoxical *coincidentia oppositorum* of beneficent and maleficent aspects that archetype comprises ceases to puzzle.

In the words of Jung (1959: 332), 'archetypes are not determined as regards their content but only as regards their form'. Thus the *Ewig-Weibliche*, Northrop Frye says (1971: 322 f.), sometimes 'presides over ... a sacramental spiral leading up to deity', as with Beatrice in the *Divine Comedy*, Gretchen in *Faust*, or Venus in Lucretius and Virgil (and, we can add, Camões), while at other times the same archetype leads in the opposite direction, like Dido in the *Aeneid* and Eve in *Paradise Lost*, 'who spirals man downward into the Fall'. Another such ambivalent materialization of this archetype appears in Cesare Pavese's *nostos* of an Italian emigrant, *The Moon and the Bonfires*, in the person of Santa, a 'sacrificed and consecrated moon-figure', both whore and saint, metonymically associated with a 'great hill shaped like a woman's breast' which, Pavese says, 'is the ... body of the goddess to whom, on St John's Night, the ... bonfires ... will rise'.[36]

---

[36] Cit. Martin Seymour-Smith, '*La luna e i falò*', in *An Introduction to Fifty European Novels* (London, 1979), 463 f. Santa's body is ritually burnt after her execution by the Partisans; at the end of the novel the site is described as like the bed of a bonfire (Midsummer Night bonfires are the subject of the first part of Ch. 6 below).

With these examples we may now turn to Western iconography, still bearing in mind the principle of overdetermination by the tautological superimposition of equivalent symbols. To this category belong the various symbolic attributes by which Venus is customarily accompanied: her dolphins, fish, and scallop-shells, and the waves and foam of her native element, which serve as her iconographic identification.

The metaphoric and metonymic allusiveness of the goddess's attributes is insistent. The common etymology of δελφίς ('dolphin') and δελφύς ('womb') is well known, and at Delphi the tripod of the pythoness (yet another significant etymology) had dolphin-shaped feet. The symbolism of the fish, 'abyssus féminisé et maternel', is discussed at length by Durand (1969: 243−7). That of the scallop-shell, and of shells in general, has already been referred to above;[37] and the most casual examination of Botticelli's *Birth of Venus* discovers the extraordinary breast-shaped waves surrounding the shell from which the goddess has just emerged. It is a psychologically puzzling fact that in Classical Greek iconography 'the sexual elements are . . . dissociated from the god and placed around him' (Delcourt, 21).

Eve, too—another typically ambiguous manifestation of the Great Mother—is almost invariably shown accompanied by the serpent, often depicted with the head and breasts of a woman, as in Raphael's *Temptation* painted for the Pope's apartments (Clark, fig. 83). Eve thus becomes fused and confused with her attribute, just as Venus ends by being identified not only by but with her own, on acquiring the tail of a fish or dolphin and becoming a siren. As Eve for Man, the serpent is for her the initiator, the transmitter of hidden knowledge: in principle a positive function that 'confère au serpent . . . un rôle initiatique, et somme toute bénéfique' (Durand 1969: 368).

Surprisingly, Jung (1959: 333) immediately forgets his own *ex cathedra* pronouncement and goes on to classify dragons, large fish, and serpents among the unequivocally 'bad' manifestations of the maternal archetype; but in alternative traditions the serpent coiled round the World Tree is nothing less than the faithful guardian of its fruit of immortality or wisdom, which he may grant or deny to the pilgrim who seeks it, according to his deserts. Serpents also guard the tree the Golden Fleece hangs on, and the one that bears the golden

---

[37] See 'The Magic Mountain', in Ch. 4, above.

apples of the Hesperides, as Guénon recalls (111 f.), pointing out that a serpent is often found coiled round other symbols of the *axis mundi* as well, such as the mountain, where both in its sinuous form and in its function as the guardian of hidden treasure it is clearly the same as the spiral path that leads to the mountain-top through perils and ordeals.

Well deserved as the knowledge finally won may be, however, it remains an equivocal reward. When the sirens of the *Odyssey* offer the hero the absolute knowledge of which they hold the secret, he, cannier and more cautious than Adam, is wise enough to realize that the absolute—whether that of gnosis, such as the sirens promise, or of the erotic, which Calypso had offered him—is too much for anyone who is not a god.

More than one critic (among them John Finley, for the *Odyssey*, and Fergusson for the *Divine Comedy*) has remarked on the psychological difference between the prudent Odysseus portrayed by Homer and Dante's Faustian Ulysses, who challenges his companions, with the noble admonition 'fatti non foste a viver come bruti, / ma per seguir virtute e canoscenza', to accompany him on a last fatal voyage to shipwreck on the rocks of the cosmic mountain. It is worth quoting the passage of Cicero that may have suggested this attitude to Dante (cf. Singleton, ii. 460 f.):

Mihi quidem Homerus huiusmodi quiddam vidisse videtur in iis quae de Sirenum cantibus finxerit. Neque enim vocum suavitate videntur aut novitate quadam et varietate cantandi revocare eos solitae qui praetervehebantur, sed *quia multa se scire profitebantur,* ut homines ad earum saxa *discendi cupiditate adhaerescerent.* Ita enim invitant Ulixem . . . : *scientiam pollicentur . . .*

It was not the sweetness of the sirens' songs, then, that led men on to their rocks, but their own greed for the knowledge the sirens professed to have, and promised to share. Here, indeed, Dante and Camões alike coincide not with Homer, in his intuitive pre-Classical fear of hubris, but rather with the more modern and Western line of Virgil, who in the *Georgics* (2. 477 ff.) asks the Muses to reveal to him the secrets of the 'grande machina',

> . . . caelique vias et sidera monstrent,
> Defectus solis varios, lunaeque labores,
> Unde tremor terris, qua vi maria alta tumescant
> Obicibus ruptis, rursusque in se ipsa residant,

Quid tantum Oceano properent se tinguere soles
Hiberni, vel quae tardis mora noctibus obstet

—finally exclaiming: 'Felix qui potuit rerum cognoscere causas!'[38]

THE *ÍNSULA DIVINA*

The features common to the innumerable divine and human representatives of the Magna Mater, each with maternal, initiatory, and erotic elements in varying proportions, form a network of such complexity as to defy analysis (not least because in the last analysis they perhaps include not only Eve but most of her daughters). In *The Lusiads*, however, the most important relationship that begins to transpire is not between goddess and goddess, or goddess and woman, but between the goddess and the island whose inhabitant and tutelary spirit she is.

The surprising phallic shape of the Navel of the Earth identifies it as a *mise en abyme* of the Mountain: 'not only the mountain . . . is worshipped as the Great Mother but also rocks representing it—and her. . . . Numinous sites . . . experienced in *participation mystique*' with her—'mountain, cave, stone pillar, and rock'—are all equally her manifestations; and stones, including 'the *omphaloi*, the navel stones . . . we find in so many parts of the world', are 'among the oldest symbols of the . . . Goddess' (Neumann 1974: 44; 260).

Such 'numinous sites' include by definition both the island and the cosmic mountain which is a synecdoche of it, as it is itself of the sea. In Camões's poem, Yvette Centeno points out, 'the island is an "ínsula divina" emerging from "the midst of the waters" like Venus herself'. The union with Tethys, as representative of the goddess, is at the same time 'the mystical . . . union with . . . the primal One that takes the form of the waters'; and it is to this 'union with . . . the sea that [Gama] owes his vision of the *machina do mundo*': for the hero (which is as much as to say, for the poet), 'it is love that opens his eyes' (Centeno 1981: 27). Hence the necessity—even in Cháng An, even on the distant peak of the Kun Lún range—of situating the Earthly Paradise too 'no meio das águas'.

The most ancient representation of Aphrodite yet found in her first

---

[38] Identical 'Questions about the Heavens', or *Tian Wén* (and many more, to a total of 163), had already been asked in an anonymous Chinese poem of the 4th c. BCE: see the discussion of the solar and lunar discs in the Countess of Dài's portrait, above.

adoptive country, the half-Asiatic, half-European island of Cyprus, is a 'navel'. More exactly, a simple conical stone (cf. Delcourt, 43; 51). The astonishing power of survival that the fortunately incorrigible conservatism of religious art in all times and cultures seems to confer on its favourite iconographic motifs—'ces formes [qui], définies avec une puissante netteté et comme frappées dans une matière très dure, traversent le temps sans en être affectées', as Henri Focillon called them[39]—is exemplified by the persistence, as late as Imperial Roman times, of this extremely archaic motif, literally incised in the 'matière très dure' of Cypriot coins depicting the sanctuary of Aphrodite at Paphos, with this same navel-stone, already surrounded by the doves that had in the meantime become established as attributes of the goddess (cf. Grigson, 157 and fig. 9).

Other examples have been found in the Lebanon, in Pamphylia, and in Galatia; but also—more significantly, because it is once again a *mise en abyme*—on the terraces of Mount Sinai, already itself conical; 'which suggests that the Great Moon Goddess was worshipped on this Mountain... in the form of a cone, before Moses received the Tables of the Law there' (Harding, 39 ff. and figs. 1–3).

In fact, not only was Venus represented iconographically in that form, but even the sites chosen for her temples, no doubt with the intention of establishing an allusive or sympathetic association with her, habitually coincided with places conspicuously characterized by the 'sexual' form of a conical hill or a cleavage or cavern among rocks (Vincent Scully, *The Earth, the Temple and the Gods* (New Haven, Conn., 2nd edn., 1979), ch. 6). Nor is this tendency peculiar to the West: for Japanese shamanism an entire island or mountain, by virtue of its wooded and conical appearance, can attract the numen and become the permanent abode of the divinity seduced by its sexually inviting shape. Shrines may also take the form of small earth mounds

---

[39] Focillon (cit. Poulet, 1). The great morphologist of art clarifies *en passant* the difference between the archetype, variable in content but fixed in form, and the iconographic motif, which consists either in the variation of forms *vis-à-vis* a content or of content *vis-à-vis* a form, some forms being like moulds that impose unexpected meanings on their sucessive contents, while at other times a stubbornly fixed meaning takes over forms to whose creation it was unrelated: see *The Life of Forms in Art*, tr. Beecher Hogan and George Kubler (New York, 1948), 4 f. Focillon's example of the second possibility is relevant to our context: to reproduce the serpent's coils, sympathetic magic devised the serpentine: 'a sign that became a form' and ended (in traditions such as the Islamic or the Celtic) by 'coiling around the ancient iconography and devouring it'.

crowned by a tree: miniature replicas of the sacred mountain, intended to serve as invitation (or bait) for the divinity (Blacker, 39; 80). This mound-and-tree complex, a combination of two sexual symbols as well as of two forms of the *axis mundi*, is recognizable as yet another example of the overlapping of symbols found in pictorial representations of the World Mountain with the World Tree growing from its summit.

Recalling now the archetypal mountain of the Earthly Paradise, faithfully reproduced in Camões's Isle of Venus, we are less likely to be surprised by the curious fantasy recorded in the letter Columbus addressed to Ferdinand and Isabella, giving his view that the Earth was not round after all, as he had been led to believe, but pear-shaped; and that the hemisphere he had just discovered was not exactly a hemisphere but shaped rather like a breast, with the Earthly Paradise situated on the nipple:

Yo sienpre leý qu'el mundo, tierra y agua, era espérico ...; agora ví tanta disconformidad ... [que] me puse á tener esto del mundo, y fallé que no era redondo ..., salvo que es de la forma de una pera que sea toda muy redonda, y en un lugar d'ella fuesse como una teta de muger ..., y qu'esta parte d'este peçón sea la más alta y más propinca al çielo ..., en esta mar Ocçéana, en fin del oriente ... adonde acaba toda la tierra y islas.... D'esta media parte non ovo notiçia Ptolomeo, ni los otros que escrivieron del mundo, por ser muy ignoto.[40]

Admiral Morison, Columbus's learned and meticulous biographer, has explained the miscalculations that might have caused his error; but it seems more natural to assume 'a deeper impulsion ..., so that Columbus, seeking the aboriginal site of human generation, would nostalgically imagine it as a maternal archetype'.[41] If his modest pride in the disparity between book-learning and knowledge based on experience alone—'saber so dexperiencias feyto', as Camões was to call it—makes one think of *The Lusiads*, the reduction of the *axis*

---

[40] 'I have always read that the world—land and water—was a sphere.... Now I have seen such irregularity ..., I began to think this about the world: I find it is not round ..., but the shape of a quite round pear, and in one place like a woman's breast ..., and this nipple part is the highest and nearest to Heaven ... in this Ocean sea, at the furthest East ... where all the land and the islands end.... Of this middle part Ptolemy had no knowledge, nor the others who wrote about the world, for it [sc. the world] was largely unknown.'

[41] Harry Levin, *The Myth of the Golden Age in the Renaissance* (London, 1970), 183 f.

mundi to a maternal and/or erotic breast is not without its poetry and its deep truth.

To that poetry and that truth Camões too was sensitive. The eroticized description of the arrival on the Isle of Love is not unique in his work: his first Elegy describes the 'furious white foam' of the sea on the Moroccan coast possessing and penetrating the land, which languorously yields its 'côncavas entranhas' to the salt waves that cover it. What is portrayed by the imagery in this passage—all 'curves, recesses, protuberances, undulations, and softness', one Camonian scholar comments—'all this is Venus'[42] (plus, perhaps, a hint of the voluptuousness attributed by the traditional Iberian stereotype to Moorish women).

Such images are not hard to find in the work of modern poets (cf. Reckert 1973: 20): the special virtue of older or more exotic examples of gynaecomorphic symbolism is their greater pre- or extra-theoretical innocence, unaffected by the feedback that may lead visual or verbal artists, influenced by psychology, anthropology, sociology, and art history, to produce what they believe is expected of them.

The prestige of works such as those of Neumann or Harding, transformed into canonical texts and cult objects by the feminist movement, makes the old innocence difficult and a degree of scepticism essential. If it is still possible to attribute a vision like Masson's *Cascade* or Reddick's *Landscape Figure* to direct intuition, the same can probably not be said for Charles Roff's photograph 'Cave 1' (Adam, 21), in which a sphinx-like nude, her knees parted, sits at the entrance to an enormous V-shaped cavern that reproduces on a monumental scale what she is at no pains to conceal.

For the Anglo-Italian scholar Guido Almansi, the existence of such images in widely separated culture areas 'sembra rivelare la presenza di schemi simbolici archetipici. . . . L'immensa forma femminile supina sarebbe . . . una opzione interpretativa del paesaggio.'[43] In

---

[42] António José Saraiva, *Luís de Camões* (Lisbon, 1959), 63. A few lines further on, four other familiar motifs reappear: the mountain, the hero, the trees with magic fruit, and the serpent that guards them: 'I climb the mount that Theban Hercules / did cleave apart from Calpe's lofty rock / . . . / and gaze out from the summit whence he saw / the grove of the Hesperides, and slew / the serpent that would not have let him pass'. These same motifs—cleft mountain, serpent, and orchard—are all found in Camões's own coat of arms (Moura 1987: 96 f.). Only the hero is missing, and the poet has accordingly put himself in the picture.

[43] *L'Estetica dell'Osceno* (Turin, 1974), 192 f. The diversity of 'ambiti culturali' Almansi considers to extend from Hogarth to D'Annunzio is even greater than he supposes.

reality what Camões is doing in the octaves that lead up to the vision of the Island is something more ambitious (and stranger) than the mere versifying of an archetype, or the exploration—as in Baudelaire's sonnet 'La Géante'—of an 'option for interpreting landscape'. The opening scene of the Island episode points in fact towards a hierogamy, and to a hierogamy on a scale not just heroic but cosmic.[44]

The idea of sacred marriage arises in response to the need to formulate in ritual or hieratic terms the interdependence of eros and gnosis. On a purely human level, the erotic liturgy of Tantric Buddhism, for instance, aims in the most concrete manner at 'producing, through the active participation of a man and a woman purified by gnosis, the drama of the universe' (Tucci, 126). Similarly, but now within the parameters of Mesopotamian and Western mythology, whenever the 'marriage' of Inanna/Ishtar/Aphrodite to Dumuzi/Tammuz/Adonis is reproduced in the ritual union of a hero with a goddess, the act serves to regenerate the world (Eliade 1954: 26).

Camonian specialists do not always bear in mind that the poet's literary culture included not only the pagan classics and Renaissance Humanism[45] but also—no less than that of other Humanists such as his compatriots André de Resende, Barros, or Heitor Pinto—Christian Latinity. In that alternative tradition, M. H. Abrams points out (165 ff.), the goal of life conceived as a journey, and specifically in the 'fundamental trope of life as a pilgrimage . . . , was represented, as a rule, by New Jerusalem, which is at the same time a city and a woman; and the ardent desire to attain that goal was often expressed . . . in terms of an invitation to a wedding'; while Augustine's *Confessions*, for their part, provided a model for the kind of Christian narrative whose action consists in a voyage in search of a land that is the dwelling of a woman of irresistible erotic enchantment, and ending in a marriage.

This same topos also occurs in patriotic contexts, associated with those of the *laus Patriae* and the *laus civitatum*. For Isidore of Seville,

[44] Of the 'chymical wedding' or alchemical hierogamy, Jung (1968: 461) remarks that 'An essential feature of the royal marriage is . . . the sea-journey'.

[45] A Humanist work that appears to have escaped the *Camonistas'* net is Francesco Colonna's *Hypnerotomachia Poliphili* of 1467 (Venice, Aldo Manuzio, 1499). This romance, 'celebrated if little read', and likely because of its linguistic difficulty to remain 'un libro chiuso e di scarsi lettori' (Salvatore Battaglia, *La letteratura italiana: Medioevo e Umanesimo* (Milan, 1971), 428 f.), anticipates to a certain extent the atmosphere, the spirit, and even some of the concrete details of the Isle of Venus.

for example, Mater Hispania is sucessively desired and wedded by
the Roman empire and kidnapped and loved by that of the Visigoths,
whose own 'effort and skill' had legitimated them as the successors
of the original spouse: 'te iam pridem ... Roma caput gentium
concupivit, et ... spoponderit, denuo tamen Gothorum ... gens
post multiplices in orbe victorias certatim rapuit et amavit'. But the
etymologist saint is merely following in the footsteps of St Cyprian of
Carthage, and possibly in those of the Romano-British chronicler
Gildas as well; and later the Arabs were similarly to personify the
cities they desired to conquer as brides to be courted and won.[46]

Camões's originality, then, like all originality, is rooted in the
fertile humus of a pre-existing tradition, which in this case is both
literary and iconographic. And it does not consist exclusively either in
form (the 'gynaecomorphization' of geography and geology) or in
content (the Classical topos of the nuptials of a goddess with a hero),
but above all in the novel way in which this form and this content are
fused in an unprecedented *Gestalt*. This fusion is achieved by the use
of two related compositional techniques: the successive *mise en abyme*,
in three concentric circles, of the same archetype of hierogamy; and
the symbolic overdetermination implied by the essential identity of
the contents of the three circles.

The first and smallest of these contains the individual 'wedding' of
Gama and Tethys, as the hierarchical figures in whom the collective
entities of sailors and nymphs are summed up. The communal union
of these two groups in turn forms the larger circle in which that of
the representative couple is inscribed. To the marriage by proxy that
unites the historical Portuguese hero with the delegate of Venus,
however, and to the union of the representatives of the historical
Portuguese community with those of the kingdom of Love over which
Venus presides, there necessarily corresponds another circle, with
another union: this one *sub specie aeternitatis*, and only expressible in
telluric imagery like that used to describe the voyagers' arrival at the
Island.

It is in the context of the old prelapsarian, pre-theoretical innocence,
like that of Adam and Eve (or Gama and Tethys) on the mount of the
Earthly Paradise, that the reader of the final cantos of *Os Lusíadas*
gradually becomes aware of the true relation between Venus herself

---

[46] Cf. Reckert 1967: 24 f. and n. 13. On the late Antique and medieval Latin *laudes
civitatum* see Curtius, 157.

and the 'Ilha alegre, & namorada' that is her creation and her domain. As we picture the prow opening the sea, the *enseada Curva*, the blond shells and fair hillocks (with the *valle ameno* dividing them), the delightful scented pomes and pyramidal pears and lovely lemons (all of which, surely, and not only the last, 'Estão virgíneas tetas imitando'), the tangled bush, and the purple lily—the feeling that begins to dawn on us, intuitively and subliminally triggered by that description, is that a strange and prodigious metamorphosis has occurred: that just as happened with her dolphins and doves, what has taken place is a convergence or imaginative fusion of Venus with her insular 'attribute': a fusion, in the crucible of Camões's verbal alchemy, of the Island with its mistress, who had prepared and adorned it 'in the heart of deepest Ocean', after first creating it in her own metaphoric and metonymic image.

What the great synaesthetic overture to the Island episode really presages is the transcendental union, outside Space and Time—a true marriage of *Yáng* and *Yin*—of the metaphysical entity called Portugal and Venus *tout entière*: a Venus who is both the water of the sea and the island that emerges from it, and who, herself an epiphany and a source of epiphanies, represents not only Love but Wisdom.[47]

---

[47] Cf. Centeno 1981: 20–6. For Neumann (1974: 47; 260), 'the natural elements . . . connected with vessel symbolism include both earth and water . . . : the mixture of . . . earth and water is primordially feminine'.

III. THE HORIZONS OF SILENCE

For Yvette Centeno

6

LIMITS AND THRESHOLDS
(LIMINALITY IN SOME
MODERN POETS)

A transgressão: é esse o meu limite
toda a arte é limite
toda a arte é limiar

Y. K. Centeno

As early as the reign of Augustus, popular etymology equated *līmes* with *līmen*: ends with beginnings.[1] The equation may have been prompted by cyclical ideas of Time; but it is a wise saying that there are no false etymologies, and in this case (on however shaky historical grounds), *vox populi* spoke with the intuitive authority of poetry.[2]

The poetic intuition that dead ends are potential thresholds is typically expressed in images of confinement or exclusion and of attempts to escape or transcend them. If the ultimate image is the circle, ultimate confinement is in the self, in the infinite regress of the mirror, and ultimate transcendence that of the self through union with another self, when (in Petrarch's words, echoing Plato and echoed in turn by John of the Cross and Camões) 'l'amante ne l'amato si transforma'. And if the vision of life as rounded with a sleep—of the circle of birth and death as a *coincidentia oppositorum*— is less spatial than temporal, since Einstein the distinction between Time and Space—between events and objects—no longer holds.

---

[1] See Ernout and Meillet s.vv., and cf. Durand 1981: 35–79. On philosophical and religious aspects of *līmes* and *līmen* since Classical antiquity see Eco 1992: 26–8, and cf. Durand 1981: 35–79; on van Gennep's anthropological concept of liminality, as adapted by Victor Turner, see Leach. Chs. 4 and 5, above, touch on aspects of liminality with specific relation to poetry.

[2] Vindicated from the perspective of Classical poetry by Frederick Ahl, and from that of Dante by M. U. Sowell (*Cauda Pavonis*, NS 7: 1 (Spring 1988), 10 f.). From that of physics, 'il faut attendre Einstein ... puis Hubble ... pour que l'expérimentation sépare nettement la *fin* et la *limite*' (Durand 1981: 36).

With Heisenberg the last boundaries go, and the metaphysical intuition of the poets is at last ratified by physics as objects too lose their contours and merge into one another. But the self still remains firmly locked within the circle of language; and from this there is perhaps no escape, since consciousness—the awareness of self—is primarily a linguistic construct, and language, as a moment's reflection suffices to make clear, primarily a vehicle not for communication but for thought.[3]

The first section of this chapter amounts in effect to an extended footnote to a footnote (ch. 1, n. 12) in Yvette Centeno's and my *Fernando Pessoa* (1978). In it I shall draw on the work of Pessoa and two of his contemporaries to illustrate (1) the imagery of limitation of the self (whether by confinement or by exclusion); (2) some of the strategies that have been resorted to in the attempt to transcend it; and (3) the alternative of resignation to it as a fact of life. Imposing a limitation of my own at the outset, I shall confine my examples, as in Chapter 1, to a single theme: in this case a Midsummer Night's theme.

MIDSUMMER MIRRORS, BONFIRES OF ST JOHN

Fernando António Nogueira Pessoa, whose centenary in 1988 was celebrated on both sides of the *mar português* with characteristic Luso-Brazilian commemorative fanfare, is by common acclaim (not without some injustice to three or four other plausible contenders) the major modern poet of the Portuguese language. Indeed, as he said, it was his language he regarded as his true *Pátria*,[4] since he felt himself to be one of those Portuguese who had nothing left to do once the sea route to India had been discovered; and was furthermore a Joachimite Fifth-Monarchy man.

---

[3] 'Da quando il linguaggio fa la sua comparsa nell'universo, l'universo assume il modo di essere del linguaggio, e non può manifestarsi se non seguendone le regole' (Calvino, 202). The relation of consciousness to language and to the self is studied from neurological, psychological, and philosophical perspectives in recent works such as those of Arbib, Dennett 1988, Elster, Kolm, Ornstein, Popper, Steedman, etc. listed in the Bibliography; cf. 'Further Reading', in Hofstadter and Dennett, 465–83. For an impartial overview (by a believer in the possibility of artificial intelligence) see Dennett 1987; for a powerful refutation of 'AI', Penrose.

[4] A contemporary parallel can be found in Czesław Miłosz, in whose birthplace, 'the city without a name' (in fact with three: Vilnius, Vilna, or Wilno), Lithuanian, Russian, and Yiddish were all in competition with Polish—which, as the poet's 'faithful mother tongue', itself became for him 'my native land; I lacked any other' (1988: 216 f.).

Pessoa's lifelong involvement with a conglomeration of esoteric doctrines—from the cabbala to Joachim of Flora and Freemasonry, and from Theosophy to the Rosy Cross, astrology, and the shaggier fringes of occultism—make him look at first glance like a Portuguese version of Yeats, whom he imprudently dismissed in 1917 as 'flotsam washed up from the wreck of English Symbolism' (an embarrassing visitation a dozen years later by Yeats's 'unspeakable mad person' Aleister Crowley was perhaps a judgement). But it is not easy to picture him among the gazelles and wild swans at some Lusitanian Lissadell or Coole: neither his solidly middle-class background nor his temperament (one could see him looking typically diffident on the old hundred-escudo note, while the one-time flotsam appears with unmistakable aplomb on a much higher Irish denomination) would have made him an obvious candidate for invitation to great houses; and in fact his customary role at festivities would seem to have been that of the uninvited, as in his 'heteronym' Alberto Caeiro's Midsummer Night poem:

> Noite de S. João para além do muro do meu quintal.
> Do lado de cá, eu sem noite de S. João.
> Porque há S. João onde o festejam.
> Para mim há uma sombra de luz de fogueiras na noite,
> Um ruído de gargalhadas, os baques dos saltos.
> E um grito casual de quem não sabe que eu existo.
>
> 265
>
> St John's Eve on the other side of my garden wall.
> On this side myself, without any St John's Eve.
> St John's Eve is where they celebrate it:
> For me there's a shadow of bonfires' glow in the night,
> A burst of laughter, clicking of heels,
> And the casual shout of someone who doesn't know I exist.

Here the image is simultaneously one of confinement by the wall and of exclusion from the festival. This being one of the two most magically liminal of the year—that of the summer solstice—what is perhaps unexpected is the lack of any attempt to turn the barrier into a threshold; but Pessoa's *œuvre* as a whole makes it clear that this apparent resignation is in reality only a pretext for a consistent policy of defensive isolation from human contact. Build walls round who you dream you are, he advises; and make yourself a double being, so

well guarded that none who stare and pry can see more of you than
they would of a walled garden:

> Cerca de grandes muros quem te sonhas.
> Depois . . .
>
> .   .   .   .
>
> Faze de ti um duplo ser guardado;
> E que ninguém, que veja e fite, possa
> Saber mais que [de] um jardim de quem tu es.
>
> 194

If walls bar the poet from the celebrations on the other side,
these are themselves a metaphor for everything he is excluded from:
happiness; love; the whole festival of life, which (according to Álvaro
de Campos, another of his heteronyms) is one big fairground, with
nothing but booths and saltimbanques: 'uma grande feira, e tudo são
barracas e saltimbancos' (517).

Solitude in the midst of a festive crowd was the intended theme of
Act V of Pessoa's unfinished Faust play, in which the dancing goes
on at a festival while the dying Faust lies unattended (p. 727). It is
surely no accident that out of some two dozen poems of Pessoa's
mentioning *festas*, the only one referred to by name[5] is precisely that
of St John, which reappears in one of his 'folk' quatrains (p. 595) as
the subject of a laconic and disenchanted observation that

> No dia de S. João
> Há fogueiras e folias,
> Gozam uns e outros não
> Tal qual como os outros dias.
>
> On the feast day of St John
> There are bonfires and merry-making.
> Some are merry, others not—
> Just like any other day.

The summer solstice, as the night when young girls dream of their
future husbands, is liminal above all in its link with a major rite of
passage; but to Pessoa the otherness of other selves poses a threat to
his own, and the mere thought of their possibly having claims to

---

[5] Not counting a quadra (p. 590) that brings in all three 'Santos populares' of June:
Anthony, John, and Peter.

make on him is intolerable.[6] His walls—the 'grandes muros', the 'muro do *seu* quintal', the 'parede sem porta' (456) where Álvaro de Campos waits in vain for the non-existent gate to open; even the closed window behind which 'when there's a *festa* outside there's one inside' (491)—all these are functionally identical; and their ultimate function is defensive: at some times covertly and at others even overtly, the heteronyms being among other things a convenient device for enabling the poet to 'feel everything in every way' (445; 666), however contradictory.

For Pessoa's real concern is in fact less with otherness than with identity:[7] with drawing the line, or establishing the frontier, not just between self and non-self but between the different selves he finds within his own self: 'Between me and what, in me, is who I suppose I am, an endless river runs':

> Entre mim e o que em mim
> É o quem eu me suponho,
> Corre um rio sem fim.

> 160

If not even God has unity, he asks (664), how can I?: implicitly justifying the fragmentation of his own not into a trinity but into a whole spectrum of heteronyms, each with a different life history, poetic style, and thematic repertoire. But all the repertoires, paradoxically, have in common a rejection of the 'alma com fronteiras': a denial, that is, of the individual. Constitutionally unable (or temperamentally unwilling) to transcend the boundary of self by union with another self, however, he is obliged to resort to the fissiparous creation from within his own self of the necessary otherness. Necessary—but of course not, in the event, sufficient.

Giorgos Seferis, born a dozen years after Pessoa, and like him uprooted in adolescence from the country of his childhood, holds a place of comparable if less solitary eminence in modern Greek poetry. In his 'Bonfires of St John' ("Φωτιὲς τοῦ Ἄη Γιάννη"), attributed to the heteronym Stratis Thalassinos, the liminality of Midsummer Night, with its practices alluding to the rite of passage

---

[6] Cf. Y. K. Centeno, 'Ophélia-bébézinho ou o horror do sexo', in Centeno 1985, and 'Fragmentação e Totalidade em "Chuva Oblíqua"', in Reckert and Centeno; also my 'Alexander Search, entre o Sono e o Sonho', ibid. 93 f.
[7] So much so, indeed, that for L. Perrone-Moisés (1) 'any study of Fernando Pessoa is an investigation of identity'.

from the authority of the father to that of a husband—provides him, under the pretext of a reflection on folk customs and superstitions such as hydromancy, catoptromancy or mirror-divining, and the interpretation of ashes, with the opportunity for an implicit comment on the eternal condition of women in traditional society:

> Our fate, spilt lead, can't change
> there's nothing to be done.
> They have spilt the lead into the water under the stars and may the
>   bonfires burn.
>
> If you stand naked before the mirror at midnight you see
> you see the man moving in the mirror's depths
> the man who by your fate will rule your body
> in loneliness and silence, the man
> of loneliness and silence
> and may the bonfires burn.
>
> .   .   .   .   .
>
> It is the children who light the bonfires and cry out before the flames in
>   the hot night
>
> .   .   .   .   .   .
>
> But you . . .
>
> .   .   .   .   .   .
>
> heard from far off the human voice of loneliness and silence
> inside your body
> that St John's Night
> when all the bonfires went out
> and you studied the ashes under the stars.[8]

The solitary confinement Seferis evokes is not, like Pessoa's, in the inescapable prison (or impregnable fortress) of the self, but one imposed on the self from without, as much by the weight of unquestioned tradition and the tyranny of society as by that of the imagined future husband.[9] The shift from the woman's to the poet's voice after the first stanza not only signals his empathy with her as another self, but at the same time allows him to observe objectively her subjective resignation, and by inference to question the Fate which, once the spontaneous and unthinking joy of the children is no

---

[8] 126; I have made minor changes in the English. For the full Greek text see the Textual Appendix.

[9] These three forces are respectively instrumental in the destruction of Pavese's whore-goddess Santa and her two sisters.

longer an option, and the fire in her own blood has died down to ashes, she will have no choice but to accept.

My other example comes from a poet two years Pessoa's senior, but who outlived him by more than thirty. Manuel Bandeira, like Pessoa, knows the feeling of exclusion from the Midsummer Night festivities; but he projects it both backward and forward in time: back to the days when, unlike the children in Seferis's poem, he was still too young to participate in the merry-making, and forward to the time when, like the people he remembers from his own now distant childhood, he too will be 'dormindo profundamente':

Quando ontem adormeci	When I went to sleep yesterday
Na noite de São João	On St John's Night
Havia alegria e rumor	There was gaiety and noise
Estrondos de bombas luzes de Bengala	The sound of bombs Bengal lights
Vozes cantigas e risos	Voices singing laughter
Ao pé das fogueiras acesas.	Beside the burning bonfires.
No meio da noite despertei	In the middle of the night I woke
Não ouvi mais vozes nem risos	I heard no more voices or laughter
Apenas balões	There were only fire balloons
Passavam errantes	Wandering through the sky
Silenciosamente	Silently
Apenas de vez em quando	Only from time to time
O ruído de um bonde	The sound of a tram
Cortava o silêncio	Would cut through the silence
Como um túnel.	Like a tunnel.
Onde estavam os que há pouco	Where were the ones who a while ago
Dançavam	Were dancing
Cantavam	Singing
E riam	And laughing
Ao pé das fogueiras acesas?	Beside the burning bonfires?
—Estavam todos dormindo	—They were all sleeping
Estavam todos deitados	They were all lying down
Dormindo	Sleeping
Profundamente	Soundly
Quando eu tinha seis anos	When I was six
Não pude ver o fim da festa de São João	I couldn't see the end of the feast of St John
Porque adormeci	Because I fell asleep
Hoje não ouço mais as vozes daquele tempo	Today I no longer hear the voices of that time

Minha avó	My grandmother
Meu avô	My grandfather
Totônio Rodrigues	Totônio Rodrigues
Tomásia	Tomásia
Rosa	Rosa
Onde estão todos êles?	Where are they all?
—Estão todos dormindo	—They are all sleeping
Estão todos deitados	They are all lying down
Dormindo	Sleeping
Profundamente.	Soundly.

i. 210

For Fernando Pessoa, St John's Night, by virtue of its associations with sexuality—and therefore with the consciousness of identity and otherness—is of all the celebrations he feels excluded from the one most charged with potential menace for his own precarious sense of self: a self at once protected and imprisoned by the defences with which he has hedged it about. And precarious perhaps in part because (despite occasional protestations to the contrary) he was both culturally and linguistically an *apátrida*. On this reading, his atavistic fear of any invasion of his intimacy, and therefore of his very identity—a fear rationalized philosophically as a quasi-Buddhist resolve to escape from the vicious circle of procreation, birth, and death—could be seen as partly a product of that stateless condition.

For Seferis, the immemorial rituals of the solstice call to mind a plight as much social as personal, but one he is enabled, by the distancing process of using different voices, to present both from the social perspective of the sympathetic but detached observer and from the personal one of the unavoidably involved participant. For Manuel Bandeira, finally, what the annual return of the Midsummer Night festivities suggests is, in a quite uncomplicated and straightforward way, the familiar and inescapable circle of birth and death.

Bandeira and Seferis alike were among the many Western poets of their generation to be attracted to the haiku. The Brazilian poet himself experimented with the form as well as translating four of the micropoems of Bashō; and Seferis, as we shall see in the next chapter, wrote a sequence of sixteen of his own. As for Pessoa, Leyla Perrone-Moisés has extracted from the poetry of his heteronym Alberto Caeiro more than twenty 'accidental' haikus which, if metrically imperfect, are nevertheless perfectly in keeping with the spirit of the genre in theme and expression: far more so, certainly, than any of Pessoa's almost three hundred *quadras ao gosto popular*, with their *faux-naïf* sententiousness. I should like to think all three of these poets might have recognized, in the five haikus that follow, something like an ultimate distillation of what they themselves were saying in their own longer poems.

In the first, the poet—the eighteenth-century Buddhist nun Sogetsu—needs do no more than hint at the lonely darkness at the end of the Japanese Feast of All Souls or Lantern Festival, when, like Seferis's bonfires and the *balões* drifting through the night sky over Bandeira's Recife, the lanterns have all gone out:

Bon-odori	After the dancing,
ato wa matsu kaza	the wind in the pines;
mushi no koe	the voices of insects . . .

IH 116

The point would not be lost on Sogetsu's readers that the Festival of Lanterns is also the Festival of the Dead, and that each successive year's lanterns and dancers must in their turn drift away into the shadows of what is always, in Pessoa's words, the same 'noite antiquíssima e idêntica', leaving behind only the timeless sounds of Nature.

It is not inconceivable that a well-read Buddhist nun might have had at the back of her mind the ancient Chinese 'Rites for the Souls' (fourth century BCE), which form the coda to the even more ancient 'Nine Songs' (*Jiŭ Ge*):[10]

> The rites are done now; the drums beat together.
> The flower wands are passed on: new dancers take our place.
> Lovely maidens sing their songs solemnly and slowly.
> Orchids come in springtime, chrysanthemums in autumn,
> ever and again until the end of time.

---

[10] My version conflates those of Owen (1989: 111) and Hawkes (1959: 44). The shamanistic *Nine Songs*, like the *Shi Jing*, had from the 2nd c. BCE been provided with Confucian interpretations to make them respectable. On the 17th–18th c. revival of Japanese interest in Confucianism and archaic Chinese poetry see Shūichi Katō, *A History of Japanese Literature*, ii, tr. D. Sanderson (London, 1983), 54–70. Even the old custom of writing verse in Chinese (cf. Ch. 2, n. 34, above) was revived as a genteel accomplishment occasionally resulting in true poetry: see Burton Watson, *Japanese Literature in Chinese* (New York, 1975–6) and *Kanshi* (Berkeley, Calif., 1990). The 8th-c. poet Qián Qǐ once heard from his window someone reciting what might be a rarefied echo of our ancient song: 'The music is over; the people disappear. / Above the river the peaks are green'.

In any case, the seventeen syllables of Sogetsu's haiku seem to anticipate and concentrate—though without Pessoa's characteristically Western existential anguish—the feeling of solitude and of intimations of mortality that in more diffuse form pervades such lines of his as 'Quanta alegria onde os outros são / E dançam bem!' (175) or 'Alegria alheia . . . Nas ruas da feira / Deserta' (79.3), or most of all, perhaps, this poem written in 1930 on the day after the Feast of St James, with which it may possibly have a tenuous connection:

Depois que todos foram	When everyone had gone
E foi também o dia,	And the day departed too,
Ficaram entre as sombras	Among the shadows were left
. . . . .	. . . . .
Eu e a minha agonia.	Myself and my agony.
A festa fora alheia	The festival was for others
E depois que acabou	And when it was over and done
Ficaram entre as sombras	Among the shadows were left
. . . . .	. . . . .
Quem eu fui e quem sou.	The selves I was and I am.

639

The life cycle of the haiku, spanning the almost six hundred years from the early thirteenth to the late eighteenth century (with an eclectic revival beginning towards the end of the nineteenth), roughly coincides with that of the sonnet. Of my four remaining specimens, the first two are respectively by Buson and his seventeenth-century predecessor (and Bashō's exact contemporary), Sodō:

Shi-go-nin ni	On four or five
tsuki ochi-kakaru	still dancing
odori kana	the moon has begun to set.

Hk iv. 28

For the earlier poet, as for Pessoa, the shadows and solitude after the festival are implicit reminders of the divided self:

Ware wo tsurete	Taking me along,
waga kage kaeru	my shadow returns home
tsukimi ka na	after the moon-viewing.

Hk iii. 403

The other two haikus are by the last (and only modern) master of the form, Masaoka Shiki, who died at about the time when the fourteen-year-old Fernando Pessoa—home on holiday from Durban High

School after six years in Natal, and beginning to feel his way back into his native language—was writing his first Portuguese verses on the Azorean island of Terceira:

Hito kaeru	Going home alone:
hanabi no ato no	after the fireworks,
kuraki kana	the darkness!

Hk iv. 23

If that might be the voice of Pessoa (and a possible alternative translation of the first line would in fact be 'when everyone had gone'), Shiki's other poem could equally well have been signed by either Giorgos Seferis or Manuel Bandeira:

Sabishisa ya	Loneliness:
hanabi no ato no	after the fireworks,
hoshi na tobu	a falling star.

Hk iv. 24

TO LEARN FROM STONE

Things, as much as selves—objects, no less than subjects—have their identities; but to them this presents no problem, and Pessoa, in the persona of Caeiro (272), invokes their enviable autonomy as evidence that consciousness is no criterion of worth:

Cada cousa é o que é

. . . .

Às vezes ponho-me a olhar para uma pedra.
Não me ponho a pensar se ela sente.
Não me perco a chamar-lhe minha irmã.
Mas gosto dela por ela ser uma pedra,
Gosto dela porque ela não sente nada,
Gosto dela porque ela não tem parentesco nenhum comigo. . . .

Every thing is what it is.

. . . . . .

Sometimes I'll look at a stone,
I don't start wondering, does it feel anything?
I don't waste my breath calling it my sister.
But I like it for being a stone.
I like it because it doesn't feel anything,
I like it for having no kinship with me at all. . . .

That all phenomena are unique, singular, unrepeatable—that 'things are real, and all different from each other', as Caeiro says—is not only a tenet of both Taoism and Zen but one implicit even in the Western esoteric tradition, from Giordano Bruno and van Helmont to Leibniz, who formulated it as the 'identity of indiscernibles'.[11] Where Pessoa got it from is anyone's guess; and his image for it is no less a topos: one recalls such other fiercely autonomous stones as Dámaso Alonso's *terca piedra*, with its frenzied muteness or immobile cry—'frenética mudez o inmóvil grito'—which nevertheless

expresa duramente,	expresses with its hardness,
llega a decir su duelo	telling its woe
a fuerza de silencio atesorado.	by dint of hoarded silence.

1970: 51

Or like the *galet* minutely and lovingly described by Francis Ponge (98), who does, unlike Caeiro, recognize a 'parentesco' with it, because its very individuality—the product of literal, geological fragmentation—gives it the status of an honorary person: 'la pierre à l'époque où commence pour elle l'âge de la personne, de l'individu, c'est-à-dire de la parole'.

In contrast with Ponge and in common with Caeiro, Alonso feels the otherness of the object, but strives, unlike him, to penetrate the barrier between it and himself and call into being—whether through the senses or by recourse to language—the non-existent relationship. These lines are from a poem entitled simply 'Cosa' ('Thing'):

Cuando la mano intenta poseerte
siente la piel tus límites:
la muralla, la cava
de tu enemiga fe, siempre en alerta.
Nombre te puse, te marcó mi hierro

.   .   .   .   .

(era tu sombra lo que aprisionaba).
Al interior sentido
convoqué contra ti. Y, oh burladora,
te deshiciste en forma y en color,

---

[11] Calvino (81) attributes this *mathesis singularis*, or 'scienza dell'unicità d'ogni oggetto', to Barthes; in fact it is somewhat older. To a Taoist, Valéry's apparently contradictory pronouncement (300: 'Le Vide et le plein') that 'Les objets ne sont indépendants qu'en apparence. Leurs distances, leurs non-contacts sont apparences' would itself be contradictory only *en apparence*.

en peso o en fragancia.
¡Nunca tú: tú, caudal, tú, inaprensible!

¡Ay, niña terca,
ay, voluntad del ser, presencia hostil,
límite frío a nuestro amor! . . .

                    1970: 60

When my hand would possess you,
skin feels your limits:
the wall, the moat
of faithful enmity, ever on guard.
I thought to name you, brand you with my iron

      .   .   .   .

(it was only your shadow that I caught).
I called up inner meaning
in aid against you. Mocking,
you shattered into form
and colour; weight or fragrance.
Never yourself; fluid, unseizable!

Ah, stubborn girl,
ah, will to be: hostile presence,
cold limit to our love! . . .

In a well-known poem by perhaps the most important poet to have
remained in Poland through the Stalinist period, Zbigniew Herbert,
the recalcitrant object is typified—as earlier for Alonso—by a stone,
or more exactly a pebble:[12]

kamyk jest stworzeniem	the pebble
doskonałym	is a perfect creature
równy samemu sobie	equal to itself
pilnujący swych granic	guarding its limits
wpełniony okładnie	filled exactly
kamiennym sensem	with stony meaning
. . . . .	. . . . .
jego zapał i chłód	its ardour and coldness
są słuszne i pełne godności	are just and full of dignity
. . . . .	. . . . .
—Kamyki nie dają się oswoić	—Pebbles don't let themselves be tamed

[12] Herbert 1961: 59; English version after Miłosz (Herbert 1985: 108), slightly
modified (full Polish text in the Textual Appendix).

do końca będą na nas patrzeć   to the end they will look at us
okiem spokojnym bardzo jasnym   with a calm, very clear eye

Ponge values the stone for its kinship with man; Caeiro because it has none. Herbert, as Czesław Miłosz has said (1983: 23), implicitly contrasts it with man, who is not always equal to himself; who does let himself be tamed; who once tamed can no longer look his fellows calmly in the eye; and who 'is characterized by a limitless striving to transcend all limits' instead of 'guarding' his own (whether in Alonso's sense of defending them or in that of keeping decently within them). 'Kamyk'—Miłosz rightly says—is both a political and an eschatological poem.

In a curious verbal parallel with Alonso, Herbert (1985: 24) praises a stool for 'with great immobility explaining by dumb signs' its own genuineness, so that 'at last the fidelity of things opens our eyes'. 'Objects'—he surmises in a prose poem with that title—'do this from pedagogical considerations, to reprove us for our instability' (1985: 63).

'Pebble', like 'Objects', speaks about the things named; 'Stool', like 'Cosa', addresses the object directly (and even with an endearment). In Wisława Szymborska's 'Conversation with a Stone', dumb signs and frenzied muteness at last yield to dialogue as the stone condescends to submit to interrogation; but the *límite frío*—the cold barrier of otherness—remains firmly in place, and even the note of hostile mockery is present:

> I knock on the stone's door.
> —It's me, let me in,
> I want to come inside
> and look round.
>
> .   .   .   .
>
> —Go away, says the stone;
> I'm shut tight.
> You can smash us stones to pieces;
> we'll still be shut tight.
> You can even grind us to dust;
> we won't let anyone in.
>
> .   .   .   .   .   .
>
> —I only mean to stroll round your palace
> and then go and visit a leaf and a drop of water.
> I haven't much time to do all those things:
> my mortality ought to move you.

—I'm made of stone, says the stone,
I have to keep a straight face.
Go away,
I have no muscles to laugh with.

    .   .   .   .   .   .

—I hear there are great empty halls inside you,
unadmired, uselessly beautiful,
hollow-sounding, echoing to no footsteps.

    .   .   .   .

—Great empty halls, the stone says:

    .   .   .   .   .   .

beautiful, perhaps, but beyond the reach
of your poor senses.
You can examine me, never experience me.

    .   .   .   .

If you don't believe it, says the stone,
go ask the leaf, it will tell you the same as I do;
ask the drop of water, it will tell you the same as the leaf.

    .   .   .   .

I knock on the stone's door.
—It's me, let me in.

—I *have* no door, says the stone.[13]

Variations on a single theme, centred on a single objective correlative and composed by contemporaries and compatriots, would normally suggest influence. The earlier appearance of the same theme and motif in a major poet of a kindred language would seem to reinforce this hypothesis. Osip Mandel'shtam's first book of poems, published in 1913, was *Kamen'* ('Stone'); his last recorded words, to a fellow gulag inmate as they sat by a heap of stones they had been carrying, were 'my first book was *Stone*, and my last will be stone, too'.[14] Of Mandel'shtam it has been said that stone 'became his image, hardness and design his consolation';[15] and in an essay contemporaneous with that first book he had already spoken of 'the mute

---

[13] 'Rozmowa z kamieniem', in *Wielka liczba* (Warsaw, 1976), 90 ff. (full Polish text in the Textual Appendix).
[14] Nadezhda Mandelstam, *Hope Against Hope* (1970), tr. Max Hayward (3rd edn., Harmondsworth, 1983), 475.
[15] Seamus Heaney, 'Osip and Nadezhda Mandelstam', in *The Government of the Tongue* (London, 1988), 78.

eloquence of the granite block', and of stone as 'itself the discoverer of the dynamic potential concealed within it'.[16]

Appearances can deceive, however; and in the Polish poets the motif may derive not from intertextuality (Mandel'shtam's works were out of circulation for most of the relevant period) but from the common intuitive choice of a symbol embodying the complementary aspects of an experience shared with their Russian predecessor: on the one hand the claustrophobic atmosphere of Stalinism and the inscrutability of its agents; on the other the strategic imperatives of secrecy and self-sufficiency, resilience and resistance, and stubborn, stony silence under extreme duress.

For the Brazilian João Cabral, as for Pessoa—and to some extent Alonso[17]—the motif is more personal. The opening lines of Cabral's *Pedra do Sono* were written in Recife, the seamy and steamy metropolis of the *Nordeste*, in 1939; the concluding ones of *A Educação pela Pedra* in the more aseptic purlieus of Berne a quarter of a century later. In the interim he had produced the remarkably homogeneous and self-contained body of verse that established him as the most original and influential poet of his generation in Brazil: an *œuvre* whose unifying aim—to apprehend and express the concrete reality of the objects it contemplates—he sums up in the images of *sun* (which 'strips them of all shadow'), *water* (which 'frees their own light'), and *stone*, respectively the epitomes of luminous clarity and of order: 'a ordem que vês na pedra'. As well as order, stone is form and outline (Mandel'shtam's 'hardness and design'[18]); *dureza* and *duração*—or consistency and persistence (Alonso's 'will to be').

These are intellectual virtues. Recalling Alonso's scale of styles based on their relative proportion of conceptual, affective, and imaginative or sensory elements, we shall not be surprised to find in Cabral a preponderance of the conceptual and sensory over the affective. Nor, in a poet who speaks of moments of heightened

---

[16] 'The Morning of Acmeism', in Mandel'shtam 1977: 129.

[17] The discussion of Cabral that follows is in part an abridgement of my 'João Cabral: From *Pedra* to *Pedra*', *Portuguese Studies*, 2 (1985–6), 166–84. As for Alonso, the existential 'terror vital' that haunted him all his life was exacerbated by the horrors of two successive wars and the indignities of the Franco regime, resulting in the explosion of pent-up anguish of *Hijos de la ira* (1944).

[18] Many of the Russian's poems concern famous buildings, in whose design the 'dynamic potential' latent in stone is most fully realized; while two of Cabral's metaphors for a poet are 'architect' and 'engineer'.

perception 'when to look is to touch', that his sensory imagery mostly refers to the two senses best suited to engaging with *objects*. This predilection was no doubt encouraged by his reading of Ponge, who had found that 'la contemplation d'objets précis . . . porte des fruits' quite different from those of 'les rêves . . . , indéfinis, informes, et sans utilité' (176 f.). To exorcise the formless shadow world of dreams and discover his own identity—which is the same as to say a voice and a language of his own—Cabral will limit his vocabulary ruthlessly to 'the same twenty words / revolving round the sun / that cleans them of whatever is not knife': lean, sharp words, like *água, pedra, sol*. This sun, the metaphor for a constant theme, is to burn away the last impurities of the already sublimated vocabulary that orbits round it, driven by the controlled energy of syntax. The lines quoted are the paradigm—metaphor, theme, vocabulary, syntax—of a whole poetic language, which Cabral now sets himself to learn, in a course of object-lessons, from stone:

> Uma educação pela pedra: por lições;
> para aprender da pedra . . . ,
> captar sua voz inenfática, impessoal
> (pela de dicção ela começa as aulas).
> A lição de moral, sua resistência fria
> ao que flui e a fluir . . .
> a de poética, sua carnadura concreta;
> a de economia, seu adensar-se compacta . . .
>
> 130
>
> Learning from stone, lesson by lesson:
> to learn from stone . . . ,
> catch its unemphatic, impersonal voice
> (it starts with elocution).
> Its lesson in morals is its cold resistance
> to whatever flows, and to flowing . . . ;
> in poetics, the concreteness of its flesh;
> in economics, its dense compactness . . .

'The form of an object', D'Arcy Wentworth Thompson said (11), is a 'diagram of forces.'[19] *Orbit, dance, game*—Cabral's images for the

---

[19] Wentworth Thompson, who mentions Leonardo da Vinci on his first page, may have been familiar with Leonardo's intuition that 'L'aria è piena d'infinite linie rette e radiose, insieme intersegate e intessute . . . , rapresentando a qualunche obieto la vera forma della lor chagione'.

behaviour of words in poetry—correspond to regular, reciprocal motion, like the to-and-fro movements we have seen in other poets. But in Cabral this kinetic imagery is a constant, and represents a transition between conventional metaphor and what may be called metaphorical syntax. More than the objects compared, what interests him is the relations he can discover or invent between them; and the comparison itself depends on the superimposition of a difference on an analogy.

The formula for this device is simply 'A has in common with B certain characteristics X, plus another, Y, which B lacks'; but variations on it can give rise to comparisons of great originality and complexity, as when the indifference (A) by which a woman defends her intimacy resembles a cage (B) or a blouse (C) enclosing (X) her, while simultaneously transforming the whole universe outside her into an infinite cage (B') or strait-jacket (C') for the man whom, as a barrier excluding him from access to her, it thus also paradoxically 'encloses' or imprisons (X').[20]

What is common to all Cabral's paradoxes and oscillatory movements—metrical and syntactical as well as semantic—is that they represent alternative but equally valid perspectives on the same phenomenon. This multiple perspectivism culminates in four poems 'Written with the Body', and exploring different aspects of the same woman. The first says her essence can only be grasped 'as a whole: never in detail'; in the second, the dichotomy of part and whole is replaced by that of far and near; and the third develops the idea that to be clothed is the reciprocal and not the opposite of being unclothed: a paradox the fourth shows to be a variant of the inside–outside or open–shut duality (as in 'Woman dressed in a cage') which is as typical of Cabral's spatial imagery as are to-and-fro or in-and-out movements on the kinetic level.

It is the third poem that is most relevant at this point. Here the stock metaphor of silk for a woman's skin prompts Cabral to portray the act of love by an analogy between being embraced by her and

[20] An example of the basic formula is 'Imitação da Água' (above, Ch. 4), in which a woman lying down (A) recalls in several respects (X) a wave (B), but one with the special quality (Y) of being able to suspend indefinitely its moment of breaking, mounting up through a series of run-on lines that describe it from ever-changing perspectives as it advances and retreats in successive anadiploses until its pent-up energy is finally released: not only the woman but the poem itself is an 'imitation of water'.

being clothed. This way of being clothed, however, implies not only literal nakedness but the casting off even of personal identity in a mutual abandonment of self. Dressed only in the silk that is his beloved's body, the lover feels more naked than ever, his skin dissolving as he puts on hers, which then too melts away, leaving not even silk; and the two bodies end by becoming indistinguishable from each other in their common nakedness: 'nudez comum, sem mais fronteira'.[21]

The perspectivism of such poems, predicated on the indeterminacy of subject and object and on an ambivalence (or plurivalence) seen as inherent in the phenomenon observed, allows Cabral to dignify the object of observation by recognizing its right to be alternatively this *and/or* that for this *and/or* that observer. At the same time the mutuality of the relation observer–observed makes every object, as co-participant in the observation, a subject as well; so that 'tudo acabe confundido', with no more frontiers left. Cabral's whole mature *œuvre* is in fact a continual abolition of frontiers between apparently different phenomena which his intuition seizes as identical: a confusion, or fusion, of poetic 'making' with love-making; of a woman's essence with that of a landscape; of natural history with its social corollaries;[22] in short, of ontology with epistemology (and sociology).

The poet's quest for his own inner identity thus proves inseparable from a quest for the Other—but an Other likewise seen from the inside: from her, or his, or its own centre. The goal of this quest is indeed possession: but a fundamentally cognitive possession, effected from within the object possessed. It makes no difference whether this is a stone or a poem, a woman or a whole community, like the *retirantes* in their harrowing trek across Pernambuco from the

---

[21] Cabral, 56 f. In what I have called metaphorical syntax the syntagma alone assumes functions normally shared with lexical and morphological elements; here the syntax is not metaphorical but onomatopoeic, playing a role normally exclusive to phonology. The mutual nature of the surrender is conveyed mimetically by the successive permutations of *ela roupa/sêda ela, ele assume/ela empresta, pele dêle/pele dela/pele emprestada*, etc.; and the embrace itself by the grammatical intertwining of the ideas 'being clothed' and 'feeling naked'. In this poem (Portuguese text in the Textual Appendix) we seem to be hearing, as Baudelaire did in the musical syntax of *Tannhäuser*, 'tout le dictionnaire des onomatopées de l'amour'.

[22] Cabral's three almost exclusive themes (superficially heterogeneous but in his poetry predictably inseparable by any frontiers) are eroticism, artistic creativity, and the long-suffering rural population of his native North-East.

drought-ravaged backlands to Recife: to grasp the essence of the Other necessarily entails entering it.

It is no wonder, then, that Cabral habitually presents the cognitive act in quasi-sexual terms, as an act of penetration to a living centre, hidden and persistently sought, which even when attained continues by its nature to be for ever elusive and ambiguous. Poems are a poet's way of knowing; and as Robert Frost said, 'the figure a poem makes is the same as for love'. In the poetry of João Cabral, as in Camões's Isle of Venus, *eros* and *gnosis* are one.

BIS REPETITA PLACENT

To create *ex nihilo* not being given to mortals, so-called artistic creation ought rather to be known as composition, consisting as it does in the combining of pre-existent signifiers—linguistic, visual, plastic, or auditory—selected from among 'les mots et les choses' that make up our mental and physical environment, for the realizing of forms that were previously no more than potentialities.

'Les choses', because the materials used in this process of putting together may as well be a block of marble, a palette of paints, or a gamut of impalpable sound waves, as words. And if it is indeed with words and not ideas that poems are made, even the ideas are in greater or lesser degree pre-existent. The only thing that is really creative, then (and this is no small achievement), is the way the materials selected are combined to produce, as in a chemical reaction, a hitherto *non*-existent structure.

The words 'selected' and 'combined' are reminders that if the materials involved in this structure are of necessity drawn from our *circunstancia vital* (in Ortega's terms), and therefore belong (in Roman Jakobson's) to the 'axis of selection', the structure itself is syntagmatic, being composed not just of words but of sequences of words; and hence belongs to the 'axis of combination'.

The prefabricated materials for the construction of a text thus include, as well as ideas and words, syntagmas—which may be anything from a banal formula in the common domain, such as 'I love you', to a lengthy quotation from a literary source. If the hero of a play reinforces his declaration of love by reciting the sonnet 'So are you to my thoughts as food to life', the resulting fourteen-line syntagma, regarded as a single complex signifier, will have a signified that is no longer Shakespeare's but that of the author of the play.

The 1940s film *Ruggles of Red Gap*, in which Charles Laughton, taunted by a rowdy band of cowboys, reduces them to silence by reciting the Gettysburg Address, is a concrete example.

This points to a semiological conclusion: if the original meaning of the Gettysburg Address is for ever the property of Abraham Lincoln, and that of the sonnet for ever Shakespeare's, their new meanings belong by right to the authors of the real film and the hypothetical play. It follows that a signified is the product not only of a signifier, but of a signifier in a context; and from this conclusion another and more important one follows.

We have no trouble in granting that a word—the most rudimentary form of conceptual signifier—is the property of all the speakers of the language it occurs in. But once signifiers are recognized as contextual, it is clear that any signifier, however complex, is no less legitimately the property of all and sundry than is a single word. The *reductio ad absurdum* of this truth we owe to Borges, who takes it to its logical conclusion (since it is absurd only in practice, and not in logic) in 'Pierre Menard, author of *Don Quixote*'. Menard's 'admirable ambición', it will be recalled, was to rewrite Cervantes's novel word for word and line for line, but with a new and 'almost infinitely richer' signified which, because of the different circumstances of its composition, was to make Menard's *Quixote*, even incomplete, 'la obra más *significante*' of our time.

What this implies is that in any text only the signified is ever *created*: the signifiers are always given. Obviously so in the case of words, which are provided by the language written in (or the form of it appropriate to the genre, period, or audience concerned, which admits some and excludes others according to stylistic decorum: *sermo nobilis* or *humilis*; colloquial or formal register). Obviously, too, in the case of morphemes, the minimum units of conceptual signification, and in that of the tonic or metrical accents, light or dark vowels, rough or smooth consonants, and other hypomorphemic microsignifiers that function only subliminally, on the affective or imaginative level.[23] That even the sometimes very extensive syntagmas (or hyperlexical macrosignifiers) taken over bodily from other earlier texts—'intertextuality' is the current euphemism—create radically new complex signifieds of their own, if less obvious, is no less true.

[23] The latter include the 'visual microsignifiers' referred to in Ch. 1, n. 9, and the corresponding text.

The essence of verse is repetition, from that of the most subliminal phonetic microsignifiers to that of whole stanzas as refrains. The regular recurrence of accents or beats (metre) and that of sounds (rhyme) are the norms of ancient and modern Western versification respectively. The repetition of words, lines, or stanzas is a still older and more widespread practice, being the basis both of parallelism and of the refrain. What makes this repetition neither poetically nor significatively superfluous is that it is only the signifiers that are repeated. Where signifieds are concerned, every subsequent enunciation subtly alters the focus and perspective of the one before, which can therefore not properly be said to be repeated.[24]

In the Introduction I spoke of a book as both a unique and tangible object and an 'infinitely repeatable' text. Calvino (171 f.) draws an analogy with the ancient wooden shrines of Japan, such as that at Ise, repeatedly rebuilt while the resident numen remains constant (see above, Chapter 4): in Japan 'l'antico è ciò che perpetua il suo disegno attraverso il continuo distruggersi e rinnovarsi degli elementi perituri . . . ; così i versi d'una poesia si tramandano nel tempo mentre la carta delle pagine su cui saranno via via trascritti va in polvere'.

This comparison of poems, surviving through the centuries while the books in which they are successively reprinted crumble away, to the divinities who (like texts, as it were) continue to inhabit their successively rebuilt sanctuaries, calls for qualification. While the Sun Goddess arguably remains the same despite the repeated demolition and reconstruction of her dwelling,[25] the poem—as a signified—changes not only from printing to printing, accompanying the evolution of the literary canon (Eliot's 'tradition'), but according to the circumstances of the individual reader.

A story (Owen 1989: 53–5) told by the Táng poet Bó Ju Yì (Po Chü-i) illustrates the essential unrepeatability of any text. A friend,

---

[24] For Jakobson (1973: 234), 'l'essence, en poésie, de la technique artistique réside en des retours réitérés'; but even such a cultivator of reiterative syntax as Gertrude Stein had her doubts about 'the question of repetition and is there any such thing . . . I am inclined to believe there is no such thing . . . And really how can there be' (300). If there cannot, the question of plagiarism ('and is there any such thing') then arises: some caution in defining it is in order, at least, in view of the *cause célèbre* of D. M. Thomas's *The White Hotel* and *Ararat*, trial balloons with which the author seems to have been intent on provoking accusations of plagiarism by his silent appropriation of very large blocks of easily recognizable 'borrowed signifiers'.

[25] Though even this is open to question, since the nature and functions of deities too are subject to periodic reinterpretation.

posted to a remote and dreary provincial town, finds written on a wall there one of Bó's quatrains, composed years before at a drinking party of young men in the capital in praise of a singing-girl. Before becoming an anonymous graffito, inscribed perhaps by another exile recalling girls and parties and friends of his own youth in the far-off capital, it may have been sung to other girls at other parties as an inducement and prelude to casual love, or by the girls themselves in self-praise. Now 'the poem returns to its author; but like a child who has grown up and had experiences the parents can never know, it is changed'. The new depth it has meanwhile acquired comes from just these unknowable experiences: its meaning for the friend, an exile himself; its meaning for successive hearers, passing from mouth to mouth as a singing-girl does from man to man; its meaning even for the poet, as he recalls the now almost forgotten moment of its composition:

the author . . . no longer has authority over the poem . . . : his long-ago intentions . . . are . . . now only a part of what [it] has become. . . . The poem is no longer [an] infinitely repeatable text . . . : [it] has become its particular inscription on that broken wall in T'ung-chou. . . . And the fact that the wall will crumble . . . will not simply be the loss of one copy of a poem that can be written down again and again . . . [but] the loss of the last trace of one intense and mysterious moment . . . [that] we can never know . . .

ICONOGRAPHIC EXCURSUS

Working in the temporal medium of language, Cabral, with his repeated syntactical spiralling round the object of attention to view it from every possible angle, necessarily presents simultaneous perspectives serially; Picasso, having learnt from palaeolithic cave paintings of bison the art of presenting serial ones simultaneously, sums up in a single spatial composition his own repeated observations of the horse in *Guernica*. In contrast, it is the persistence of spatial form through temporal flux that is expressed in Turner's views of Norham Castle, begun with a pencil sketch in 1797 and continuing at one- to fourteen-year intervals with six watercolours and two series of sketches until his final statement on the subject, the great oil of 1840–5, where the castle at last melts into the landscape, dissolving in pure light and colour.

Still closer in method to Cabral are Monet's thirty views of Rouen cathedral. Unlike Turner's series, spanning almost half a century,

Monet's, though dating from two visits to Rouen in 1892–3, is diachronic only in representing the passage of time from dawn to dusk. Monet's practice, implying 'that no single image could convey the full complexity of what it represented and that all variations on a motif had equally valid claims to being "true" '[26] also links him to the Eastern aesthetic principles he was consciously applying at the same time in the designing of his garden at Giverny, with the Japanese bridge that was to be the subject of two other series of paintings. It is not that Monet's perspectives or brushwork owe any significant debt to Japanese models (nor could they well have done, Western knowledge of these being at the time confined almost entirely to the block prints of the *Ukiyo-e* school); it is rather that Impressionist doctrines happened to agree at a deeper level than that of technique with an attitude that had long prevailed in East Asia.

This can be summed up as a relative indifference to distinctions considered fundamental in the West: between art as product and art as process; between finished and unfinished; unitary and fragmentary; large and small; transcendental and trivial; solid and flowing; permanent and ephemeral: distinctions historically blurred by Buddhist and Taoist awareness of the relativity and impermanence of everything in the phenomenal world. Moreover, while Phidias and Praxiteles were not received in polite Greek society because they worked with their hands, East Asia has seen no need for a hierarchy of fine and applied or decorative arts such as pottery, calligraphy, gardening, flower arrangement, or even the brewing and drinking of tea.[27]

Among contemporary artists (like the Italian Fausto Melotti[28]) who have made a point of using 'ignoble' or perishable materials, the sculptor Andy Goldsworthy says of his own work that ephemerality 'reflects what I find in nature and . . . not . . . an attitude towards art. . . . That art should be permanent or impermanent is not the

---

[26] Jack Flam, 'Monet's Way', *NYRB* 17 May 1990, 9.

[27] This long-established and unselfconscious cultural tradition clearly left no room either for irony like that of the great pastry-cook Carême, who declared that 'the Fine Arts are five in number: painting, music, sculpture, poetry, and architecture—of which the principal branch is confectionery'; or for the frivolous ostentation of the Roman banquets where the tables were decorated with *trionfi* sculpted in marzipan, meringue, sugar, ice, jelly, or even butter (cf. Jennifer Montague, *Roman Baroque Sculpture* (New Haven, Conn., 1989)).

[28] One of his works, reproduced by Calvino (84 f.), is entitled 'Gli effimeri' (a punning allusion to mayflies: *effimere*).

issue. My sculpture can last for days or a few seconds—what is important ... is the experience of making.'[29] The most ephemeral of all materials is surely snow; but when working at the North Pole, Goldsworthy discovered that in Arctic conditions 'snow is ... sand and ice is slate': an experience that made him 'realize how rhythms, cycles and seasons in nature ... work ... at different speeds in different places' (158). Having worked in Japan as well and found the atmosphere congenial to his methods, he is likely to have realized too that awareness of the relativity not only of time but of matter, in its inevitable subjection to time, was no new discovery for the East.

NO FRONTIERS BUT HORIZONS

In the West the will to permanence has since Classical times been expressed in the ideal of a *monumentum aëre perennius*. The still older topos of vainglory, however, serves as a sobering reminder that even the most durable of monuments is eventually prey to *tempus edax rerum*, and as a final lesson to be learnt from stone:

... sozinha	... alone,
aprender a lição	to learn the lesson
que a pedra ensina	stone teaches:
não a eternidade	not eternity
a solidão	but solitude[30]

The Japanese, on the other hand—as one of the most distinguished Western students of Japan points out—'have not only been content with impermanency but ... eagerly sought it'.[31] The transience of beauty has been a topos in the West at least since Horace; in Japan it is the beauty of transience that is the stuff of poetry and painting alike.

---

[29] Goldsworthy, 141; 147. One of his constructions is made of old roof slates arranged so that the shapes appear to alter with the movement of the sun and the viewer: an effect recalling (as well as Monet's dawn-to-dusk cathedral views) the chamber in the Alhambra through whose pierced roof the sun projects onto the floor images of silver coins which as the day advances gradually turn to gold.

[30] Centeno 1979: 9.

[31] Keene, 19. Another experienced observer of the Japanese scene speaks of 'a culture that values, above almost anything else, the melancholy beauty of evanescence' (Ian Buruma, *TLS* 20–6 Apr. 1990). Extrapolating from Keene, Steven Heine ('From Rice Cultivation to Mind Contemplation: The Meaning of Impermanence in Japanese Religion', *HR* 30–4, May 1991) studies this phenomenon in the wider context of traditional Eastern agrarian societies.

This 'most peculiarly Japanese of aesthetic principles: that beauty is indissolubly bound to its perishability', is made explicit by the thirteenth-century Buddhist monk Kenkō, who also exemplifies both the fastidious Japanese distaste for regularity and symmetry (see above, Ch. 1, n. 20) and the corresponding regard for the fragmentary or unfinished, remarking that 'leaving something incomplete ... gives ... the feeling that there is room for growth' (as if to say, for making the limit a threshold).[32]

In the last analysis, what is reflected in all these attitudes is the absolute relativity of space, time, and matter in the Taoist and Buddhist teachings that are the substratum of Chinese culture and of those ultimately derived from it. The richest and most innovative of these, partly owing to the presence of a third spiritual current, Shinto, is that of Japan, where time has typically been 'believed to exist only in relation to movements or space ..., [and] space ... perceived as identical with the events or phenomena occurring in it'.[33] The Japanese language itself, 'rather than construct[ing] a ... linear narrative order ..., carries internal gaps and pauses ... filled with ... emotional energy. A ... cause/effect narrative order ... continually dissolves ... into these spaces.'[34]

Such spaces are called in Japanese *ma*: a word also defined as 'interval', 'blank', or, perhaps most significantly, 'gap'. The concept of *ma* is fundamental to that of the *kami*, the deities which in popular Shinto are not anthropomorphic beings but 'formless energy that comes and goes': a view that 'emphasize[s] the dynamic, processual, ephemeral ... character of sacred reality'.[35] In Japanese mythology

---

[32] Kenkō, p. ix. Two of the most impeccably canonical works of Japanese prose, the *Makura no Sōshi* or 'Pillow Notes' (*c.*1000 CE) of Sei Shōnagon and Kenkō's own *Essays in Idleness*, consist entirely of fragmentary musings and anecdotes: a formless form in which Prof. Keene (Kenkō, p. xvi) suggests readers 'took pleasure not only in moving from one to another of the ... subjects treated but in tracing subtle links joining the successive episodes': a pleasure clearly related to the 'coolness' of Japanese itself as a linguistic medium.

[33] Isozaki Arata, in Isozaki *et al.*, *'Ma': Space-Time in Japan* (New York, 1979), 13 (cit. Pilgrim, 256). This idea suggests a corollary to Leibniz's dictum that space is no more than the relative position of objects: i.e., that time is no more than the relative position of events.

[34] Kemmochi Takehiko, *'Ma' no nihonbunka* (Tokyo, 1982), 13–32 (cit. Pilgrim, 260). It is interesting to contrast this typically Japanese syntax with the paratactic strategies, referred to earlier, of that other cool medium, Chinese.

[35] Pilgrim, 268 f. The Japanese attitude to secular reality displays a corresponding 'sensitivity to the ... processual world ... of ... shadows, moon and mist' (Okuno Takeo, *Ma no kozō* (Tokyo, 1983), 397–415, 430–3, cit. Pilgrim, 268), which

even solid objects, such as stones (or the trees and pillars that universally represent the *axis mundi*), contain *ma* into which the gods temporarily descend.[36] As well as the infinitely expandable crystal grotto-heavens of Taoism, enclosed in microcosmic geodes, these stones inevitably call to mind the 'great empty halls' concealed inside Szymborska's *kamień*. But their closest Western parallel is Borges's 'Aleph' (i. 623 ff.): 'one of the points in space that contain all points . . . ; the place where all places . . . are present, seen from all angles', and within whose 'diameter [of] two or three centimetres . . . , is all cosmic space, undiminished in size'. The Aleph is in fact 'el microcosmo de alquimistas y cabalistas'—and, we might add, of Taoist sages. *Sub specie aeternitatis et infinitatis*, a snowflake and a galaxy are of equal size, and equally long-lasting.

As a spatial or temporal gap between things or events, *ma* 'deconstructs all boundaries as mind-created . . . order imposed on the chaos of experience' (Pilgrim, 257). The original meaning of χάος, for the pre-Socratics, was precisely 'gap'; and for Taoism the emergence of order from primal chaos was in fact a fall from grace, redeemable only through chaos regained. What is possibly the earliest statement of the self-evident truth that boundaries do not exist in reality but are imposed on it[37] adds the rider that they are created not by the mind alone but by words: 'Sameness, because of words, became differentiated'. As Liu points out, the passage goes on to regret that although it is words that make the boundaries between things, we have to use them to say so; recognition of this impasse leads naturally to the Taoist 'principle of saying more by saying less, or . . . saying all by saying nothing',[38] which in turn leads both to the

'represent the moving . . . , ephemeral condensation of . . . the . . . living energy of *kami*' (Matsuoka Seigow, 'Aspects of *Kami*', in Isozaki *et al.* 57, cit. Pilgrim, 262).

[36] Cf. Pilgrim, 262, and Isozaki, in Isozaki *et al.* 13 (cit. Pilgrim, 263).

[37] Zhuang Zǐ, ch. 27. The chronology of this Taoist classic is problematical, the oldest parts dating from *c.*300 BCE; a Buddhist maxim also of uncertain age states that 'between thing and thing [or event and event] there is no boundary' (*shì shì wú ài*). In the East, the *coincidentia* of opposites is not a coming together but a simultaneous coexistence: a non-dialectical continuum. Thus, not only are the Japanese, as we have seen above (Chs. 1, n. 20, and 4, n. 16), averse from symmetry and 'the clear-cut oppositions . . . required for parallelism', but in Japanese even the signifier and signified 'are not taken to be different so much as versions of each other' (Miner 1990: 93).

[38] Liu 1988: 12; 43; 56. On Zhuang Zǐ's rooted distrust of words see Ch. 7, n. 12 and corresponding text.

condensation and miniaturization we have found at the heart of Eastern aesthetics and to the equally basic philosophical goal of emptiness, which in terms of language means silence.[39]

That the goalposts are continually moved further away—that the goal of silence is in practice a horizon—is obvious. If the first word on the subject comes from a classic of Taoism, the last so far, which perhaps comes as close as is humanly possible to the horizon of silence, is by a contemporary Zen Buddhist poet, the late Takahashi Shinkichi:[40]

> The wind blows hard among the pines
> towards the beginning
> of an endless past.
> Listen; you've heard everything.

[39] And of music: for the musicologist Wilfrid Mellers (*TLS* 31 July 1987), John Cage's 'notorious silent piece . . . fulfils the kabbalistic prognosis that the ultimate end of music is silence, when matter, inherent . . . in the human voice as well as in . . . instruments, dissolves away'. John of the Cross, in mystic ecstasy, heard the solitary sonority of this ultimate silent music—'la música callada, / la soledad sonora'; that Cage's philosophically valid experiment fails to work as as 'music' is proof enough that in the material world the goal of silence can only be theoretical.

[40] *Triumph of the Sparrow*, tr. Lucien Stryk and Takashi Ikemoto (Urbana, Ill., 1986), 13: lines that sound like a distant echo of Pound's (*Cantos*, 120: 803):

> I have tried to write Paradise
> Do not move
> Let the wind speak
> that is Paradise

7

BEYOND CHRYSANTHEMUMS

La señorita
del abanico
va por el puente
del fresco río.

Los caballeros
con sus levitas
miran el puente
sin barandillas.

Lorca

BORGES (iii. 299) confesses to a 'culto del Oriente' which, in his view, the peoples of that 'miscellaneous Orient' do not themselves share (whether with him or with each other, he omits to say). Among those who do not share it one could safely include the poet Ō-oka, whose purposely demystifying line I have appropriated for my title.

It is Borges, too, who holds that the only genuine Europeans are by the same token the Americans, North and South, since the natives, preoccupied with their patriotic obligation to be first of all Dutch or Danish, Polish or Portuguese, cannot see the wood that is the West for the great rooted blossomers growing in their own gardens.[1] When I say 'the West', then, I shall in principle mean the world-wide community of nations that speak an originally European language—a 'white language', like that of the frock-coated gentlemen and their tall blonde ladies in Lorca's 'Canción china en Europa' (GL 297).

In practice I shall leave out of account the English- and French-

---

[1] Borges would have known Eliot's remark that 'the final ... consummation of an American [is] to become ... a European—something ... no born European, no person of any European nationality, can ever become' (David Cheshire, *TLS* 29 May 1992). Eliot's example of this consummation was Henry James; Borges and Eliot himself are others.

speaking areas of the world, whose literary relations with the East have already been studied in some depth and detail, and concentrate as before on the Iberian and Ibero-American countries, for which much critical and historical groundwork still remains to be done. Octavio Paz (1970: 18–27), summarizing Japanese influences on Hispanic poetry, notes this lacuna in the Spanish-language domain; in the Portuguese-speaking world (with a few exceptions also confined to Japanese[2]) the position is not significantly different.

When it comes to the 'misceláneo Oriente' I shall similarly continue to limit myself to its two easternmost components, China and Japan, which (together with Vietnam and Korea) make up, like 'the West', a cultural οἰκουμένη that for all its variety is still recognizably *one*.

THE DREAM IN THE GLASS

The *one* is defined by contrast with the *other*: the West mirrors itself in the enigmatic visage of the East ('enigmatic', 'exotic', 'inscrutable', are among the epithets we use to avoid making the effort that would be needed to get behind the looking-glass).

'Things', the great fifth-century theoretician of Chinese poetry Liú Xiè said, 'do not exist in isolation...; on the contrary, they are naturally completed by their antitheses.'[3] It therefore follows that there can be no totality—not even that of the individual self—that is not already a *coincidentia oppositorum*. This is what is hinted at in mimetic fashion by the mirror-like inversion of alternatives and the repeated intertwining of vowel sounds[4] in this Portuguese micropoem by Yvette Centeno (1984: 34):

o que é	what is
o eu	my self:
é o outro?	the other?

---

[2] Of the seven relevant items listed in the Bibliography (under Campos, Franchetti, Horta, Janeira, and Perrone-Moisés), three are concerned with Fernando Pessoa and (significantly, in the light of the preceding chapter) with the question of personal identity.

[3] *Wén xin* 7.8a, cit. Owen 1985: 61 (the text reads 'Shì bù gu lì...xiang xu, zì rán chéng duì'; I have slightly modified Owen's translation).

[4] These are limited to *e* (open and close), *o*, and *u* (with the corresponding semivowels [i] and [w]), in the order [u–ⁱε / u–eʷ / ε–u–o–u / u–ⁱε / u–o–u / ε–u–eʷ].

o que é	what is
o outro	the other:
é o eu?	my self?

But the same poet had already pointed out earlier (1974: 73) that even the *opposita* themselves exist only as functions of their own contextual antitheses:

> Se a realidade é outra
> a realidade é múltipla.
> 'Outro' não tem limites.

So much so, indeed, that the *outro* often turns out to be nothing more than a distorted and internalized mirror image of the *eu*—as Jung held, and Rimbaud, anticipating him, tacitly recognized when he declared 'Je est un autre'.[5]

Borges invites us to observe a cat. Or rather, a whole series—a *regressus ad infinitum*—of cats, always the same cat, who is in turn observing

> ... himself in the lucid moon of the looking-glass.
> Who is to tell him the other observing him
> is nothing more than a dream in the looking-glass?

The fact is, for Borges, that all these multiple cats are only 'semblances an eternal archetype / concedes to Time'. And 'mirrors themselves are not more silent' than another cat—likewise one and many, and 'master / of a domain enclosed like a dream'—whom the protagonist of the story 'El Sur' strokes in wondering realization that 'that contact was an illusion, and that they were separated as if by a pane of glass, because Man lives in Time... and the magical animal... in the eternity of the instant'.[6]

What happens is that Man, in interrogating the mirror, creates at the same time both his own identity and an alterity which, by opposing itself to that identity, defines it. As Plato said in the first *Alcibiades*, the eye that would know itself must first view itself in the mirror of another eye. Otherwise (and here the words come from a

---

[5] *Œuvres complètes*, ed. A. Adam (Paris, 1972), 250 (Letter to P. Demeny). The implications of this *obiter dictum*, often quoted out of context, are studied in that of the 'identity problem' in Centeno 1982: 55–63.

[6] 'Beppo' (iii. 297); 'A un gato' (ii. 513); 'El Sur' (i. 525). On infinite regress in facing mirrors see Durand 1969: index, s.vv. *avalage* and *redoublement*, and cf. Hofstadter 1985: 489–94.

venerable Zen manual of meditation) life is 'like an eye that sees, but does not see itself'.[7] Or that sees nothing but itself; which is what Antonio Machado seems to be suggesting both in these lines (307) attributed to his *alter ego* Abel Martín—

Mis ojos en el espejo	My eyes in the looking-glass
son ojos ciegos que miran	are blind eyes that observe
los ojos con que los veo...	the eyes that I see them with...

—and in these (268) in which he speaks in his own persona:

El ojo que ves no es	The eye that you see is not
ojo porque tú lo veas:	an eye because you can see it:
es ojo porque te ve.	it's an eye because it sees you.

The entire universe, conceived of as an 'actividad consciente', is for Abel Martín (306) 'the great eye that sees all by looking at itself'; and it is specifically to the East that Machado, speaking again in his own voice (388), relates this idea of an active and awakened consciousness:

Hombre occidental,	Western man,
tu miedo al Oriente, ¿es miedo	your fear of the East: is it fear
a dormir o a despertar?	of sleeping, or waking up?

Before the West can obey the Delphic commandment that under-lies its whole mental history—γνῶθι σαυτόν—it has first, then, to mirror itself in the eye (which turns out not even to be 'slant'[8]) of the East. Only then shall we be in a position to recognize that, far from being limited to the willow-pattern quaintness that delighted the *caballeros enlevitados* and *altas rubias de idioma blanco* of a century ago, the civilization of the East is perfectly serious, and neither picturesque nor in any meaningful sense 'exotic' at all, even in the light of the Euro-American criteria it implicitly denies, subtly skews, or at times—like any other mirror—even inverts.

To plot the trajectory from *fin-de-siècle* exoticism to recognition of this fact by the educated Western public would take a specialist in cultural history.[9] My aim is simply to register the fact and try to account for its recent more general recognition. To this end I shall

---

[7] *Zen Rinkushū* (compiled before 1574), cit. *Hk* i. 13.

[8] Physiologically speaking, this Western misapprehension (which has been known to deceive even royalty) is due to the epicanthic fold.

[9] For Anglo-Japanese relations this gap has been partly filled by Toshio Yokoyama, *Japan in the Victorian Mind: A Study of Stereotyped Images of a Nation 1850–80* (London, 1987).

again draw on evidence consisting mainly of parallel micropoems in Chinese, Japanese, and a variety of Western languages—now with greater emphasis on the poetry of the twentieth century—and illustrating (in addition to the poetic process of condensation, which privileges intensity over extension) the concept of the *coincidentia oppositorum*, or rather, of the 'non-dialectical treatment of essential duality' (Plaks, 303; cf. above Ch. 6, n. 37), and two symbolic motifs frequently used to realize that concept: the mirror image and its variant, the shadow.

Together with the brevity of the poems themselves, this thematic and symbolic restriction will make it possible, as the theme of solitude and the symbolism of citrus fruit did in earlier chapters, to delimit a manageable corpus or universe of data. If in the case of condensation it might be legitimate to think of an Eastern 'lesson', what I shall chiefly be concerned with here, rather than such influences as there may happen to be, is the *con*fluence of two highly complex literary currents which for many centuries flowed in widely separated channels, receiving tributaries of the most diverse origin, before at last themselves merging and mingling in a great *coincidentia*.

The most significant thing about any mirror image is what might be called its ontological ambiguity. It is a particular extension of this ambiguity (together with an unusual amount of both inherent and acquired symbolic meaning) that makes water, more than glass or metal, the natural and obvious mirror for use in symbolic contexts; because liquid is a reflecting medium by nature prone to ever-changing distortions and disturbances that exacerbate the uneasiness provoked by what is already in itself the most disquieting property of all reflections: their inversion of the object reflected.

BASHŌ'S POND

The best-known poem in the Japanese language is in all probability a haiku by the acknowledged supreme master of that supremely con-densed genre, Bashō (1644–94): the contemporary haiku scholar Hiroaki Satō, collecting English versions of it, stopped at one hundred. Here is version 101:

Furuike ya	The old pond.
kawazu tobikomu	A frog plunges in
mizu no oto.	(sound of the water).

Hk i. 340

Buson (1716–84), the second of the four canonically consecrated masters of haiku both in time and in reputation, transforms his predecessor's purely auditory experience into a visual one:

> Oborozuki   Hazy moonlight.
> kawazu ni nigoru   Troubled by the frog,
> mizu ya sora.   both water and sky.
>
> *Hk* i. 72

The scene that Bashō merely intuits, on the evidence of concentric sound waves, Buson visualizes, transforming these into ripples in the water that in turn trouble the reflection of the moon (itself already blurred by mist) which the poet, with his back to the real moon above him, is contemplating in the pond.

The haiku itself often creates, as here, concentric waves in our subconscious. As the author of one of Satō's hundred translations[10] puts it (in haiku form):

> my mind was still
> till Bashō's frog
> made it ripple.

If the frog's sudden plunge demonstrates that the pond has not only surface but depth as well, the reflection of the moon projects us upward towards the opposite, unplumbed depths of the heavens; and the sudden troubling of that image brings home to us the fragility and transience of the contingent world of the 'ten thousand things'. A haiku by Sora, Bashō's companion on his walking tour of the 'Narrow Road to the Deep North', blends the visual and the auditory:

> Ike no hoshi   Stars of the pond . . .
> mata hara-hara to   Once again the patter
> shigure ka na.   of autumn rain!
>
> *Hk* iv. 223

We might imagine these stars to be a metaphor for the raindrops pattering on the surface of the water; but in fact what is going on here is rather more complicated—and odder: in the transcendental world of Buddhism, the innumerable sparks of light the rain ignites in the water are rigorously *identical* to the stars whose place they take, extinguishing their reflection.

---

[10] William Flygare, in Satō Hiroaki, *One Hundred Frogs* (Tokyo, 1983), 167.

The two great East Asian languages of culture are characterized, as we have seen, by an intrinsic ambiguity that at the same time as it makes every signifier a potential medium for expressing plural meanings also makes the languages themselves what Marshall McLuhan called 'cool media': that is to say that to be intelligible they demand from the recipient of the 'message' an active collaboration in its decoding. David Slawson (54) gives a concrete example of this process as applied to Japanese teaching methods: 'the traditional form of verbal communication in Japan has not been the explicit, exoteric style we value so much . . . , but rather has tended toward the esoteric . . . : for the transmission to be completed, the student's mind must be ready to receive it.'[11]

In addition to this inherent tendency, however, the literary tradition of both Chinese and Japanese has systematically cultivated ambivalence (or rather, plurivalence) as an expressive virtue and a conscious stylistic resource. It is hard not to see in this a philosophical conviction that no signifier can ever either fully or exactly reproduce the signified it ostensibly pursues, and that therefore nothing is to be gained by straining to make it do so: a suspicion of the signifier that can be traced as far back as the semiotic doctrine of the Taoist sage Zhuang Zǐ, in the fourth century BCE: 'Nets are for fish: catch the fish and forget the net; snares are for rabbits: catch the rabbit and forget the snare; words are for ideas: catch the idea and forget the words. Oh, where can I find somebody to talk with who has forgotten the words?'[12]

Some verses from Czesław Miłosz's 'On reading the Japanese poet Issa' admirably illustrate the multiplicity of interpretations, all equally admissible, that plurivalence as a stylistic resource permits. Is it really a Japanese landscape that is evoked in the haiku Miłosz quotes as an epigraph? Or is it not rather the Lithuanian

---

[11] The example refers specifically to the teaching of garden design, but Slawson quotes a general formulation of the principle in terms of 'high-context' and 'low-context' communication, the former 'one in which most of the information is . . . in the physical context or internalized in the person, while very little is in the coded, explicit . . . part of the message', and the latter the exact opposite (Edward T. Hall, *Beyond Culture* (Garden City, NY, 1976), 79). McLuhan's 'cool media' could thus be defined as those in which high-context communication is the norm.

[12] Zhuang Zǐ, ch. 26 (my translation). Zhuang Zǐ (otherwise Chuang-tzu), as we saw in the preceding chapter, was equally suspicious of the reality behind the ideas the signifiers were meant to catch, and, having once dreamt he was a butterfly, wondered afterwards whether he was not in fact a butterfly now dreaming it was Zhuang Zǐ (ibid., ch. 2).

village where he spent summer holidays as a young man, among real, solid, known people, all with names of their own? Or Berkeley, California, where he now lives, surrounded by other people with other names, no longer Polish but American? It is of course all these places, or any other that the poet's, or any individual reader's, memory or imagination allows him to glimpse through the white mists of ambiguity—or of San Francisco Bay:

> *A good world—*
> *dew drops fall*
> *by ones, by twos*

A few strokes of ink and there it is.
Great stillness of white mist,
waking up in the mountains,
geese calling,
a well hoist creaking,
and the droplets forming on the eaves.

Or perhaps that other house.
The invisible ocean,
fog until noon
dripping in a heavy rain from the boughs of the redwoods,
sirens droning below on the bay.

Poetry can do that much and no more.
For we cannot really know the man who speaks

.   .   .   .

And whether this is the village of Szlembark
above which we used to find salamanders in the wet grass,
gaily coloured like the dresses of Teresa Roszkowska,
or another continent and different names.
Kotarbiński, Zawada, Erin, Melanie.
No people in this poem. As if it subsisted
by the very disappearance of places and people . . .[13]

The paradigm of the contrary tendency in Western languages would be that hottest of hot media, French, lovingly shaped over the past five centuries by a tireless passion for lucidity and exactness. It is precisely this that accounts for the frivolous infatuation of a Barthes, in his eagerness to discredit *la clarté française* as a supposed instrument of economic subjugation jealously monopolized by the

---

[13] Miłosz 1988: 30 f.: 'Czytając japońskiego poetę Issa (1762–1826)'; full Polish text in the Textual Appendix. Issa was the third of the canonical haiku masters, preceded by Bashō and Buson and followed by Shiki.

bourgeoisie, with the supposed 'empty signifiers' of Japanese language and social organization.[14]

Less experienced than Eastern literature in the relentless pursuit of ultimate concision, that of the West—the product of languages which, if not always with the single-minded devotion of French, have in general aimed at unequivocal intelligibility—only occasionally manages to combine terseness and inclusiveness to the same extent as the following micropoems from widely distant parts of Europe.

One of Giorgos Seferis's 'Sixteen haikus' (88) neatly captures the precise moment when a reflection is eclipsed:

Στάξε στὴ λίμνη	Spill in the lake
μόνο μιὰ στάλα κρασί	only a drop of wine
καὶ σβήνει ὁ ἥλιος.	and the sun goes out.

Giuseppe Ungaretti's best-known poem, on the other hand—the distich 'Mattina' (65), the original title of which was 'Cielo e mare'—shows the poet mirroring himself simultaneously in the immensity of both:

> m'illumino
> d'immenso

Of the two themes, *cielo* and *mare*, the celestial or solar one is suggested onomatopoeically by the sparkling of the front vowels *mi . . . mi* in m'i*llu*mino; the marine by the unfurling of the long syllables *im-men*; and the horizon that simultaneously unites and divides them, by the inversion *mi/im*. In the definitive title, '*Matti*na', the initial *m* and the stressed *i*, followed by *n*, anticipate the *m*s, *i*s, and *n*s of the poem itself.

Another distich also by Ungaretti (145), a simple *imagiste* snapshot in the Poundian manner, records a murky lake's 'offence' in failing to reflect the heavens:

> Inanella erbe un rivolo,
> Un lago torvo il glauco cielo offende.

---

[14] See my '*Império dos Signos* ou Imperialismo dos Significantes?' Far from being empty, the signifiers of Japanese (and Chinese) are so packed with a multiplicity of different meanings that the problem—to the extent that it is one—is to choose among them. On the medieval Western esteem (then shared even by France) for 'la expresión enigmática, capaz de movilizar . . . la inteligencia del lector y forzarla . . . a un trabajo de creación interpretativa', see Rico, 688.

A brook makes ringlets in the grass,
A turbid lake offends the glaucous sky.

Yvette Centeno, in 'Shepperton' (1984: 46), recalls the solitude of the Thames on a cloudy November night:

no rio	in the river
só peixes solitários	only lone fish
só uma lua	only a moon
a que nunca se vê	one never sees
só barcos sem pessoas	only boats with no people
só água sem maré	only water with no tide

The central word in the poem, *nunca* ('never'), with exactly the same number of syllables before as after it, is the axis of the obsessive pulse of phonemes of deprivation—*só, solitário, só, só, sem, só, sem*—which echo the endless lapping of tiny waves against the deserted landing-stage. Leyla Perrone-Moisés has called *sem* ('without') 'a preposição Zen *par excellence*'; and Michael Riffaterre, studying the Symbolist motif of the mirror without backing, has shown that *sans*, in the set phrase 'miroir sans tain', works as a semantically autonomous 'sign of lack', evoking the blurred images produced by an imperfect reflecting surface.[15] The solitary fish of Centeno's nocturnal meditation, as invisible as the moon behind its veil of cloud, only give away their presence by the ripples they leave in their wake, thus revealing that this dark mirror too, like the old pond in Bashō's most famous haiku, conceals an unexpected dimension of depth.

Paul Celan, in three intense and dramatic lines (1978: 74) equating human beings, in an almost Buddhist manner, with lofty poplar trees, speaks of other dark waters mirroring them to their death amid the paradoxical radiance of a black reflection:

Ihr hohen Pappeln—Menschen dieser Erde!
Ihr schwarzen Teiche Glücks—ihr spiegelt sie zu Tode!
Ich sah dich, Schwester, stehn in diesem Glanze.

Celan was of course a notoriously hermetic poet. If inclusiveness as well as terseness is taken to be a condition of successful condensation, it must be granted that this poem, in omitting or suppressing the no doubt too harrowingly autobiographical clues that could have

---

[15] See respectively Perrone-Moisés, 130, and Michael Riffaterre, *Semiotics of Poetry* (1978; 2nd edn., London, 1980), 32–9.

made it more accessible (the poet, who had no sister, called by that name a friend who died in Auschwitz) has sacrificed inclusiveness— perhaps even intelligibility—for the sake of intensity.

In Borges, on the contrary, the essential biographical datum—that of his own blindness—is never far from the surface. His poem 'Los espejos' (ii. 192) is inclusive in the further sense that it amounts almost to a compendium of the metaphysics of mirrors, which he contends exist, like shadows, only to remind man that he is no more than a vain reflection: 'para que el hombre sienta que es reflejo / y vanidad'.

The East, too—whether Buddhist, Taoist, or Shintoist—is well known to set little store by the individual self; and it may not be without significance that in every one of the 'mirror poems' we have seen up to this point—Western no less than Eastern—it is not the figure of the poet himself that is reflected but what is above, behind, or around him: so to speak, his context in the natural world. The Portuguese poet David Mourão-Ferreira (1985: 14) synthesizes this attitude in 'Templo Xintoísta':

Aqui aprende a pedra	Here the stone learns
a ser igual à flor	to be equal to the flower
Aqui a flor se adestra	Here the flower trains
a ser igual ao pássaro	to be equal to the bird
E nós a ser por dentro	And we to be, within,
pássaro pedra flor	bird stone flower
noutra onda do Tempo	on another wavelength of Time
noutra espécie de Espaço	in another species of Space

Curiously, this last couplet contains effects not dissimilar to those in Ungaretti's 'Mattina', both in the prolonging of the wave, represented by the long sounds *nd* and *mp* in *onda* and *Tempo*[16] (foreshadowed by *aprende* and the *nt* of *dentro*), and in the expansion of Space suggested by the reiterated whistling of the sibilants *s*, *ss*, *c*, and *ç*, throughout the poem.

Seferis was only one of a number of Western poets of his own and succeeding generations to be attracted to the haiku, with its capacity for condensation similar but superior to that of the typical folk

---

[16] The onomatopoeic combination of nasal + occlusive to suggest rolling or undulating motion (a constant in Portuguese from the 13th to the 20th c.: cf. Reckert 1984), is as old as Homer's line (*Odyssey*, 11. 598), admired by Aristotle (*Rhetoric* 12–34), about the stone of Sisyphus rolling downhill.

couplets of Greece, or the Portuguese quadras cultivated (with in-
different success) by Pessoa. Antonio Machado, Borges, Mourão-
Ferreira, and Centeno, as well as Seferis, have all themselves written
haikus.[17] But it is the Greek poet who, thanks to our acquaintance
with his Midsummer Night poem, has provided us with what is
perhaps a unique opportunity to observe *in fieri* the actual process of
condensation whose end product is a haiku. In this one, another of
his "Δεκαέξι Χαϊ-καϊ" (90), he distils the essence of the longer
poem to show us once again the same archetypal woman at a later
stage, when the destiny she foresaw has been fulfilled:

Συλλογισμένο	Pensive
τὸ στῆθος της βαρύ	her breasts heavy
μὲς στὸν καθρέφτη.	in the mirror.[18]

REPERCUSSAE IMAGINIS UMBRA

Unlike that of the East (or of the Western mirror poems we have
been studying), the mainstream Western tradition, flowing from
Ovid, is individualistic when not indeed egoistic. Or more precisely,
narcissistic, since the first recorded victim of an identity crisis
was Narcissus himself, plunging his arms 'in medias... aquas' in
his frenzy to embrace the mere shadow of a reflected image: the
'repercussae... imaginis umbra'. A haiku by Machado (268) en-
capsulates his dilemma:

Ese tu Narciso	That Narcissus of yours
ya no se ve en el espejo	can't see himself any more
porque es el espejo mismo.	in the glass: he *is* the glass.

And his example, as another micropoem by Yvette Centeno (1984:
64) implies, is still valid as a warning not to jump to conclusions:

não chego a saber	I can't make out
quem és	who you are:

---

[17] The most recent work of Centeno, who has long been attracted to the Chinese
Taoist tradition, is *Os 64 Trigramas*, included in the forthcoming *O Templo Interior* and
consisting of haikus, regular and 'false' (cf. n. 22, below), with references to Bashō and
Zen, but with a title alluding to the 64 hexagrams (derived from 8 trigrams) of the
Taoist *Yì Jing*.

[18] The original states what translation can only hint at: that it is the breasts
themselves that are 'pensive'.

| tu mesmo | yourself, |
| ou reflexo meu? | or my own reflection? |

So like the story of Narcissus and at the same time so different that it might be called its mirror image is the legend that tells how Lǐ Bó, on one of his almost programmatic binges, drowned while attempting to embrace not his own reflection (as could have been expected, given his notorious egocentrism), but that of the moon in the river. But as Empson says—in a poem aptly entitled 'Bacchus'[19]—who can tell if even Narcissus may not, as in our previous mirror poems, 'use his pool as mirror for the skies?' The Taoist quest for the *elixir vitae* often led adepts who felt pressed for time to experiment with the short-cut of alcohol; and drunkenness in China (like the 'simplicity' of the Court fool in the West) was also a convenient pretext, sanctioned since the third century by the example of the celebrated Seven Sages of the Bamboo Grove, for otherwise inadmissible irreverences and disrespect for Authority. In Lǐ's case it may be supposed that instead of sinking he ascended directly to the heaven of those Taoist Immortals to whom he was habitually compared; for in the illusory world of mirrors, as in that of the devotees of Hermes Trismegistus, that which is above is as that which is below.

Thus, in a poem by Borges (i. 67), the tops of a boat's masts lose themselves among the stars, while the stars in turn descend like doves 'from the patio where the cistern is an inverted tower between two skies'. This interpenetration of earth and sky, in which the two end by becoming mutually and inextricably fused, recalls, in addition to Yvette Centeno's nocturne beside the Thames and certain drawings of Escher's,[20] those verses from the *Romancero gitano* (GL 413) in which Lorca speaks of

Un solo pez en el agua	A single fish in the water
que a las dos Córdobas junta:	that joins the two Cordovas:
blanda Córdoba de juncos,	soft Cordova of reeds,
Córdoba de arquitectura.	Cordova of architecture.

Lorca, as a *Granadino*, might equally well have thought of the Patio of the Myrtles in the Alhambra, where the tremulous light of the candles in the galleries on either side of the central reflecting pool,

---

[19] *Collected Poems* (1955; London, 1984), 43.
[20] Such as 'Three Worlds', 'Puddle', or 'Rippled Surface', in Hofstadter 1979: 246 and 256 f. as well as in Escher's *Complete Graphic Works* (London, 1992).

flickering in the water ruffled by the breeze and by the invisible fish beneath the surface, collaborates in belying the deceptive solidity of the surrounding architecture, and with it the whole transitory universe of phenomena.

Both Cordova and Granada, if no longer part of the Middle East, are still at least middling Eastern in spirit; and while this motif (along with its philosophical implications) appears only sporadically in the West, it has the status of a topos in the East because of the traditional recognition of the mirror as what is now called an interface: a kind of membrane, permeable from both sides, that both joins and separates them, as in Buson's haiku about the hazy moon in the river, or Sora's about the stars and the raindrops. Or this one, by Onitsura (1660–1738):

> Tobu ayu no   In the depths of the leaping trout's
> soko ni kumo yuku   river, look: the clouds
> nagare ka na.   are flowing!
>
> *Hk* iii. 253

Going back now more than a thousand years before Onitsura, here—in his less familiar role as poet—is Yáng Dì, last emperor of the Suí dynasty of China at the beginning of the seventh century: that same emperor whose Magic Mountain or 'island' made such a profound impression on the Japanese envoys to his court:

> [The] evening river [is] smooth [and] untroubled;
> [the] spring flowers [are] just [in] full bloom.
> Flowing waves go, taking [the] moon;
> Tide waters come, bringing [the] stars.[21]

Those stars which a millennium later in Sora's haiku were to merge with the raindrops, in the emperor's quatrain have become the heavenly equivalents of the flowers, and these the earthly counterparts of the stars. But stars and flowers alike, when their time comes, will be borne away just as the moon now is. And as was the emperor himself when his grandiose public works programme had brought ruin to the imperial treasury and a premature end to the Suí dynasty, ushering in the Táng, and the six hundred years' Golden Age that

[21] Hans H. Frankel, *The Flowering Plum and the Palace Lady* (New Haven, Conn., 1976), 15.

was to produce the first two of the accepted 'three perfect creations' of Chinese art: Táng poetry and Sòng painting (Míng porcelain being traditionally regarded as the third).

Heaven and Earth, then, are seen to be at base merely two interchangeable dreams. Once this is accepted—and it very early was in the East—it even becomes possible to be light-hearted about it, as in this haiku by Ryōta (1707–87):

> Mizu no tsuki   The moon in the water
> mondori utsute   turns a somersault
> nagare keri.   and drifts away.
>
> *Hk* iii. 376

No less illusory than the rest of the universe of mere phenomena, obviously, is personal identity; this is the message of the early seventeenth-century Chinese poet-sage Hóng Zì Chéng (*Hk* i. 72):

> Hearing [the] sound of [a] bell [in the] silent night
> [I] wake [from a] dream within [this] dream.
> Seeing [the] shadow of [the] moon [in the] clear pool
> [I] glimpse [the] self behind [this] self.

In the next-to-last line I have purposely translated the character *yǐng* as 'shadow', rather than 'reflection', to emphasize the fact that Chinese (like Japanese—and like Ovid's Latin) makes no distinction between the two.

Yvette Centeno (1974: 404) goes still further than the Míng poet, denying reality even to the 'self behind the self', which is revealed as yet another mask, in infinite regress:

> Que máscara é essa
> que por trás das pessoas se adivinha?

In contrast, one of Borges's characters says, on the eve of death, 'In the mirror of this night I see at last / my unsuspected and eternal face' (ii. 246), while on another occasion the poet himself calls death 'the mirror / in which I shall see no one, or another' (ii. 217).

Is there, then, only one way out of the self, with its irremediable solitude? The transcending of that shadowy and insubstantial self is no doubt a prerequisite to the discovery of the Bergsonian *moi fondamental*, which Antonio Machado (273) says cannot be actively sought, because it is only to be found in the form of the other:

> No es el yo fundamental   It's not the *moi fondamental*
> eso que busca el poeta,   the poet seeks,
> sino el tú esencial.   but the essential *you*.

That is, the other as complement, in love. For Machado's *persona* Abel Martín (313), 'the great incentive to love ... [is] the metaphysical thirst for what is essentially other.... The lover would renounce, in love, whatever is a mirror, because he would begin to love in the beloved what by its essence can never reflect his own image.'[22] As Yvette Centeno implies (1974: 151), love cannot be the reflection of the self in others, but only its continuation:

> O amor: continuação nos outros
> de nós mesmos.

This definition is confirmed in a triptych of 'false haikus' by Mourão-Ferreira (1980: 24), the last with a pair of symbols recognizable as *yin* and *yáng*:[23]

> Ao meio-dia em ponto   At midday sharp
> entre a sombra e o corpo   between shadow and body
> o encontro   the encounter
>
> A seguir ao sol posto   Just after sundown
> entre a sombra e a sombra   between shadow and shadow
> reencontro   re-encounter
>
> Nada menos efémero   Nothing less ephemeral
> que uma taça e um ceptro   than a chalice and a sceptre
> no deserto   in the desert

This defiant affirmation of permanence—a challenge hurled into the desert of solitude—sorts well with a haiku by the last of the four great masters of the genre, Masaoka Shiki:

---

[22] Machado, a true Symbolist poet (as J. M. Aguirre, refuting critical dogma, has shown), did not overlook the motif of the *miroir sans tain* and the world of tedium that strips it of its silver: 'mundo sin encanto.../ que borra el misterioso azogue del cristal' (109); cf. Aguirre 1982: 207–10; 333 ff.

[23] Or rather (since the haiku is a Japanese form), *in* and *yō*. By a coincidence the poet was unaware of, the Japanese for 'shadow', *kage* (which we have already met), can be written with either of two characters, one of which is the same as *in* (*yin*). Mourão-Ferreira's own description of his haikus as 'falsos' refers to the irregular syllabic scheme 7—7—4 (instead of 5—7—5); but genuine (and indeed classical) Japanese haikus exist with schemes of 6—8—5, 8—7—5, 5—10—5, and even 10—7—5 (cf. *Hk* i. 375).

Akikaze ya   Autumn wind . . .
ikite aimiru   We're alive! We see each other,
nare to ware.   you and I!
Hk iii. 314

A NEW PARADIGM?

From the collection of micropoems we have been examining, what general conclusions can be drawn? First of all, that a radically concentrated and condensed poetic form automatically imposes, or at least favours, a number of stylistic and rhetorical procedures such as allusion, paradox, ellipsis, ambiguity, aphoristic form, the symbol in preference to metaphor or simile, etc. Second, that such procedures, and the condensation itself that they permit or facilitate, correspond to certain habits of thought, feeling, and expression that are historically (though of course not necessarily) associated with the East, and constitute as a whole a poetic language that, like any other language, not only reflects but also moulds and conditions the thought it expresses. And third, that it therefore follows that this language, when adopted by the West, perforce involves ways of thinking and feeling which, when not identical, are at least analogous to those that originally gave rise to it.

Among these the most significant is perhaps the privileging of relation over what is related: so to speak (in semiotic terms), of the axis of combination over that of selection; of syntax over the word. Or of the *Ruah* of Genesis—the Spirit, moving on the face of the waters—over the static *Logos* of the Gospel.[24] In short, the privileging of *operation* over *substance*, since as Dante said,

Ogne forma sustanzïal . . .

. . . .

specifica vertute ha in sé colletta,
la qual sanza operar non è sentita,
né si dimostra mai che per effetto . . .[25]

It is not enough to affirm, with Mallarmé, that a poem is made of words: there is room for so few of them in the seventeen syllables of a Japanese haiku, or the twenty of a classical Chinese jué jù, that

---

[24] Pre-Vulgate translations of the Greek NT (followed by Erasmus) render Λόγος not by *Verbum* but by *Sermo*: an altogether more dynamic concept.
[25] *Purg.* XVIII. 49–53: 'Every substantial form . . . has within itself a specific virtue, / which without operating is not perceived, / and never shows itself but by effect.'

the current of meaning has to percolate imperceptibly through the interstices between them (and if Mallarmé himself spaced them out with such care in the 'Coup de dés', it was surely to facilitate just that invisible circulation).

But MacLeish's formula 'A poem should not mean, but be' will not quite do either; because as well as meaning and being, the Oriental micropoem professes also to *operate*, setting up, like Bashō's frog, a wake or bow-wave that can go on expanding indefinitely in the reader's mind. It is for this reason that it constitutes a textbook example of Umberto Eco's *opera aperta*; and this timeless and accidental 'modernity' (or even modishness) may in part account for the attraction it exerts on some contemporary Western poets.

The way from a quaint 'Far East' (far from where?) to the real East Asia is proving a long and rocky road; that it is not yet altogether adequately signposted is clear from the proliferation of martial arts, do-it-yourself acupuncture, instant Zen, and the *Yi Jing* as a parlour game. In so far as the road map has been properly read, however, it now seems possible to recognize a development akin to Thomas Kuhn's scientific paradigm shift. The relativistic and anti-positivist tendency that has come to dominate the sciences in the course of the century increasingly characterizes the arts as well. If physics suppresses the frontiers between bodies ('substantial forms', Dante would call them), reconciling itself to the impossibility of distinguishing between them, or between them and their 'operation' (are they particles? waves? superstrings?), or of specifying simultaneously their position in both time and space—or, for that matter, of tracking the chaos of a tornado in Texas back to its ultimate source in the fluttering of a butterfly in Brazil—this new approach to the reality 'out there' has analogues in the new philosophies and psychologies that dissolve, both synchronically and diachronically, the human personality; in Picasso's simultaneous multiple perspectives and the unfocused faces in the paintings of Francis Bacon (both implicitly subversive of temporality); in the silences of John Cage (under the influence of Japanese music); or in the alternately soaring and plummetting tonal intervals of a Honegger or a Berio, among which the musical syntax floats as the ether used once to float among the stars.

In psychology, at least, it might be thought that the apparent new departures represent essentially a return, *mutatis mutandis*, to the mental schemes of the pre-Renaissance West: schemes which (like those still characteristic of Japan, where they have never been abandoned) define and value the human being much more in terms of his role in society than as an individual. At the interface of philosophy and the arts, deconstruction disperses personal identity into 'a kind of Magellanic cloud of interactive and changing energies ..., moments of compacted consciousness..., around an even more indeterminate central region or black hole of the...unconscious' (Steiner 1986: 11).

Where the arts specifically are concerned, however, only a radical change of *Weltanschauung*, I think, can explain the confluence of the Eastern thematic, symbolic, and stylistic mainstream with the work of poets who, like Celan, owe little or nothing to its direct influence, and have reached the same destination by other roads such as, for example, the cabbala and Hasidism. If Celan's refutation of absolute Space[26] recalls Taoist relativism, that of Time is no more uncompromising in Borges, and that of the time-bounded self no more total in any Buddhist sage, than in half a dozen chilling lines by another poet, born only thirty miles from Celan (and ten years later), but who chose to write in another language.

Paul Celan (1920–70) was born in Cernăuţi—earlier Czernowitz, and now the Ukrainian Černovtsy—and Dan Pagis (1930–86) in Rădăuţi: two towns of the Austro-Hungarian crown land of Bukovina incorporated in Rumania[27] in 1918, and whose population of Rumanians, Ukrainians, Austrians, and Jews had continued to use German as the *lingua franca* of culture.[28] Both survivors of the Nazi extermination camps, Celan opted for Paris, while keeping German, and Pagis for Israel and Hebrew. The six short lines of his poem condense the whole history of human suffering, from Genesis to the

---

[26] The traces, in his late poems, of hermetic doctrines of silence and relative Space, and of the 17th-c. theosophist Jacob Böhme's concept of the *Ungrund* or bottomless abyss (which Celan also calls *Sternschlupf,* or 'star hole', evoking the black hole of astrophysics), are analysed in Centeno 1989.

[27] The Ceauşescu regime's attempt to impose the form *Romania* (traditionally the collective designation for the original Romance-speaking areas of Europe) having failed everywhere but in the English-speaking countries, I have retained the normal English name.

[28] The aura of social prestige that clung to German among local Jews is brought out in *For Every Sin* (tr. Jeffrey M. Green (London, 1989)), by the Israeli novelist Aharon Appelfeld, also a *Czernowitzer.* For a vivid evocation of the simultaneously cosmopolitan and provincial Cernăuţi of *l'entre deux guerres* see Gregor von Rezzori's ironically titled *Memoirs of an Anti-Semite* (= *Memoiren eines Antisemiten* (Munich, 1979)), tr. Joachim Neugroschel and the author (London, 1983), and its sequel *The*

Apocalypse, in a single unfinished message 'Written in Pencil in the Sealed Goods Van':[29]

כָּאן בַּמִּשְׁלוֹחַ הַזֶּה

אֲנִי חַוָּה

עִם הֶבֶל בְּנִי

אִם תִּרְאוּ אֶת בְּנִי הַגָּדוֹל

קַיִן בֶּן אָדָם

תַּגִּידוּ לוֹ שֶׁאֲנִי

Kan mišloah hazé	Here in this carload
aní Havá	I Eve
im Hébel bni	with my son Abel
im tirú et bni hagadól	If you see my elder son
Qayín ben Adám	Cain the son of Adam
tegídu lo še aní	tell him I

To make poems after Auschwitz, Theodor Adorno held, was barbarous. For Celan, on the contrary, poetry meant a way of breathing again, a proclamation, from within mortality itself, of the eternal: 'Dichtung: das kann eine Atemwende bedeuten...: diese Unendlichsprechung von lauter Sterblichkeit' (1961: 81; 85).

Adorno's outburst, with its unselfconscious revelation of ignorance of the very nature of poetry, is quite likely nothing more than an echo of Lenin's well-publicized view that in a society as cruel and corrupt as that of the tsars it was not possible to listen to Beethoven. In any case there are those, like Celan and Pagis, who have earned the right to think the making of poetry even more necessary after the Holocaust than before, and assumed in full awareness the obligation to make it.[30] And not only to make it, but to make it in accordance with the canons of the new (and fortuitously 'Oriental') paradigm.

Snows of Yesteryear (= *Blumen im Schnee* (Munich, 1989)), tr. H. F. Broch de Rothermann (London, 1990).

[29] *The Penguin Book of Hebrew Verse*, ed. T. Carmi (Harmondsworth, 1981), 575.

[30] It has been observed that the young Adorno, still undecided whether to become a philosopher or a composer, already betrayed his lack of 'the artist's feeling for physical life, for its sounds, smells and surfaces' (R. Jennett, reviewing Adorno's book on Alban

In the context of that paradigm, and in the face of the responsibility and seriousness of such poets, the narcissistic *japoniaiserie* of a Barthes seems a provincial anachronism, disagreeable less because it plays with serious things than because it does not know how to play seriously: because narcissism is the negation of that forcible, painful, but necessary splitting of the self that—as Borges and Machado saw—it is the mirror's natural mission to effect; while Borges's own *sombras chinescas* represent that specialized form of *coincidentia oppositorum*, the paradox: a highly responsible and serious verbal game (and one that, as it happens, is an integral part of the theory and practice of both Zen and Tao).

In the playful verses García Lorca wrote for his small goddaughter back in the Twenties, and which are prefixed to this chapter as an epigraph, the *caballeros enlevitados* and their tall blonde wives gaze at the doll-like Chinese maiden with the fan, her world so alien they can feel only idle curiosity. But even in Lorca's still unabashedly picturesque toy poem, we may be sure that whoever it is the *señorita del abanico* sees reflected in the cool river as she looks over the edge of the bridge without railings, it will not be Madam Butterfly. The *imaginis repercussae umbra* that looks back at her is more likely to resemble the eighth-century Japanese

> Maiden walking alone on the great vermilion bridge
> over the Katashiwa, trailing her crimson skirt,
> her cloak dyed blue with mountain indigo.
>
> Has she a husband young as the green grass?
> Or does she sleep as lonely as an acorn?
>
> How I wish I could ask her...
> (Oh, not to know her bower!)[31]

Whereof one may not speak, thereof must one remain silent? I have called the new paradigm welcomed by many poets in the West a 'fortuitously' Oriental one. It is not always so. If Miłosz, for instance, appears to mistrust the nebulous vagueness of Issa's haikus at the same time as he is attracted by the expressive advantages

Berg in *TLS* 27 Feb. 1992); cf., above, Ch. 2 n. 36. After reading Celan, however, Adorno himself felt obliged to concede that in some circumstances it might, after all, still be permissible to write poetry (cf. Amy Colin, *Paul Celan: Holograms of Darkness* (Bloomington, Ind., 1991), 17).

[31] *MYS* 658. By now we are unlikely to be surprised to find again, even in a very different context, a man who is 'dying to find out where it is' a woman has her 'bower' (cf. the Alentejan quadra transcribed above in Ch. 2, n. 27).

of that 'great stillness of white mist', his own commitment to Orientalism (in a quite non-Saidian and non-appropriative sense) had in fact already been assumed from the moment when, faced with 'the difficulty of finding a formula for the experience of elemental cruelty', and feeling, like Adorno, that 'next to the atrocious facts, the very idea of literature seems indecent, and one doubts whether certain zones of reality can ever be the subject of poems or novels' (1983: 21), he concluded that since the language of poetry could never confront the world of genocide and the camps head-on, he must learn to confront it, so to speak, slantwise. It is this he gives us to understand when he confesses how—precisely because he has gone '*beyond* chrysanthemums and November mist'—

> . . . I changed
> My opinion about poetry, and how it came to be
> That I think of myself today as one among the many
> Merchants and craftsmen of the Empire of Japan
> Composing verses about cherry blossoms,
> Chrysanthemums, and the full moon.[32]

---

[32] Miłosz 1981–8: 47: 'Nie więcej' ('No more'); full Polish text in the Textual Appendix.

POSTSCRIPT

The publishers have asked what led me to write this book. When I was twenty I said I proposed to spend my declining years translating Chinese quatrains into Portuguese. Later concluding that translation is impossible (a conclusion borne out by my attempts in the foregoing pages), I spent the next forty teaching, not poetry—another impossible proposition—but some possible ways of reading and thinking about it in its Iberian and Latin American varieties. In the meantime its East Asian manifestations have remained a permanent if semi-clandestine obsession.

The book is thus the result of a lifetime's love affair with the poetry of four languages: with the subtly nuanced phonemes of Portuguese and the springtime freshness of thirteenth-century cantigas; with the energy and sententiousness of Castilian and the tenderness of sixteenth-century villancicos; with the unemphatic cadences of Japanese and the fastidious discretion of haiku and tanka in their probing of the most evanescent moods and feelings; and with the unique concreteness and particularity of that philosophically most fascinating of all languages, Chinese, that allow it, in the jué jù, to come so near its unattainable goal: by saying nothing, to say all.

TEXTUAL APPENDIX

ANONYMOUS

Η Χιώτισσα

Κάτω 'ς τὸ' 'γιαλό', κάτω 'ς τὸ περιγιάλι,
—Κάτω 'ς τὸ' 'γιαλὸ' κοντή,
Νεραντζοῦλα φουντωτή.

Πλένουν Χιώτισσαι(ς), πλένουν παπαδοποῦλαι(ς),
—Πλένει Χιώτισσα κοντή,
Λεμονίτσα φουντωτή.

Καὶ μία Χιώτισσα, μικρὴ παπαδοποῦλα,
—Καὶ μία Χιώτισσα κοντή,
Νεραντζοῦλα φουντωτή.

Πλένει κι' ἁπλώνει καὶ μὲ τὸν ἄμμο' παίζει,
—Πλένει κι' ἁπλώνει, κοντή,
Λεμονίτσα φουντωτή.

Κι' ἄρμενο' περ(ν)ᾷ χρνσό', παλαμισμένο',
—Κι' ἄρμενο' περ(ν)ᾷ, κοντή,
Νεραντζοῦλα φουντωτή.

Ἔλαμψε κι' αὐτό, κ' ἔλαμψαν τὰ κουπία του,
—Ἔλαμψε κι' αὐτό, κοντή,
Λεμονίτσα φουντωτή.

'Φύσηξ' ὁ βορέας, μαῖστρος τραμουντάνα,
—'Φύσηξ' ὁ βορέας, κοντή,
Νεραντζοῦλα φουντωτή.

Κι' ἀνασήκωσε τὸ ποδοφούστανό' της,
—Κι' ἀνασήκωσε, κοντή,
Λεμονίτσα φουντωτή.

Καὶ τῆς 'φάνηκεν ὁ ποδαστράγαλός της,
—Καὶ τῆς 'φάνηκε, κοντή,
Νεραντζοῦλα φουντωτή.

Κ' ἔλαμψ' ὁ 'γιαλός, κ' ἔλαμψ' ὁ κόσμος ὅλος,
—Κ' ἔλαμψ' ὁ 'γιαλός, κοντή,
Λεμονίτσα φουντωτή.

JOÃO CABRAL DE MELO NETO

Escritos com o Corpo—III

Quando vestido unicamente
com a macieza nua dela,
não apenas sente despido:
sim, de uma forma mais completa.

Então, de fato, está despido,
senão dessa roupa que é ela.
Mas essa roupa nunca veste:
despe de uma outra mais interna.

É que o corpo quando se veste
de ela roupa, da seda ela,
nunca sente mais definido
como com as roupas de regra.

Sente ainda mais que despido:
pois a pele dele, secreta,
logo se esgarça, e eis que ele assume
a pele dela, que ela empresta.

Mas também a pele emprestada
dura bem pouco enquanto véstia:
com pouco, ela toda, também,
já se esgarça, se desespessa,

até acabar por nada ter
nem de epiderme nem de seda:
e tudo acabe confundido,
nudez comum, sem mais fronteira.

ZBIGNIEW HERBERT

Kamyk

kamyk jest stworzeniem
doskonałym

równy samemu sobie
pilnujący swych granic

wypełniony dokładnie
kamiennym sensem

o zapachu który niczego nie przypomina
niczego nie płoszy nie budzi pożądania

jego zapał i chłód
są słuszne i pełne godności

czuję ciężki wyrzut
kiedy go trzymam w dłoni
i ciało jego szlachetne
przenika fałszywe ciepło

 —Kamyki nie dają się oswoić
 do końca będą na nas patrzeć
 okiem spokojnym bardzo jasnym

HORIGUCHI DAIGAKU

風景

桃色の尖った屋根が　ああ　見えかくれ
島番の一つ家の尖った屋根が見えかくれ
こんもりした谷間の木蔭に
島のなかほど　おお　美学の中心
やさしい曲線がふつくらと三つに流れ
褐色の羊歯がしげつて
日当りのいい三角小島
牛乳の海に浮いた
ああ　美しい　やはらかい
うねり　波うち　また　よれる
ああ　女体の曲線は

CZESŁAW MIŁOSZ

Czytając Japońskiego Poetę Issa
(1762–1826)

Dobry świat: rosa
kapie po kropli,
po dwie.

Parę kresek tuszem i staje się.
Wielka cichość białej mgły,
przebudzenie w górach,
gęsi krzyczą,
żuraw skrzypi u studni,
krople z okapu chaty.

Albo może ten inny dom.
Niewidoczny ocean,
mgła do południa
rzęsistym deszczem kapiąca z gałęzi sekwoi,
syreny buczące w dole na zatoce.

Tyle może poezja ale nie więcej.
Bo nie wiadomo kim jest naprawdę ten kto mówi,
jakie jego ścięgna i kości,
porowatość skóry,
jak siebie czuje od środka.
I czy to jest wioska Szlembark
nad którą w mokrych trawach znajdowaliśmy salamandry
jaskrawe jak suknie Teresy Roszkowskiej,
czy inny kontynent i inne imiona.
Kotarbiński, Zawada, Erin, Melanie:
nikogo z ludzi w tym wierszu. Jakby trwał
samym zanikaniem okolic i ludzi.

Kukułka kuka
dla mnie, dla góry,
na zmianę.

Siedząc pod swoim daszkiem na skalnym progu,
słuchając jak szumi wodospad w parowie,
miał przed sobą fałdzistość leśnej góry
ze słońcem zachodzącym, które jej dotykało,

i myślał: jak to jest, że głos kukułki
zawsze zwraca się to tam, to tu,
mogłoby tego nie być w porządku rzeczy.

> *Nigdy nie zapominaj*
> *chodzimy nad piekłem*
> *oglądając kwiaty*

Wiedzieć i nie mówić:
tak się zapomina.
Co jest wymówione wzmacnia się.
Co nie jest wymówione zmierza do nieistnienia.
Język jest zaprzedany zmysłowi dotyku.
Ciepłem i miękkością trwa nasz ludzki rodzaj:
króliczek, niedźwiadek i kotek.

Tylko nie dygotanie o mroźnym świcie,
strach idącego dnia
i bicz dozorcy.
Tylko nie zima ulic
i na całej ziemi nikogo
i kara, świadomość.
Tylko nie

Nie Więcej

Powinienem powiedzieć kiedyś jak zmieniłem
Opinię o poezji i jak to się stało,
Że uważam się dzisiaj za jednego z wielu
Kupców i rzemieślników Cesarstwa Japonii
Układających wiersze o kwitnieniu wiśni,
O chryzantemach i pełni księżyca.

Gdybym ja mógł weneckie kurtyzany
Opisać, jak w podwórzu witką drażnią pawia
I z tkaniny jedwabnej, z perłowej przepaski
Wyłuskać ociężałe piersi, czerwonawą
Pręgę na brzuchu od zapięcia sukni,
Tak przynajmniej jak widział szyper galeonów
Przybyłych tego ranka z ładunkami złota;
I gdybym równocześnie mógł ich biedne kości
Na cmentarzu, gdzie bramę liże tłuste morze,
Zamknąć w słowie mocniejszym niż ostatni grzebień
Który w próchnie pod płytą, sam, czeka na światło

To bym nie zwątpił. Z opornej materii
Co da się zebrać? Nic, najwyżej piękno.
A wtedy nam wystarczyć muszą kwiaty wiśni
I chryzantemy i pełnia księżyca.

Ō-OKA MAKOTO

Kage no naka de

'Taikyoku ni aru hoshi to hoshi no kinchō ga
kono ippon no ki o odoraseru no yo',
Jūichigatsu no kiri to kiku no kanata kara kita
onna ga yū.

.   .   .

Kono ki wa Meiōsei ni aru boku no kokyō no
kogawa ni sodatta ki ni chigainai—
ano hoshi no mei no kodō ga
boku o sore no taikyoku ni tatsu ni suru
sakeya mo naku.

onna to boku no mae de
ippon no ki ga yuruyaka ni odotte iru.

影の中で

「対極にある星と星の緊張が
この一本の木を踊らせるのよ」
十一月の霧と菊の彼方から来た
女が言ふ。

海から湧いたやうに木は
露をびつしり幹に孕み
ときどき樹根を上に振りあげ
色とりどりの鳥の卵を払ひおとす
だが新しい曙はそのたびに来る。
この木は冥王星にある僕の故郷の
小川に育つた木にちがひない――
あの星の謎の鼓動が
僕をそれの対極に立つ星にする　避けやうもなく。

女と僕の前で
一本の木がゆるやかに踊つてゐる。

GIORGOS SEFERIS

Φωτιὲς Τοῦ Ἅη Γιάννη

Ἡ μοίρα μας χυμένο μολύβι δὲν μπορεῖ ν' ἀλλάξει
δὲν μπορεῖ νὰ γίνει τίποτε.
Ἔχυσαν τὸ μολύβι μέσα στὸ νερὸ κάτω ἀπὸ τ' ἀστέρια κι' ἅς
ἀνάβουν οἱ φωτιές.

Ἄν μείνεις γυμνὴ μπροστὰ στὸν καθρέφτη τὰ μεσάνυχτα
βλέπεις
βλέπεις τὸν ἄνθρωπο νὰ περνᾶ στὸ βάθος τοῦ καθρέφτη
τὸν ἄνθρωπο μέσα στὴ μοίρα σου ποὺ κυβερνᾶ τὸ κορμί σου
μέσα στὴ μοναξιὰ καὶ στὴ σιωπή, τὸν ἄνθρωπο
τῆς μοναξιᾶς καὶ τῆς σιωπῆς
κι' ἅς ἀνάβουν οἱ φωτιές.

Τὴν ὥρα ποὺ τέλειωσε ἡ μέρα καὶ δὲν ἄρχισε ἡ ἄλλη
τὴν ὥρα ποὺ κόπηκε ὁ καιρὸς
ἐκεῖνον ποὺ ἀπὸ τώρα καὶ πρὶν ἀπὸ τὴν ἀρχὴ κυβερνοῦσε τὸ
κορμί σου
πρέπει νὰ τὸν εὕρεις
πρέπει νὰ τὸν ζητήσεις γιὰ νὰ τὸν εὕρει τουλάχιστο
κάποιος ἄλλος, ὅταν θά 'χεις πεθάνει.

Εἶναι τὰ παιδιὰ ποὺ ἀνάβουν τὶς φωτιὲς καὶ φωνάζουν μπροστὰ
στὶς φλόγες μέσα στὴ ζεστὴ νύχτα (Μήπως ἔγινε ποτὲς φωτιὰ
ποὺ νὰ μὴν τὴν ἄναψε κάποιο παιδί, ὧ Ἡρόστρατε)
καὶ ρίχνουν ἀλάτι μέσα στὶς φλόγες γιὰ νὰ πλαταγίζουν (Πόσο
παράξενα μᾶς κοιτάζουν ξαφνικὰ τὰ σπίτια, τὰ χωνευτήρια
τῶν ἀνθρώπων, σὰν τὰ χαϊδέψει κάποια ἀνταύγεια).

Μὰ ἐσὺ ποὺ γνώρισες τὴ χάρη τῆς πέτρας πάνω στὸ
θαλασσόδαρτο βράχο
τὸ βράδι ποὺ ἔπεσε ἡ γαλήνη
ἄκουσες ἀπὸ μακριὰ τὴν ἀνθρώπινη φωνὴ τῆς μοναξιᾶς καὶ τῆς
σιωπῆς
μέσα στὸ κορμί σου
τὴ νύχτα ἐκείνη τοῦ Ἅη Γιάννη
ὅταν ἔσβησαν ὅλες οἱ φωτιές
καὶ μελέτησες τὴ στάχτη κάτω ἀπὸ τ' ἀστέρια.

WISŁAWA SZYMBORSKA

Rozmowa z kamieniem

Pukam do drzwi kamienia.
—To ja, wpuść mnie.
Chcę wejść do twego wnętrza,
rozejrzeć się dokoła,
nabrać ciebie jak tchu.

—Odejdź—mówi kamień.—
Jestem szczelnie zamknięty.
Nawet rozbite na części
bedziemy szczelnie zamknięte.
Nawet starte na piasek
nie wpuścimy nikogo.

Pukam do drzwi kamienia.
—To ja, wpuść mnie.
Przychodzę z ciekawości czystej.
Życie jest dla niej jedyną okazją.
Zamierzam przejść się po twoim pałacu,
a potem jeszcze zwiedzić liść i kroplę wody.
Niewiele czasu na to wszystko mam.
Moja śmiertelność powinna cię wzruszyć.

—Jestem z kamienia—mówi kamień—
i z konieczności muszę zachować powagę.
Odejdź stąd.
Nie mam mięśni śmiechu.

Pukam do drzwi kamienia.
—To ja, wpuść mnie.
Słyszałam, że są w tobie wielkie puste sale,
nie oglądane, piękne nadaremnie,
głuche, bez echa czyichkolwiek kroków.
Przyznaj, że sam niedużo o tym wiesz.

—Wielkie i puste sale—mówi kamień—
ale w nich miejsca nie ma.
Piękne, być może, ale poza gustem
twoich ubogich zmysłów.
Możesz mnie poznać, nie zaznasz mnie nigdy.

Całą powierzchnią zwracam się ku tobie,
a całym wnętrzem leżę odwrócony.

Pukam do drzwi kamienia.
—To ja, wpuść mnie.
Nie szukam w tobie przytułku na wieczność.
Nie jestem nieszczęśliwa.
Nie jestem bezdomna.
Mój świat jest wart powrotu.
Wejdę i wyjdę z pustymi rękami.
A na dowód, że byłam prawdziwie obecna,
nie przedstawię niczego prócz słów,
którym nikt nie da wiary.

—Nie wejdziesz—mówi kamień.—
Brak ci zmysłu udziału.
Żaden zmysł nie zastąpi ci zmysłu udziału.
Nawet wzrok wyostrzony aż do wszechwidzenia
nie przyda ci się na nic bez zmysłu udziału.
Nie wejdziesz, masz zaledwie zamysł tego zmysłu,
ledwie jego związek, wyobraźnię.

Pukam do drzwi kamienia.
—To ja, wpuść mnie.
Nie mogę czekać dwóch tysięcy wieków
na wejście pod twój dach.

—Jeżeli mi nie wierzysz—mówi kamień—
zwróć się do liścia, powie to, co ja.
Do kropli wody, powie to, co liść.
Na koniec spytaj włosa z własnej głowy.
Śmiech mnie rozpiera, śmiech, olbrzymi śmiech,
którym śmiać się nie umiem.

Pukam do drzwi kamienia.
—To ja, wpuść mnie.
—Nie mam drzwi—mówi kamień.

TAKAMURA KŌTARŌ

……パルテノンや、ノオトルダムが鼻についたら、

チャウチンも、フジヤマも、

広重も春信も芭蕉も蕪村も、……

それや白紙の贅もいいでせう。

タンカも、ハイカイも、

御勝手次第におつまみなさい。　……

あなたと一緒に風流遊びは出来ませんよ。　……

安つぼい早悟りの大道へ坐らせようとしても、

どうも失敬しますよ。　……

ほんとを言ふと、

──ジャポン、ジャポン、ジャポン、ジャポン、ジャポン──

ああ、うるさいんです。

Select Bibliography

(Excluding works fully identified in the text and notes)

ABBOT, G. F. (1900), *Songs of Modern Greece* (Cambridge).

ABRAMS, M. H. (1971), *Natural Supernaturalism: Tradition and Revolution in Romantic Literature* (New York).

ADAM, MICHAEL (1980), *Womankind: A Celebration* (London).

AGUIRRE, J. M. (1965), *Ensayo para un estudio del tema amoroso en la primitiva lírica castellana* (Saragossa).

—— (1982), *Antonio Machado, poeta simbolista* (1973; 2nd edn., Madrid).

—— and HAUF, A. (1969), 'El simbolismo mágico-erótico de "El infante Arnaldos"', *Romanische Forschungen*, 81: 1/2, pp. 89–118.

AHL, FREDERICK (1985), *Metaformations: Soundplay and Wordplay in Ovid and Other Classical Poets* (Ithaca, NY).

ALÍN, JOSÉ MARÍA (1968), *El cancionero español de tipo tradicional* (Madrid).

ALONSO, DÁMASO (1946), *La poesía de San Juan de la Cruz* (1942; Madrid). Repr. in *Obras completas*, ii (Madrid, 1973).

—— (1958), 'Un siglo más para la poesía española' (1950; 2nd edn.) in *De los siglos oscuros al de Oro* (Madrid).

—— (1970), *Hijos de la ira* (1944), ed. E. L. Rivers (Barcelona).

—— (1989), *Poesía española: Ensayo de métodos y límites estilísticos* (1950), in *Obras completas*, ix (Madrid).

—— and RECKERT, STEPHEN (1958), *Vida y obra de Medrano*, ii (Madrid).

ALVAR, MANUEL (1966), *Poesía tradicional de los judíos españoles* (Mexico City).

ARBIB, MICHAEL A. (1985), *In Search of the Person* (Amherst, Mass.).

ASENSIO, EUGENIO (1970), *Poética y realidad en el cancionero peninsular de la Edad Media* (2nd edn., Madrid).

AUERBACH, ERICH (1959), '*Figura*' (1938), in *Scenes from the Drama of European Literature* (New York).

BACHELARD, GASTON (1967), *La Poétique de l'espace* (1957; 5th edn., Paris).

BANDEIRA, MANUEL (1958), *Poesia e Prosa* (Rio de Janeiro).

BAUSANI, A. (with PAGLIARO, A.) (1960), *Storia della letteratura persiana* (Milan).

BLACKER, CARMEN (1975), *The Catalpa Bow: A Study of Shamanistic Practices in Japan* (London).

BORGES, JORGE LUIS (1989), *Obras completas*, 3 vols. (Buenos Aires).

BOWRA, C. M. (1962), *Primitive Song* (London).

BRENAN, GERALD (1957), *The Literature of the Spanish People* (New York).

BROOKE-ROSE, CHRISTINE (1958), *A Grammar of Metaphor* (London).

CABRAL DE MELO NETO, JOÃO (1968), *Poesias Completas 1940–1965* (Rio de Janeiro).

CALVINO, ITALO (1984), *Collezione di sabbia* (Rome).

CAMÕES, LUÍS VAZ DE (1980), *Os Lusíadas* (Lisbon, 1572), facsimile in A. G. da Cunha, *Índice Analítico do Vocabulário de 'Os Lusíadas'* (2nd edn., Rio de Janeiro).

CAMPBELL, JOSEPH (1956), *The Hero with a Thousand Faces* (1949; New York).

—— (1982), *The Mythic Image* (1975; Princeton, NJ).

CARR, G. LLOYD (1984), *The Song of Solomon: An Introduction and Commentary* (Leicester).

CELAN, PAUL (1961), *Der Meridian* (Frankfurt).

—— (1978), *Gedichte*, i (Frankfurt).

CENTENO, Y. K. (1974), *Irreflexões* (Lisbon).

—— (1976), *A Simbologia Alquímica no 'Conto da Serpente Verde' de Goethe* (Lisbon).

—— (1978), *Símbolos de Totalidade na Obra de Hermann Hesse* (Lisbon).

—— (1979), *Algol* (Oporto).

—— (1981), 'O Cântico da Água em *Os Lusíadas*', in Y. K. Centeno and S. Reckert (eds.), *A Viagem de Os Lusíadas: Símbolo e Mito* (Lisbon), 11–32.

—— (1982), *A Alquimia do Amor* (Lisbon).

—— (1984), *Perto da Terra* (Lisbon).

—— (1985), *Fernando Pessoa: O Amor, a Morte, a Iniciação* (Lisbon).

—— (1989), 'Celan e Böhme: Meditações do Abismo', in *Actas del VI Simposio de la Sociedad Española de Literatura General y Comparada* (Granada), 155–60.

—— (forthcoming), *O Templo Interior: Poesias Escolhidas 1961–1991*, ed. and introd. Stephen Reckert (Cintra).

CHANG KANG-I SUN (1986*a*), 'Description of Landscape in Early Six Dynasties Poetry', in Lin and Owen, 105–29.

—— (1986*b*), *Six Dynasties Poetry* (Princeton, NJ).

CHEN, XIAOMEI (1992), 'Occidentalism as Counterdiscourse: "He Shang" in Post-Mao China', CI, 18, 4, Summer.

CHENG, FRANÇOIS (1977), *L'Écriture poétique chinoise* (Paris).

—— (1979), *Vide et plein* (Paris).

—— (1980), *L'Espace du rêve: mille ans de peinture chinoise* (Paris).

—— (1986), 'Some Reflections on Chinese Poetic Language and its Relation to Chinese Cosmology', in Lin and Owen, 32–48.

CHEVALIER, JEAN, and GHEERBRANT, ALAIN (1982), *Dictionnaire des symboles* (1969; 2nd edn., Paris).

CLARK, KENNETH (1960), *The Nude: A Study of Ideal Art* (2nd edn., Harmondsworth).

COLEGRAVE, SUKIE (1979), *The Spirit of the Valley: Androgyny and Chinese Thought* (London).

COLUMBUS, CHRISTOPHER (1933), in *Selected Documents illustrating the four voyages of Columbus*, ed. C. James (Hakluyt Society, 2nd ser., LXX, London), ii. 29–31.

COMITO, TERRY (1978), *The Idea of the Garden in the Renaissance* (New Brunswick, NJ).

COOK, THEODORE ANDREA (1979), *The Curves of Life* (1914; New York).

COOPER, ARTHUR (1985), 'Exploring Etymographic Origins of Chinese Characters', unpublished paper, British Association for Chinese Studies.

—— (forthcoming), *Heart and Mind: Ancient Language-Making as Recorded in the Chinese Script* (Oxford).

CURTIUS, ERNST ROBERT (1953), *European Literature and the Latin Middle Ages* (= *Europäische Literatur und lateinisches Mittelalter* (Berne, 1948)), tr. W. R. Trask (Princeton, NJ).

DANTE ALIGHIERI (1921), *Opere* (testo critico della Società Dantesca Italiana, Florence).

DELCOURT, MARIE (1980), *O Mito de Hermafrodita* (= *Hermaphrodite— Mythes et rites de la bisexualité dans l'Antiquité classique* (Paris, 1958)), tr. M. L. T. Machado (Lisbon).

DEMARAY, JOHN G. (1974), *The Invention of Dante's 'Commedia'* (New Haven, Conn.).

DENNETT, DANIEL C. (1987), 'Consciousness', in *The Oxford Companion to the Mind* (Oxford), 160–4.

—— (1988), 'Why Everyone is a Novelist', *TLS* 16–22 Sept., pp. 1016 and 1028 f.

DEYERMOND, ALAN (1979), 'Pero Meogo's Stags and Fountains: Symbol and Anecdote in the Traditional Lyric', *Romance Philology*, 33: 2 (Nov.).

DRONKE, PETER (1965), *Medieval Latin and the Rise of European Love-Lyric* (Oxford).

—— (1970), *Poetic Individuality in the Middle Ages* (Oxford).

—— (1986), *Dante and Medieval Latin Traditions* (Cambridge).

DURAND, GILBERT (1969), *Les Structures anthropologiques de l'imaginaire* [Paris].

—— (1981), 'La notion de limite dans la morphologie religieuse et les théophanies de la culture européenne', *Eranos Jahrbuch*, 49 (Frankfurt).

ECO, UMBERTO (1968), *Obra Aberta* (= *Opera aperta*), tr. of the 2nd Italian edn., with author's modifications (São Paulo).

—— (1992), 'Interpretation and History', in Eco *et al.*: *Interpretation and Overinterpretation* (Cambridge).

ELIADE, MIRCEA (1954), *The Myth of the Eternal Return* (= *Le Mythe de l'éternel retour* (Paris, 1949)) tr. W. R. Trask (New York).

—— (1964), *Shamanism* (= *Le Chamanisme et les techniques archaïques de l'extase* (Paris, 1951)), rev. edn. tr. W. R. Trask (London).

—— (1979), *Imagens e Símbolos* (= *Images et symboles* (Paris, 1952)), tr. M. A. Oliveira Soares (Lisbon).

ELIADE, MIRCEA (1984), *A History of Religious Ideas* (= *Histoire des croyances et des idées religieuses* (Paris, 1978)), ii, tr. W. R. Trask (Chicago).

ELSTER, JON, ed. (1986), *The Multiple Self* (Cambridge).

ERNOUT, A., and MEILLET, A. (1985), *Dictionnaire étymologique de la langue latine* (4th edn., Paris).

FAURE, BERNARD (1987), 'Space and Place in Chinese Religious Traditions', *HR* 26: 4 (May).

FERGUSSON, FRANCIS (1953), *Dante's Drama of the Mind* (Princeton, NJ).

FINLEY, JOHN H., jun. (1978), *Homer's 'Odyssey'* (Cambridge, Mass.).

Fleur en Fiole d'Or (1985) (= *Jin Píng Méi cíhuà*, anon., 16th c.), tr. A. Lévy (Paris).

FRANCHETTI, PAULO (1989), 'Wenceslau de Moraes e o *haiku*', *Colóquio/Letras*, 110–11 (Jul.–Oct.).

FRANZ, MARIE-LOUISE von (1959), 'The Process of Individuation', in Jung (1959).

FRENK, MARGIT (1990), *Corpus de la antigua lírica popular hispánica* (1987; 2nd edn., Madrid).

FREUD, SIGMUND (1966), *The Basic Writings*, ed. and tr. A. A. Brill (1938; repr. New York).

FRODSHAM, J. D. (1967), *An Anthology of Chinese Verse* (Oxford).

FRYE, NORTHROP (1971), *Anatomy of Criticism* (1957; Princeton, NJ).

—— (1982), *The Great Code: The Bible and Literature* (New York).

FÙ SHĚN (1960), *Chapters from a Floating Life* (= *Fóu sheng Liù jì*), tr. Shirley M. Black (London).

GERNET, JACQUES (1974), *O Mundo Chinês* (= *Le Monde chinois* (Paris, 1972)), tr. J. Silveira Lopes (Lisbon).

GLUCKLICH, ARIEL (1990), 'Images and Symbols in the Phenomenology of Dharma', *HR* 29: 3 (Feb.).

GOLDSWORTHY, ANDY (1990), *Hand to Earth*, ed. Terry Friedman and Andy Goldsworthy (Leeds).

GRIGSON, GEOFFREY (1976), *The Goddess of Love* (London).

GUÉNON, RENÉ (1975), *The Symbolism of the Cross*, tr. A. Macnab (London).

GUILLÉN, JORGE (1954), *Huerto de Melibea* (Madrid).

—— (1984), *Cántico: fe de vida (1928–50)* (Barcelona).

HARDING, M. ESTHER (1977), *Woman's Mysteries* (1955; London).

HARRISON, JANE (1957), *Prolegomena to the Study of Greek Religion* (1903; New York).

HAVARD, ROBERT (1986), *Jorge Guillén: 'Cántico'* (London).

HAWKES, DAVID (1959), *Ch'u Tz'ŭ: An Ancient Chinese Anthology* (Oxford).

—— (1988), *Classical, Modern and Humane* (Hong Kong).

HERBERT, ZBIGNIEW (1961), *Studium przedmiotu* (Warsaw).

—— (1985), *Selected Poems*, tr. Czesław Miłosz and Peter Dale Scott (2nd edn., Manchester).

HOFSTADTER, DOUGLAS R. (1979), *Gödel, Escher, Bach* (New York).
—— (1985), *Metamagical Themas* (New York).
—— and DENNETT, D. C. (1982), *The Mind's I* (Harmondsworth).
HOLBORN, MARK (1978), *The Ocean in the Sand. Japan: from Landscape to Garden* (Boulder, Colo.).
HORTA, KORINNA (1983), 'Para uma Leitura Taoísta de Alberto Caeiro' (i.e., Fernando Pessoa), *Persona*, 8.
HUMPHREY, NICHOLAS (1984), *Consciousness Regained* (Oxford).
JAKOBSON, ROMAN (1960), 'Closing Statement: Linguistics and Poetics', in *Style in Language*, ed. Thomas A. Sebeok (Cambridge, Mass.), 350–77.
—— (1973), 'Poésie de la grammaire et grammaire de la poésie' and 'Le Parallélisme grammaticale et ses aspects russes', in *Questions de poétique* (Paris).
JANEIRA, ARMANDO MARTINS (1967), *O Teatro de Gil Vicente e o Teatro Clássico Japonês* (Lisbon).
—— (1970), *Japanese and Western Literature* (Tokyo).
——.(1977), 'Zen nella poesia di Pessoa', *Quaderni portoghesi*, 1 (Spring).
JENCKS, CHARLES: see KESWICK.
Jin Píng Méi cíhuà: see *Fleur en Fiole d'Or*.
JOHN OF THE CROSS, Saint: see Alonso 1946.
JUNG, C. G. (1959), *The Basic Writings*, ed. Violet Staub de Laszlo (New York).
—— (1968), *Psychology and Alchemy* (1944), tr. R. F. C. Hull (2nd edn., London).
KARLGREN, BERNHARD (1964), *Grammata Serica Recensa* (Stockholm).
KEENE, DONALD (1988), *The Pleasures of Japanese Literature* (New York).
KENKŌ (1967), *Essays in Idleness* (= *Tsurezuregusa*, c.1331), tr. Donald Keene (New York).
KERMODE, FRANK (1973), *The Sense of an Ending* (1966; Oxford).
—— (1989), *An Appetite for Poetry* (London).
KESWICK, MAGGIE (with JENCKS, CHARLES) (1978), *The Chinese Garden: History, Art and Architecture* (London).
KITAGAWA, JOSEPH M., 'Dimensions of the East Asian Religious Universe', *HR*, 21, 2, Nov. 1991.
KLEIN, ERNEST (1979), *A Comprehensive Etymological Dictionary of the English Language* (1966–7; Amsterdam).
KOLM, SERGE-CHRISTOF (1986), 'The Buddhist Theory of "No-Self"', in Elster, 233–65.
KROLL, PAUL W. (1986), 'Verses from on High: The Ascent of T'ai Shan', in Lin and Owen, 167–216.
KUCK, LORAINE (1982), *The World of the Japanese Garden* (1968; 3rd edn., Tokyo).
LANGER, SUZANNE (1953), *Feeling and Form* (New York).

LAUFER, BERTHOLD (1974), *Jade: A Study in Chinese Archaeology and Religion* (1912; New York).

LEACH, EDMUND (1976), *Culture and Communication* (Cambridge).

LEWIS, C. S. (1958), *The Allegory of Love* (1936; New York).

LIÈ ZĬ (apocryphal attrib.) (1980), *Le Vrai Classique du Vide Parfait* (= *Zhong Xu Zhen Jing*, 3rd c.?), tr. B. Grynpas, in *Philosophes taoïstes* (Paris).

LIMA, F. C. PIRES DE (1962), *Cancioneiro* (Lisbon).

LIN SHUEN-FU (1986), 'The Nature of the Quatrain from the Late Han to the High T'ang', in Lin and Owen, 296–331.

—— and OWEN, STEPHEN, eds. (1986), *The Vitality of the Lyric Voice: Shih Poetry from the Late Han to the T'ang* (Princeton, NJ).

LIU, JAMES J. Y. (1982), *The Interlingual Critic: Interpreting Chinese Poetry* (Bloomington, Ind.).

—— (1988), *Language—Paradox—Poetics: A Chinese Perspective* (Princeton, NJ).

LOEWE, MICHAEL (1979), *Ways to Paradise: The Chinese Quest for Immortality* (London).

MABBETT, I. W. (1983), 'The Symbolism of Mount Meru', *HR* 23: 1 (Aug.).

MCCLUNG, WILLIAM ALEXANDER (1983), *The Architecture of Paradise. Survivals of Eden and Jerusalem* (Berkeley, Calif.); see the Italian edn. (*Dimore celesti*, tr. Giulia Angelini (Bologna, 1987)) for the introduction by Eugenio Battisti.

MACEDO, HELDER (1980), 'Uma cantiga de Dom Dinis', in Reckert (1980).

MACHADO, ANTONIO (1982), *Poesías completas*, (8th edn., Madrid).

MALLARMÉ, STÉPHANE (1970), *Œuvres complètes*, ed. H. Mondor and G. Jean-Aubry (Paris).

MANDEL'SHTAM, OSIP (1973), *Selected Poems*, tr. Clarence Brown and W. S. Merwin (Harmondsworth).

—— (1977), *Selected Essays*, tr. Sidney Monas (Austin, Tex.).

MERQUIOR, JOSÉ GUILHERME (1969), *Arte e Sociedade em Marcuse, Adorno e Benjamin* (Rio de Janeiro).

MIŁOSZ, CZESŁAW (1983), 'Ruins and Poetry', *NYRB* 17 Mar.

—— (1981–8), *Dzieła Zbiorowe*, i. *Poezje*, ii–iii (Paris).

—— (1988), *The Collected Poems 1931–1987* (London).

MINER, EARL (1979), *Japanese Linked Poetry* (Princeton, NJ).

—— (1989), 'Literatures, Histories, and Literary Histories', in Yang and Yue, 1–40.

—— (1990), *Comparative Poetics* (Princeton, NJ).

MOURA, VASCO GRAÇA (1980), *Luís de Camões: Alguns Desafios* (Lisbon).

—— (1987), *Os Penhascos e a Serpente* (Lisbon).

MOURÃO-FERREIRA, DAVID (1980), *Entre a Sombra e o Corpo* (Lisbon).

—— (1985), *Os Ramos os Remos* (Oporto).

MURASAKI SHIKIBU (1960), *The Tale of Genji* (= *Genji Monogatari*, *c.*1008), tr. Arthur Waley (1935; New York).

Mutus Liber (1980), (1677; 2nd edn., facsimile, Geneva, 1702) in M. Kunzle, *Mutus Liber: Le immagini dell'Alchimia* (Milan).

NEUMANN, ERICH (1973), *The Origins and History of Consciousness* (= *Ursprungsgeschichte des Bewusstseins* (Zurich, 1949)), tr. R. F. C. Hull (1954; Princeton, NJ).

—— (1974), *The Great Mother: An Analysis of the Archetype* (1955), tr. Ralph Manheim (Princeton, NJ).

NUNES, JOSÉ JOAQUIM (1926), *Cantigas d'Amigo* (Coimbra).

On the Meaning of the Golden Flower of the Great Monad (= *Tài Yi Jin Hua Zong Zhi*, anon., 8th c.?) (1947), tr. C. F. Baynes, with commentary by C. G. Jung, from the German tr. of Richard Wilhelm (London).

ORNSTEIN, ROBERT (1986), *Multimind* (London).

OWEN, STEPHEN (1975), *The Poetry of Meng Chiao and Han Yü* (New Haven, Conn.).

—— (1985), *Traditional Chinese Poetry and Poetics* (Madison, Wis.).

—— (1986a), *Remembrances: The Experience of the Past in Classical Chinese Literature* (Cambridge, Mass.).

—— (1986b), 'The Self's Perfect Mirror', in Lin and Owen, 71–102.

—— (1989), *Mi-Lou: Poetry and the Labyrinth of Desire*, (Cambridge, Mass.).

PAZ, OCTAVIO (1956), *El arco y la lira* (Mexico City).

—— (1970), Introduction to Bashō Matsuo, *Sendas de Oku*, tr. Octavio Paz and Eikichi Hayashiya (Barcelona).

PENROSE, ROGER (1989), *The Emperor's New Mind* (Oxford).

PERRONE-MOISÉS, LEYLA (1982), *Fernando Pessoa, aquém do eu, além do outro* (São Paulo).

PESSOA, FERNANDO (1981), *Obra Poética*, ed. M. Aliete Galhoz (8th edn., Rio de Janeiro; references are to poem numbers unless otherwise specified).

PETROPOULOS, D. (1954), *La Comparaison dans la chanson populaire grècque* (Athens).

PICCHIO, LUCIANA STEGAGNO (1982), *La Méthode philologique: Écrits sur la littérature portugaise*, i. *La Poésie* (Paris).

PILGRIM, RICHARD B. (1986), 'Intervals (*Ma*) in Space and Time: The Foundations for a Religio-Aesthetic Paradigm in Japan', *HR* 25: 3 (Feb.).

PLAKS, ANDREW H. (1989), 'Where the Lines Meet: Parallelism in Chinese and Western Literatures', in Yang and Yue, 293–330.

PONGE, FRANCIS (1967), *Le Parti pris des choses* (1942; Paris).

POPPER, KARL, and ECCLES, JOHN C. (1983), *The Self and Its Brain* (1977; London).

POULET, GEORGES (1961), *Les Métamorphoses du cercle* (Paris).

RAWSON, PHILIP (1973), *The Art of Tantra* (London).

RAWSON, PHILIP and LEGEZA LASZLO (1973), *Tao: The Chinese Philosophy of Time and Change* (London).

RECKERT, STEPHEN (1970), *Lyra Minima* (London).

—— (1973), '*Mudanças e Enganos*' (Os Lusíadas *como Documento Histórico, Cultural, e Literário*) (Lisbon).

—— (1977), *Gil Vicente: Espíritu y letra*, i (Madrid).

—— (1980), *Do Cancioneiro de Amigo* (2nd edn., Lisbon).

—— (1982), '*Império dos Signos* ou Imperialismo dos Significantes?', in *Leituras de Roland Barthes* (Lisbon).

—— (1984), '"Micro-significantes" na Semiótica de Camões', in *Actas da IV Reunião Internacional de Camonistas* (Ponta Delgada).

—— (1987), *Um Ramalhete para Cesário* (Lisbon).

—— (1993), 'Facing Both Ways: Some Poems from the *Cancioneiro Geral*', *Portuguese Studies*, 9.

—— and CENTENO, Y. K. (1978), *Fernando Pessoa* (Lisbon).

RICO, FRANCISCO (1973), 'Tradición y experimento en la poesía medieval: *Ruodlieb, Semiramis*, Abelardo, Santa Hildegarda', *Romance Philology*, 26: 4 (May), 673–89.

SCHAFER, EDWARD H. (1963*a*), *The Golden Peaches of Samarkand: A Study of T'ang Exotics* (Berkeley, Calif.).

—— (1963*b*), 'Mineral Imagery in the Paradise Poems of Kuan-Hsiu', *Asia Major*, 73–102.

—— (1967), *The Vermilion Bird: T'ang Images of the South* (Berkeley, Calif.).

—— (1985), *Mirages on the Sea of Time: The Taoist Poetry of Ts'ao T'ang* (Berkeley, Calif.).

SCHIPPER, KRISTOFER (1978), 'The Taoist Body', *HR* 17: 3/4 (Feb.–May).

Secret of the Golden Flower: see *On the Meaning . . .*

SEFERIS, Giorgos (1965), Ποιήματα (Athens); facsimile repr. ed. and trans. Edmund Keeley and Philip Sherrard (London, 1969) as *Collected Poems 1924–1955* (I have made minor changes in the English text).

Shi Jing (lit. 'Canon of Odes') (1967), *The Book of Poetry*, ed. and tr. James Legge (repr., New York). (Poem numbers as in Arthur Waley, tr., *The Book of Songs* (1937; 2nd edn., London, 1954).)

SHUTTLE, PENELOPE, and REDGROVE, PETER (1980), *The Wise Wound* (1978; Harmondsworth).

SIMS, JAMES H. (1972), '"Delicious Paradise" in *Os Lusíadas* and in *Paradise Lost*', *Ocidente* (Lisbon, Nov.).

SINGLETON, CHARLES S. (1970–5), *Dante Alighieri: The Divine Comedy, Translated, with a Commentary* (and the Italian text of G. Petrocchi) (Princeton, NJ).

SLAWSON, DAVID A. (1987), *Secret Teachings in the Art of Japanese Gardens* (Tokyo).

STEEDMAN, IAN, and KRAUSE, ULRICH (1986), 'Goethe's *Faust*, Arrow's Possibility Theorem and the Individual Decision-Taker', in Elster.

STEIN, GERTRUDE (1963), *Lectures in America* (1935; New York).

STEINER, GEORGE (1967), *Language and Silence* (London).

—— (1972), 'The Language Animal', in *Extraterritorial* (London).

—— (1978), 'Dante Now: The Gossip of Eternity', in *On Difficulty and Other Essays* (Oxford).

—— (1986), *Real Presences* (Cambridge).

STERN, S. M. (1953), *Les Chansons mozarabes* (Palermo).

TCHOU KIA-KIEN and GAUDON, ARMAND (1927), *Anthologie de la poésie chinoise* (Peking).

THEROS, A. (1951), *Tὰ Τραγούδια τῶν Ἑλλήνων*, i (Athens).

THOMPSON, D'ARCY WENTWORTH (1972), *On Growth and Form* (1917), abridged edn. J. T. Bonner (2nd edn., Cambridge).

THOMPSON, STITH (1955–8), *Motif-Index of Folk-Literature* (Copenhagen).

TORNER, EDUARDO M. (1966), *Lírica hispánica* (Madrid).

TRASK, WILLARD R. (1969), *The Unwritten Song* (London).

TUCCI, GIUSEPPE (1974), *The Theory and Practice of the Mandala*, tr. A. Brodrick (London).

UNGARETTI, GIUSEPPE (1982), *Vita d'un Uomo*, ed. L. Piccioni (10th edn., Milan).

VALÉRY, PAUL (1957), *Œuvres*, i (Paris).

WANG CHING-HSIEN (1974), *The Bell and the Drum. 'Shih Ching' as Formulaic Poetry in an Oral Tradition* (Berkeley, Calif.).

—— (1986), 'The Nature of Narrative in T'ang Poetry', in Lin and Owen, 216–52.

WILKINS, EITHNE (1969), *The Rose-Garden Game: The Symbolic Background to the European Prayer-Beads* (London).

WOSIEN, MARIA-GABRIELE (1974), *Sacred Dance* (New York).

YANG ZHOUHAN and YUE DAIYUN, eds. (1989), *Literatures, Histories, and Literary Histories: Proceedings of the 2nd Sino–U.S. Comparative Literature Symposium* (Shenyang).

YU, PAULINE (1987), *The Reading of Imagery in the Chinese Poetic Tradition* (Princeton, NJ).

ZHANG LONGXI (1985), 'The *Tao* and the *Logos*: Notes on Derrida's Critique of Logocentrism', *CI* 11: 3 (Mar.), 385–98.

—— (1989), 'The Myth of the Other: China in the Eyes of the West', in Yang and Yue, 188–223.

—— (1992), 'Western Theory and Chinese Reality, *CI* 19: 1 (Autumn), 105–30.

ZHUANG ZĬ (1968), *Complete Works of Chuang-tzu*, tr. Burton Watson (New York).

Index